Peter Lorre: Face Maker

Film Europa: German Cinema in an International Context
Series Editors: **Hans-Michael Bock** (CineGraph Hamburg);
Tim Bergfelder (University of Southampton); **Sabine Hake**
(University of Texas, Austin)

German cinema is normally seen as a distinct form, but this new series
emphasizes connections, influences, and exchanges of German cinema
across national borders, as well as its links with other media and art
forms. Individual titles present traditional historical research (archival
work, industry studies) as well as new critical approaches in film and
media studies (theories of the transnational), with a special emphasis on
the continuities associated with popular traditions and local perspectives.

**The Concise Cinegraph: An
Encyclopedia of German Cinema**
General Editor: Hans-Michael Bock
Associate Editor: Tim Bergfelder

**International Adventures:
German Popular Cinema and
European Co-Productions in
the 1960s**
Tim Bergfelder

**Between Two Worlds: The Jewish
Presence in German and Austrian
Film, 1910–1933**
S.S. Prawer

**Framing the Fifties: Cinema in a
Divided Germany**
Edited by John Davidson and
Sabine Hake

**A Foreign Affair: Billy Wilder's
American Films**
Gerd Gemünden

**Destination London: German-
speaking Emigrés and British
Cinema, 1925–1950**
Edited by Tim Bergfelder and
Christian Cargnelli

**Michael Haneke's Cinema:
The Ethic of the Image**
Catherine Wheatley

Willing Seduction: *The Blue Angel*,
**Marlene Dietrich, and Mass
Culture**
Barbara Kosta

**Dismantling the Dream Factory:
Gender, German Cinema, and the
Postwar Quest for a New Film
Language**
Hester Baer

Belá Balázs: Early Film Theory.
Visible Man and *The Spirit of Film*
Belá Balázs, edited by Erica Carter,
translated by Rodney Livingstone

**Screening the East: Heimat,
Memory and Nostalgia in German
Film since 1989**
Nick Hodgin

**Peter Lorre: Face Maker.
Stardom and Performance
between Hollywood and Europe**
Sarah Thomas

PETER LORRE: FACE MAKER

Stardom and Performance between Hollywood and Europe

Sarah Thomas

Berghahn Books
New York • Oxford

Published in 2012 by

Berghahn Books

www.berghahnbooks.com

Library of Congress Cataloging-in-Publication Data

Thomas, Sarah.
  Peter Lorre: face maker . stardom and performance between Hollywood
and Europe / Sarah Thomas. – 1st ed.
    p. cm. – (Film Europa: German cinema in an international context)
    Includes bibliographical references and index.
    ISBN 978-0-85745-441-6 (hardback : alk. paper) – ISBN 978-0-85745-442-3
(ebook)
  1. Lorre, Peter–Criticism and interpretation. I. Title.
    PN2287.L65T46 2012
    791.4302'8092–dc23   2011044921

British Library Cataloguing in Publication Data

A catalogue record for this book is available from the British Library

Printed in the United States on acid-free paper.

ISBN: 978-0-85745-441-6 (hardback)
E-ISBN: 978-0-85745-442-3 (ebook)

CONTENTS

LIST OF ILLUSTRATIONS

ACKNOWLEDGEMENTS

I would like to thank the Arts and Humanities Research Council for their financial support, without which this project would not have been possible. I would also like to express my gratitude to Berghahn Books and everyone involved with the publication of the Film Europa series, particularly the series editor, Tim Bergfelder, who has provided me with extensive and invaluable advice on my manuscript through the publication process. Thanks also to those who read all or part of the manuscript and gave me significant intellectual feedback: Martin Shingler, Andrew Spicer, Peter Krämer and Ed Gallafent.

The archival research that has gone into this work would not have been possible without the help and attention of Ned Comstock, Noelle Carter and the staff at the Warner Bros. Archive, University of Southern California, Los Angeles, USA, Barbara Hall and the staff at the Margaret Herrick Library, Academy of Motion Picture Arts and Sciences, Los Angeles, USA, and all the staff at the BFI Library, London, UK. I would like to extend my appreciation to them all. Central to this aspect of the book was the assistance of Luella Forbes in compiling this research; special thanks must go to her.

This book began as a PhD thesis at the University of Warwick. Therefore I would like to thank all the staff at the Film and Television Studies department there, especially Jon Burrows who supervised and supported me for many years as this project took shape. My current academic department has also been hugely supportive of my work, so I would like to thank my colleagues at the Department of Theatre, Film and Television Studies at Aberystwyth University, especially Kate Egan and Martin Barker.

I owe much to the continued support and enthusiasm of my parents for my work. And particularly thanks to my partner Adam for everything that he has done over the past eleven years to help me achieve this book and so much more.

INTRODUCTION

Peter Lorre is one of the remembered creatures of Hollywood. I say creature for he – or his screen persona – was so definitely the creation of this personality factory town; and I say remembered for so many have been forgotten – some more famous and some much better, or perhaps I should say, more careful actors. Peter was not in any way a bad actor; it's just that Hollywood's creation of him wouldn't allow him any more chances to be good than they have allowed many another.

Vincent Price (1981: 15)

Vincent Price's summation of Peter Lorre's legacy is a key observation that illustrates dominant perceptions surrounding the life and work of Lorre. Although the function of Price's reflection is to introduce a populist biographical sketch of Lorre's career by a fellow actor and friend (who co-starred with Lorre on five occasions), rather than to provide sustained critical analysis, it nevertheless makes a highly indicative statement concerning the way in which the work of performers who achieve a certain level of celebrity – as Lorre did – can be interpreted and analysed within critical discourses.[1] Price's elegiac commentary foregrounds the role played by Hollywood in the construction of this 'version' of Peter Lorre. Secondly, it recognizes that Lorre is almost wholly defined by a specific persona rather than through the actor's 'reality'. Thirdly, it remarks upon the difference between being a 'bad' actor and an actor who was used 'badly' by the Hollywood studio system. And last, it attests to the fact that the actor's public persona continued to define Lorre's fame even after his death.

However, Price's words also reflect some of the more problematic aspects of the critical discourse that surrounds Lorre: they equate the outcome of his work as an actor solely with the construction of Lorre's public persona (here defined explicitly as a screen persona), and also in how they 'blame' Hollywood for not allowing the actor to fulfil his potential because of the way this persona was used. Due to the cultural status of Lorre – as a European performer who was forced into exile in the United States as a result of the Nazis' rise to power in Germany during the 1930s – this perception of his American career implicitly paints Hollywood as a corrosive influence upon the actor, partly in contrast to his more 'artistic' endeavours in Europe. Although it does not specifically address Lorre's émigré status, Price's retrospective paean to Lorre conforms to the established perception of the actor's career: that the notoriety of his 'Hollywood' public persona adversely affected the terms of his employment and the way in which Lorre himself performed on-screen. Lorre's Hollywood acting style has been repeatedly characterized as a form of 'face-making' by contemporaries (including Vincent Price), scholars such as James Naremore (1988: 63), and – perhaps most significantly – by Lorre himself.[2] Lorre's admission that he considered himself a mere face-maker is a particularly pessimistic indictment of his American career that has continued to inform appraisals of Lorre's performative labour. Considerations of Lorre's career are informed by the underlying assumption that the most significant analyses of the actor can be achieved through a definition or exploration of his public image.

In 2005, the resonant image of Peter Lorre was repeated once more within Hollywood cinema. Playing a central role in *Corpse Bride*, the animated film directed by Tim Burton, was the character of Maggot; a creature clearly based on Lorre's public 'star' persona. Maggot also physically resembled Peter Lorre – or more accurately, the caricatured image that has come to signify him: the oversized head and bulging eyes, sickly flesh tones emphasized as green, thick lips and rotten teeth. Maggot's behaviour is framed around the gruesome: he lives inside the Corpse Bride's skull, and becomes inappropriately excited about the possibility of murdering the leading character Victor. His countenance is panicky, often urgent, and he speaks with the nasal accented whine that is central to impersonations of the actor. Retrospective representations and writings about Lorre repeatedly outline the rubrics of the public image, defining him as 'murderous', 'strange', 'monstrous', 'foreign', 'pervert', 'mad' and 'ghoulish'. From this one can observe that his persona was built around the concept of a certain type of 'evil incarnate', partly linked to an individual's compulsive, psychopathic desire to kill, and partly linked to wider horror iconography and cultural or sociological theories anchored around the 'abnormal', the 'other' or the 'monstrous'.

Maggot is an extreme abstraction of Peter Lorre – the actor – formed in light of the way Lorre has been presented for public consumption for over seventy years. Burton's creature illustrates not only the continuing cultural value that Lorre has within media forms and for audiences, but also the inherent issues that lie in the construction of public images, particularly around their creation and the impact of the actor's screen work on public perceptions. In *Burton on Burton*, the director discusses Maggot's relationship with his original source:

> Maggot is basically Peter Lorre. I always loved those few old Warner Bros. cartoons where it was him, it was a caricature of him. I never knew who he was, I hadn't seen Peter Lorre movies, but then you'd see this little weird character and go, 'I like that character'. That's what we were trying to do [on *Corpse Bride*], even with those characters who are only there for a couple of

scenes. They register as such a type – even if you don't get a chance to know the character, you get a bit more information. (Salisbury 2006: 257)

Here Burton states that Maggot is constructed from a very definite image of Lorre (Maggot *is* Lorre). Beyond this individuality, Lorre also connotes for Burton a specific 'type' of character: he becomes a familiar stereotype due to his repeated typecasting as a certain kind of abnormal creature. However, Burton also recounts how his own perception of Lorre as a 'weird' figure initially came not from seeing the actor's films, but from how that actor was represented via other means (the Warner Bros. caricatures). This offers a contrast to Vincent Price's words which defined Lorre as a 'creature' only via his screen persona. However, for both men, the key to Lorre's identity and value remains tied to his public persona: the strange murderous individual. But the disparity between the two personal memories also begs a further question: if Lorre's public image exists beyond his films then to what extent was that stereotypical public persona created by the actor's film work – and by Hollywood cinema – in the first instance?

My aim in this book is to demonstrate that critical perspectives which mirror the type of personal observations that Price and Burton have made can also be limiting. Attempts at analysing Lorre's career – and explicitly, his cinematic career – have often been impeded by the notoriety of his public persona, particularly through a failure to question where and how Lorre's persona originated. In doing so, they illustrate that analyses of performers which are restricted to an abstracted persona-led investigation of public images can be reductive precisely because the existence of that persona can adversely affect the way in which performances can be read, and can result in oversimplifications or inaccuracies about the history of a specific actor.

The man who became 'Peter Lorre' was born László Loewenstein in Rószahegy, a small central European town, which in 1904 – the year of Lorre's birth – was part of the Austro-Hungarian Empire (on the Hungarian border) and now lies within the borders of Slovakia.[3] During the First World War his family moved to Vienna, and it was here that Lorre first began to perform onstage in the early 1920s. His experiences on the Austrian stage lasted until 1924 when he found steady employment with repertory theatres, initially in Breslau, Germany, and then in Zurich, Switzerland. Lorre moved to Berlin in 1929 and achieved a notable level of success on the Berlin stage. During this period he also established a close working relationship with the playwright Bertolt Brecht.

Lorre first came to prominence on the cinema screen in 1931, when he appeared as the serial killer, Hans Beckert, who targets children in Fritz Lang's film *M*, and his career has often been characterized as having a close association with this notorious role. Lorre continued to work as a supporting actor within the German and Austrian film industries (including roles in three films with the German star, Hans Albers) until the growing

Nazi threat to Jewish personnel forced him to leave in 1934. He headed first to Paris and then to London, where he made *The Man Who Knew Too Much* with Alfred Hitchcock. In the same year, Lorre made the move to Hollywood, having secured a contract with Columbia Pictures.

Lorre's Hollywood career has been widely perceived to be an inconsistent one, in which the industry has often been accused of wasting the potential of the actor and typecasting him in a series of limiting roles that simply exploited the infamy of his earlier success in *M*. The consensus view has been that Lorre failed to maintain his initial status as a star performer and was quickly consigned to supporting roles or working on low-budget films by the end of the 1930s. Many of Lorre's most famous film appearances were made as a supporting player during the 1940s when the actor was contracted to Warner Bros.; these included *The Maltese Falcon*, *Casablanca* and *Arsenic and Old Lace*, and a long-running screen 'partnership' of sorts with both Humphrey Bogart and Sydney Greenstreet.

However, by the end of the decade, his on- and off-screen fortunes had declined to some degree, and Lorre was keen to move in a different direc-

Figure 0.1 Humphrey Bogart and Peter Lorre, *Casablanca*, 1942, Warner Bros.

tion. In 1950 he returned to Germany to star in the only feature film he directed, *Der Verlorene* (The Lost One). After this, he returned to Hollywood where his cinematic output decreased during the 1950s and 1960s. He made a number of supporting appearances and cameos, and also began a successful association with the independent producers, American International Pictures (AIP). This relationship shaped the last years of his screen career as a star of 'horror' films as a result of his performances with Vincent Price in *Tales of Terror*, *The Raven* and *The Comedy of Terrors*. Lorre died in March 1964, aged 59, having suffered ill health throughout his lifetime, including a long-standing addiction to morphine.

The image of Lorre as a psychotic and strange murderer has its genesis in *M*. However, Lorre's familiar star image itself is more than a mere rehash of the German role. Instead of drawing only from the singular figure of Beckert, it was constructed from Hollywood's relatively slow appropriation of elements from this character and through an emphasis on other aspects of Lorre's personal qualities which only became apparent upon his move to the United States, such as changes in his physical appearance and voice, or his subsequent positioning in relation to the 'normality' of American culture and society – often explained via his 'foreign' status.

Rhetoric surrounding Lorre inherently assumes a direct correlation between 'Peter Lorre' (the public persona of the actor) and the film roles played by the actor – particularly in Hollywood. However, the apparent simplicity of this monstrously murderous public image belies the complexity of the actor's screen career. Between 1929 and 1964, Lorre made seventy-nine films. Despite the apparent link between casting and public image, Lorre portrayed characters that can be wholly defined as following his strangely menacing and psychotically murderous public star persona in

Figure 0.2 Lorre caricatured as Maggot, *Corpse Bride*, 2005, Warner Bros.

only six films (approximately 7 per cent of his total screen output): *M* (1931), *Mad Love* (1935), *Stranger on the Third Floor* (1940), *The Beast with Five Fingers* (1946), *Double Confession* (1950), and his own directorial debut, *Der Verlorene* (1951). Even if one expands the boundaries of Lorre's public image beyond the psychotic and abnormal, and defines him – as many have – as an iconic genre star that specialized in horror films, the total number of films that he made which relate to this status as a horror icon remains relatively small. Only eight of Lorre's films can be explicitly placed within the horror genre: *Mad Love* (1935), *You'll Find Out* (1940), *The Boogie Man Will Get You* (1942), *Arsenic and Old Lace* (1944), *The Beast with Five Fingers* (1946), *Tales of Terror* (1962), *The Raven* (1963) and *The Comedy of Terrors* (1964).

Lorre's star image fails to account comprehensively for the remaining sixty-seven screen characters played by Lorre during his thirty-five-year career in film and other media. Therefore, I suggest a revision: since many characteristics associated with Lorre's persona have somewhat tenuous links to his cinematic performances, what Price explicitly terms Lorre's 'screen persona' might be more usefully defined as his 'extra-filmic persona'. This is a phrase that will be employed throughout this book in order to emphasize the split between substantive screen labour and a received public image. The disparity between image and screen role also challenges the argument that Lorre was typecast in his films as a direct result of his star persona. Considering Lorre's persona away from an immediate connection to his film work (and vice versa) suggests a more coherent relationship between his public image and representations of the actor within other media sources. By examining some of the major transmedial and transnational aspects of Lorre's career and public image, I will investigate the screen work and labour practices that informed Peter Lorre's employment, performances and star status between Hollywood and Europe.

There are two major discursive arenas that are illustrated, and expanded, through a close study of Peter Lorre. The first, and most widely discussed, is his position as an émigré figure who worked in Hollywood during the mid-twentieth century. Here, Lorre's significance has been traditionally explained in terms of the interplay between his European heritage (on and off screen) and the roles assigned to him by the Hollywood studio system in light of his public image, particularly in the perceived disparity between these two cultural sites and Lorre's willingness to assimilate into American culture, but only through his status as an 'outsider' or 'foreigner'.

The notoriety of Lorre's 'abnormal' public image has been explicitly linked to his cultural background, and therefore has been taken as emblematic of the function and experience of émigré European actors working in Hollywood who were cast as symbols of 'otherness', 'deviance' and 'inauthenticity', or who played roles that were dependent upon national stereotypes (Phillips and Vincendeau 2006). Furthermore, the Jewish identity of Lorre and other émigré actors has also been foregrounded within this context, whereby an indistinct 'foreign' on-screen identity worked towards blurring ethnic boundaries and 'camouflaging' the Jewishness of individual European performers (ibid.).[4] As well as the resonance born from this period of Hollywood filmmaking during the Second World War era, this can be taken as part of a wider strategy within production during the studio era in which the invisibility of Jewish identity (within European-born and American-born stars) could be seen as a deliberate feature (Jarvie 1991).[5] Partly because of this, it remains difficult to determine to what degree Lorre was perceived as Jewish by the American public, although this association was more clearly in evidence in Germany during the war as his image was circulated in German anti-Semitic propaganda.[6]

Reading Lorre merely as a 'foreigner' or 'other', his image takes on immense significance. The approach is synedochial where one part (the persona) is taken for the whole of Lorre's complex life, career, employment status, images within modes of representation, and so on. However, this type of critical rhetoric is limited because it relies upon the belief that his Hollywood films reduced the individual star to a broader stereotype of the generically alien and 'Un-American' (Vasey 1997). Instead the image of Peter Lorre as the 'monstrous other' was created and perpetuated in great part through non-cinematic discourse, and his film career was far more flexible than this insistence upon stereotypical imagery and industrial casting practice otherwise suggests.

Investigations which approach Lorre via his ideological and cultural identity as a twentieth-century émigré figure define his labour position exclusively as a European actor working in Hollywood during the studio era. As such, given the importance accorded to Lorre's European identity, many of the sustained examinations of the actor have been conducted by European writers and published in German, often drawing attention to more unfamiliar work undertaken by Lorre within German, Austrian and other contexts (Youngkin and Hoffman 1998; Beyer 1988; Omasta, Mayer and Streit 2004). Within the English language, the most notable examples of this approach are the essays written by Gerd Gemünden (2003) and Christopher McCullough (2004), and Stephen D. Youngkin's official biography of Lorre (2005).

These works reflect wider investigations and debates focused around the figure of the exile or émigré within different national and transnational contexts, and around diasporic filmmaking in general. Although they consider Lorre initially from a biographical perspective, they also illustrate more recent developments within studies of émigré figures by constructing their analyses partly through viewpoints which prioritize the professional, the aesthetic and the economic (Bergfelder 2007b). To some degree, this moves away from the more traditional approach which considers narratives of the personal experience and trauma of the exile, and maintains questions around a perceived loss of identity when placed in a different national context. These types of questions have certainly been posed about Lorre in the past, as an actor who embraced American populism and culture, seemingly at the expense of his European sensibilities and artistic integrity. All three analyses offer perceptive insights into the performative process and the way Lorre's international identity enabled the actor to combine certain European theatrical traditions and self-reflexive techniques within his Hollywood screen roles. Through this, Lorre's importance as a figure who transgresses and problematizes fixed categories within film history, such as 'national' status, is foregrounded.

However, these analyses continue to repeat the characterization of Lorre – and, by implication, the émigré in general – as a tragic figure exploited by Hollywood and forced to play the 'outsider' in order to become the 'insider'. Gemünden refuses to privilege German art cinema over Hollywood films and to define one part of Lorre's career (Europe) as more artistically significant than the other (Hollywood) in order to highlight the limitations of focusing film history within the borders of national cinemas. He suggests different ways that Weimar cinema influenced Hollywood filmmaking by reading Lorre's own performances as enactments of displacement that contain agency and resistance to Hollywood's strategies of casting émigré actors as 'othered' characters. This analysis of Lorre's non-naturalistic acting in his Hollywood films as a commentary upon his environment is highly valuable, and is an approach that will continue within this book. But to do so, Gemünden provides a monolithic view of Hollywood itself as he offers a simplistic outline of Lorre's Hollywood career that conflates Lorre's public image and marketing rhetoric with his actual employment by the studio system. His descriptions of Lorre's roles as 'only' perverts, serial killers, Nazis or psychotics is far from accurate and, whilst he attempts to reposition Lorre as a challenging and intelligent actor who critiqued the émigré experience on-screen, he also reduces aspects of Lorre's career to lazy typecasting strategies by the Hollywood studios that resulted in self-parodying performances from Lorre at the end of his career.

The implicit critique of Hollywood is also present within McCullough's and Youngkin's writing, effectively defining Lorre through a series of binary divisions: European/American, Theatre/Film, Artistry/Commerce and Persona/Person. In each case, one category is assumed to dominate wider public perceptions of the actor ('American', 'Film', 'Commerce' and 'Persona'), whereas the objective of the authors is to reveal the other category, which is constructed as having a higher cultural value ('European', 'Theatre', 'Artistry', 'Person'). In doing so, the way in which Lorre is defined uses a mode of analysis that is very much indebted to and derived from traditional theoretical approaches to stardom (even though authors rarely position Lorre as a star) in the perceived need to reveal what Lorre was 'really' like (his authentic identity as a European actor) away from the confines of his dominant public persona (the identity forced upon him by Hollywood which was then consumed by audiences).

The continued emphasis in both pieces on the way Lorre's persona effectively obscured the identity of the person behind the façade promotes the notion that there was little of artistic or cultural value within Lorre's Hollywood employment, and that the actor's career path could be seen as a tragically slow and inexorable slide towards mediocrity, in which, effectively, the crass commercialism of the Hollywood machine corrupted the 'soul' of the European artist. This view comes partly from primary sources attributed to Lorre himself – most obviously in the instances where he described his Hollywood screen work as 'just making faces' – and to those that worked with the actor, such as other European émigrés (Youngkin 2005: 260). However, the limitations associated with the way in which an actor perceives his own career in exile and constructs a particular viewpoint about it for a variety of reasons and for various audiences (such as conversations conducted within a specific cultural environment, like the émigré community), is not directly addressed. Therefore, to a certain extent, Lorre's own disparaging views about his Hollywood career, such as his belief that he was a mere 'face-maker', should be challenged.

The second discursive arena, which is no less significant even though it has received far less attention, moves away from a singular definition of Lorre as an 'actor-in-exile' only, and on to his position as a 'star performer'. Whilst analysis of the figure of the star has long been an extensive feature within film studies, Lorre has never been a focus of this discourse, apart from his position as an emblematic 'émigré star'. Lorre's lack of conventional star status but recognizable public image and complex position within the Hollywood studio hierarchy enables wider analyses between different modes of stardom (the traditional leading star, the character actor and the cult star), modes of screen performance, and the political economy around acting labour.

There are also clear parallels between developments within studies of émigrés and studies of star performers that Lorre is able to illustrate. This should not be surprising since both fields are concerned with individual actors and personalities, or groups of culturally similar and significant people. Although different in tone, the scope of recent questions raised around the historical position of the émigré are shared by scholars examining historical approaches to stardom in general. Tim Bergfelder (2007b) argues that studies of émigrés are initially significant because of the way in which these figures challenge fixed boundaries (around histories and concepts of nation, culture and, increasingly, of 'belonging'). Because they are problematic, too often they have fallen through traditional film histories and canons. But he also suggests there is a need to expand beyond the biographical approach which emphasizes personality, image and cultural legacy at the expense of other processes and exchanges that exist in relation to these figures, particularly the economic, the performative and the aesthetic. An approach such as this is reflected in Joseph Garncarz's (2006) research into German-speaking actors who played Nazis in Hollywood, which – as the author acknowledges – moves away from his original hypothesis around cultural and ideological concerns and towards labour and industrial conditions. When examining émigrés who worked in Hollywood during the 1930s and 1940s, it is important to remember these individuals' status as workers within an established economic system (and one that was purposefully internationalist and transnational in its outlook), and that creative reinvention and cultural adaptation was not only possible but also necessary. These perspectives can easily be applied to 'Lorre-the-émigré-actor', but they are equally relevant to 'Lorre-the-Hollywood-star', particularly in light of the creative and cultural adaptations that can be found within his work, not only between Hollywood and Europe, but also within the complex and mutable spaces he occupied within Hollywood itself as an actor and a star.

Within studies of stardom, the fixed boundary of 'star status' has rarely been challenged by problematic case studies which open up discussion around possible different modes of stardom, performance and labour status. As Paul McDonald (2000: 2) suggests, reading stars as images and relating those images to the social, ideological and historical conditions in which they emerged continues to dominate studies of stardom. Studies of 'the star' remain the pre-eminent way of approaching 'the actor', and work that continues to be influenced by the early approach of Richard Dyer in *Stars* (1979) implicitly positions 'stars' as separate from other actors through the significance they hold for an audience and through their economic value.

Although this approach recognizes the importance of both production and reception, the agency played by the consumer (the audience) is often foregrounded over the agency of the producer (Hollywood). This focus on consumption rather than production implicitly, but inherently, encourages the exclusion from film history of actors who achieved a certain level of fame or notoriety, or who even had a 'star' persona of sorts, but who tend not to be termed 'stars' because of the economic status they held within the industry in which they worked.[7] Analyses of cult, horror or minority 'stars', recognizable supporting actors, and performers who move up and down the filmmaking hierarchy throughout their careers – all of which apply to Lorre as much as his status as an émigré actor – prove to be challenging case studies according to theories of stardom, despite the ability of their 'star image' to be consumed by a prescribed 'subcultural', cult or niche audience. Approaches which only implicitly deal with economic contexts and the way in which the industry constructs star images for an audience to consume are rarely able to address this disparity directly.

More recent revisionist work has developed aspects of star discourse away from this earlier focus on the relationship between star personae and cultural identity, acknowledging the historical shifts in the nature of stardom within a cinematic industry which increasingly appears more flexible in its own definitions of stars, and in relation to the rise of new media forms and celebrity culture.[8] To some degree, this revision in light of developments within contemporary Hollywood and multimedia practices sidesteps a crucial historical issue pertaining to Hollywood stardom. Whilst the notion prevails that the star images of major figures from the classical Hollywood era were extra-textual, multi-medial, and able to support contradictory elements, these stars are still primarily considered in light of a singular star persona. Additionally, whilst work on contemporary stardom acknowledges the decreased significance of the cinematic product on the development of a star's persona, the relationship between film and image within examples of classical Hollywood stardom needs to be reconsidered.[9]

It is within studies of screen performance and acting that there is an explicit move to disentangle performative labour from star status and public image in order to evaluate an actor's significance.[10] The emphasis on 'acting' rather than 'stardom' has also opened up discourses away from the all-encompassing figure of the star, allowing some refocus towards supporting casts (and the process of casting in general). Analyses of screen performance have pursued a variety of aims: to prioritize alternative readings of highly recognizable screen work, to discuss existing acting methodologies and how these traditions work in conjunction with the cinematic apparatus in order to create a 'screen' performance, and to show that 'a reading of the uses of the voice and body can inform a larger understanding of any film and films in general' (McDonald 2004: 26). This type of research has confronted the notion that performance is resistant to analysis, and challenged certain critical perspectives which emphasize the ways in which a performance is created more by formal elements of filmmaking than by the actor him/herself.

Lorre's own performative strategies are a feature throughout examinations of his career – both within this book and in the essays referenced earlier – partly because of the well-documented professional and personal relationship with Brecht throughout his career. Many of Lorre's screen appearances appear to be highly visible and non-naturalistic, leading them to be read as self-reflexive articulations of resistance to his performative environment. For Gemünden, this resistance is linked to the experience of the exile in Hollywood's foreign cultural context. Throughout this book, a different path of resistance will be suggested – one that extends beyond discussions of the émigré in favour of broader Hollywood contexts. This draws upon Danae Clark's (1995: 70) argument that an articulation of, and resistance to, a capitalist system of production and exchange which encouraged consumers to ignore the presence of acting labour (such as Hollywood in the studio era), can be found with examples of screen performance through the way specific performers draw attention to the mechanics of screen acting (and therefore to their own labour) through their own chosen mode of performance.

The performative process shifts critical paradigms around the 'actor'. Clark's tentative discussion of performance is indicative of another: their role within economic and labour exchange. Increasingly, studies have moved away from seeing stars as images in order to emphasize that stars are 'workers' as well as 'stars'.[11] Whilst star studies construct stardom through a consideration of production, text and reception, the focus on consumption effectively aims to reconstruct the star as a mythic figure who becomes symbolic of particular ideologies which are reliant upon disguising (through the abstraction of the actor within a star persona) and then revealing (through the audience's desire for extra-textual knowledge) the 'reality' of the actor. The split between person/persona or reality/image places a particular emphasis on issues of authenticity, so that the consumer can find out what a star is really like. In doing so, the binary split also obscures the labour involved in the creation of the star; the performative labour of the actor, the other workers who help to construct that image of stardom, and the overall industrial and economic contexts in which performance and stardom are engineered. From this perspective, stars can be considered as a 'phenomenon of production' and the links between image, labour and capital can be considered.

Analyses of actors cannot help but identify the dual position that recognizable screen actors are caught between – as both labourers and objectified commodity images. Although a very general distinction, studies of stardom tend to examine the latter at the expense of the former, whereas screen performance studies tend to do the opposite. Barry King and Paul McDonald consider both elements equally and, most significantly, examine the relationship between the two elements, although both limit their discussion to concepts of stardom. Clark (1995) adapts this methodology to analyse the 'actor' rather than the 'actor-as-star'. Here, the emphasis is on how Hollywood studios managed both the labour and the image of the actors they employed, and of particular relevance to an understanding of Peter Lorre's career is the definitive split Clark proposes between labour and image. (This avoids issues surrounding an actor's 'real' identity – an identity whose authenticity is highly contentious.) The Hollywood studios maintained economic and political control over an increasingly fragmented acting profession through hierarchical divisions and employment strategies such as typecasting, and the construction of actors as commodified objects through the application of a particular image which was used to publicize or market the actor by the studios away from the cinema screen (ibid.: 23–24). As such, it is possible that certain personae were more closely aligned with an actor's marketable image than with their screen work. This demonstrates the problems associated with equating an actor wholly with their persona because of the way that their labour can be superseded by their dominant promotional image: a situation that, as will be explored in the following chapters, characterizes the life and career of Peter Lorre.

In order to achieve this, a detailed overview of Lorre's career is necessary. However, whilst this work takes its primary focus and structure from major periods within Lorre's chronology, it is by no means meant to represent a thorough biographical history of the actor.[12] The objective of my examination into the historical circumstances of the figure of Peter Lorre is less concerned with intimate biographical details and more with elements relating to the employment of certain types of performers that can be observed through an examination of the wider contexts that informed the outcomes of Lorre's career.

In doing so, within my work there has been an inevitable positioning of Lorre within the industrial context that most dominated his work; a move which is, to some degree, at odds with the existing critical perspectives about Lorre that focus upon issues raised by the actor's European identity and experiences. Throughout this book, I prioritize an understanding of Lorre's standing within Hollywood and, above all, purposefully define him as much as a Hollywood performer as a European émigré working in Hollywood. In addition to this overall focus on the American film industry and studio system, I also acknowledge specific elements of Lorre's formative experiences within the European stage and cinema. Whilst primarily attending to Lorre's place within a cinematic framework, I will also demonstrate that considering the film career of an actor, especially one from Hollywood's classical era, in isolation from the remaining media forms or performative arenas in which they either worked or were represented, is as problematic as a persona-based approach can be. As such, there is the recognition that transmedial contexts, as well as transnational contexts, can play a vital role within a film actor's career.

This book considers Lorre's career within a number of different contexts: in Hollywood and central Europe, onstage and on-screen, and as 'star' and as 'support'. It follows a chronological timeframe from his early stage roles in Austria and Germany during the 1920s and 1930s, to his final screen roles for the independent production company AIP in the 1960s. This timeframe covers virtually all of the classical Hollywood era, and certain industrial concerns form an important backdrop to, and influence upon, the outcome of Lorre's career.

Chapter 1 outlines the formative professional experiences of Lorre on the European stage during the 1920s and early 1930s, and considers a later film, *The Beast with Five Fingers* (1946), in light of that experimental stage training. Chapter 2 offers a close reading of Lorre's performance as the serial killer in Fritz Lang's *M* (1931), a role which is widely assumed to have defined the actor in terms of image and his later employment. It also explores the partnership between Lorre and Lang. Chapter 3 concentrates on Lorre's move to Hollywood and his employment as a leading actor between 1934 and 1941, with a focus upon the marketing strategies that were used to manage the actor's career during this time, and how these impacted upon perceptions of the actor's screen work. Chapter 4 deals with Lorre's position as a supporting actor, most notably at Warner Bros. during the 1940s, and outlines changes which occurred within his performative techniques in line with this 'reinvention'. Chapter 5 is an analysis of the only film he directed, *Der Verlorene*, within the context of his position as a returning émigré and as an exploration of how, through his roles as actor and director, the self-reflexive references to his German and Hollywood films act as a more objective filmmaking tool in the creation of political and social discourse. Chapter 6 examines Lorre's final screen roles of the 1950s and 1960s and his work within action/adventure films and horror films, and suggests that Lorre's final years are indicative of more than a 'face-maker' who resorted to a self-parodic performance style within his films. Finally, Chapter 7 considers how alternative Hollywood-based media and entertainment outlets, such as radio and caricatures, worked to create and perpetuate Lorre's public image away from the cinema screen.

Notes

1. Price appeared with Lorre in the films, *The Big Circus* (1959), *Tales of Terror* (1962), *The Raven* (1963) and *The Comedy of Terrors* (1964), and in two episodes of the (unaired) television series *Collector's Item* (1957).
2. Peter Lorre, Vincent Price, and others quoted in Stephen D. Youngkin, 2005: 449.
3. The name 'Peter Lorre' was suggested to Lázló Loewenstein by the Viennese psychodramatist, Jacob Moreno around 1922.
4. In one Hollywood film, *The Constant Nymph* (1943), which was based on a novel in which Lorre's character was Jewish, all traces of this ethnic identity were absent in the script.
5. However, as well as exploring this perspective, Jarvie also argues (within his discussion of predominantly American-born and conventional star figures) that because there were so few Jewish stars, this concealment was nullified.
6. Most famously, scenes of Lorre's performance in *M* were used within the Nazi propaganda film *Der ewige Jude (The Eternal Jew)* (1940) in order to suggest the degenerate nature of the Jewish race.
7. Both Ian Jarvie (2004) and Alan Lovell (2003) comment upon the limitations of conventional star discourse in this way.
8. John Ellis 1991; Paul McDonald 1998; Christine Geraghty 2000; Thomas Austin and Martin Barker 2003; Lucy Fischer and Marcia Landy 2004.
9. Through his analysis of Bette Davis, Martin Shingler (2006) implicitly suggests that established classical era stars need to be re-evaluated away from their all-encompassing star statuses in order to acknowledge that these performers could be equally as contentious, and support different perspectives pertaining to their career, as their more modern counterparts.
10. Naremore 1988; Alan Lovell and Peter Krämer 1999; Carole Zucker 1990; Cynthia Baron, Diane Carson and Frank Tomasulo 2004; Cynthia Baron and Sharon Marie Carnicke 2008.
11. Barry King 1987; Paul McDonald 2000; Adrienne L. McLean 2004.
12. For this, see Stephen D. Youngkin's definitive biography, *The Lost One: A Life of Peter Lorre.*

Chapter 1

LORRE AND THE EUROPEAN STAGE (1922–1931)

The initial part of this chapter will cover the non-cinematic aspects of Lorre's work, through his theatrical career (antecedent to his on-screen fame) in the experimental atmosphere of the theatres of central Europe throughout the 1920s and early 1930s, concentrating on the two figures of Bertolt Brecht and Jacob Levi Moreno – prior to the release of *M* (1931). An analysis of the developmental stages of Lorre's acting career and the potential recognition of a dominant non-naturalistic performative style preferred by the actor also enables a more balanced interpretation of his cinematic labour and experiences. The latter part of the chapter will then return to focus on film, momentarily disrupting the overall chronological structure of this book, in order to consider how Lorre's experiences in European theatre might be discerned within his American screen work, using *The Beast with Five Fingers* (1946): a performance which has variously been dismissed as unskilled, incoherent and repetitive in comparison to Lorre's more noted film appearances.

Appraisals of Lorre often underplay the value to be found in Hollywood performances such as the one in *The Beast with Five Fingers*. Instead, the performative value identified around Lorre is more firmly associated with products of European art traditions: expressionistic Weimar cinema such as *M*, and the German stage of the same period, especially productions associated with Bertolt Brecht. The figure of Brecht plays a major role when considering the performance history of Peter Lorre. It is relatively common to find references to Brecht within critical literature on Lorre, and there are two reasons for this underlying presence. Firstly, the two men had a close working relationship from 1929 onwards which culminated in a notorious production of Brecht's play *Mann ist Mann* (Man Equals Man) in 1931, and their friendship continued during their exile in Hollywood (until Brecht's return to Berlin in 1948) in spite of Brecht's apparent disdain for Lorre's American film work. Secondly, there is the significant place that Brecht occupies within twentieth-century culture and the depth of critical work devoted to examining his works and theories. Not only does the immense research conducted on Brecht's early works and his position as an exile reveal much about Lorre (by proxy), but the cultural legitimacy of Brecht as a subject also influences perceptions about Lorre as a potentially legitimate subject for serious scholarly study.

The two essays, Gerd Gemünden's 'From "Mr M" to "Mr Murder"' (2003) and Christopher McCullough's 'Peter Lorre (and his friend Bert Brecht)' (2004), both begin by invoking Brecht. In particular, they cite a poem written by Brecht and widely assumed to be about Lorre, entitled 'Der Sumpf' (The Swamp), in order to highlight the disparaging attitude of the playwright to Lorre's Hollywood work.[1] Both works aim to legitimize studies of Lorre by revealing the inherent complexities to be found in his otherwise misunderstood Hollywood performances via Lorre's own established European theatrical heritage. This is achieved by identifying how experimental techniques that were associated with Brechtian practice, such as duality or alienation, were echoed in the way that Lorre worked in Hollywood, and suggesting how subsequent screen performances can be read as allegories of exile where political and social situations are revealed. In both instances, Brecht provides an appropriately scholarly framework with which to explore the career of the screen actor.

However, it is not useful or accurate to wholly reduce Lorre's career to a direct application of Brechtian theories. To demonstrate that Lorre's work with Brecht constituted just one aspect within a ten-year period of important theatrical experimentation which saw Lorre collaborate with other significant innovators and producers, as well as establish himself as a critically rated stage performer, I will highlight Lorre's main achievements and explore his professional relationship with a second figure – Jacob Levi Moreno. Moreno was a social psychiatrist whose work was founded upon the use of group-based dramatic reconstruction and who employed Lorre's services as an actor between 1922 and 1924; in other words, at least five years before the actor met Brecht.

Jacob Levi Moreno, the Stegreiftheater and 'Psychodrama': 1922–1924

Jacob Levi Moreno (1889–1974) was a noted figure in twentieth-century social psychiatry, and was a pioneer of social psychological therapies and quantitative methodologies, including 'psychodrama', early forms of group psychotherapy, and 'sociometry'. With the financial support of his younger brother, William, Moreno first began to practise his theories of psychodrama whilst living in Vienna in the late 1910s and early 1920s, observing both the aftermath of the First World War and the interactions of children in public groups. In 1925, his emigration to the United States gave him the opportunity to combine his own teaching and research with practical counselling experience in an appropriate setting. In its early stages, the practice of psychodrama relied heavily on dramatic performance and reconstruction. In keeping with this, Moreno initially experimented with ideas of 'drama-as-therapy' and continued to maintain his career as a therapist. However, in 1922 he founded a theatrical group called the Stegreiftheater (Theatre of Spontaneity), based in Vienna. It gave gifted and unconventional actors, including Lorre, the opportunity to find employment on the stage.

In the same year, Lorre was introduced to Moreno by William, who had encountered the impoverished young would-be-actor within the city's coffee-house society. Moreno's bohemian theatrical group gave Lorre his first professional experiences of acting. As outlined by Stephen D. Youngkin (2005: 16), Moreno was drawn to the maverick performer who had 'a curious smile and an unforgettable face', just as Lorre appeared to find solace with the 'social misfits, malcontents and psychological rebels', and the natural yet unorthodox actors who were also involved in the theatre. Lorre later remembered his time with Moreno as an 'ideal school of acting' as it allowed him to develop his own natural talent through innovative practical means rather than through conventional teaching methods (ibid.: 17). It was also during this period of employment with the Stegreiftheater that, on the advice of Moreno, the young man who was born László Loewenstein took the stage name 'Peter Lorre' (ibid.: 19).[2]

The innovative nature of Moreno's theatre existed on two fronts. Firstly from a psychiatric perspective, Moreno wanted to expand his own style of therapy using group-based practical performative methodologies. Secondly, he wanted to confront what he perceived to be the stale and degraded Viennese theatre, believing his methods which favoured impromptu acting would restore a sense of immediacy, vitality and imagination to the dramatic form. The narratives of the Stegreiftheater's shows were constructed through improvizations or suggestions from the audiences, and were often informed by news stories or issues pertaining to the modern urban atmosphere. This was in keeping with Moreno's aesthetic desire to challenge theatrical traditions through the creation of an interactive theatre, where the division between spectator and actor was removed and both became involved in the construction of the drama. He perceived that this mode of performance and consumption might enable the theatre to be seen as a democratic force for social change and debate. Through the creation of this type of interactive relationship, Moreno hoped to be able to explore the shared values or prejudices of a particular social group made up from both audience members and the Stegreiftheater's actors.

Fundamental to Moreno's ideas about ways in which to combine therapy and performance was the role played by the individual within a group setting. Many of the onstage performances and rehearsal exercises were constructed around different forms of this type of social interaction. Youngkin highlights that Lorre was particularly adept at this mode of performance and he cites instances where Lorre acted as an individual catalyst whose improvizations could provoke certain 'healing reactions' in those who shared the stage with him. Through a series of interviews with Moreno's widow, Youngkin (2005: 18) also makes a connection between Lorre's experiences with the Stegreiftheater and a 'psychological' mode of performance where the actor learnt 'to be in the core of the role … [to] swap skins with another's feelings and being'. This description is reminiscent of descriptions of naturalistic modes of performance (particularly those derived from the writings of Constantin Stanislavsky), which aim to subsume the identity of the actor behind the role in order to present the 'psychological truth' of the character.

Whilst this may be an accurate summation of the desired outcome of a psychodramatic performance – whereby an audience, comprising both performers and spectators, is able to share an otherwise unfamiliar psychology or behaviour (as directed by one or more individual's performance) – it is perhaps an oversimplification both of the way that Moreno trained and directed his actors, at least in the early stages of his career as a psychodramatist when therapy was explicitly combined with professional performance, and of Lorre's own style, as evidenced by the later work of the actor. Considering the techniques employed by Moreno (particularly in the context of how they were subsequently defined and utilized within psychodramatic practices), one can determine a careful strategy which aimed to train the actor through a variety of subjective and objective exercises, during which the performers engaged with, and also remained distant from, their roles. Moreno did not merely advocate an intense understanding of one particular character on the part of the actor, as this was not a technique which lent itself successfully to social understanding or group-based psychiatric practices. Instead his aim was to focus on individual growth in and by the group. Therefore, even at this early stage in his practical research, Moreno encouraged the development of diagnostic ability and the capacity for observation and identification between all participants within a group.

Moreno used a series of exercises in order to prepare his actors for onstage performances, with the aim of encouraging his actors to comprehend contrasting and complex perspectives. Although there is no direct connection between the two (apart from the figure of Lorre), some of the exercises presaged Brecht's theories of epic theatre, particularly methods which broke down linear time into 'moments' and the use of non-verbal gestures to express abstract concepts. Specific psychodramatic rehearsal practices were later incorporated into Moreno's therapeutic teachings, and the rehearsal exercises contemporary to Lorre's involvement in the Stegreiftheater were subsequently termed 'role reversal', 'doubling' and 'mirroring' within psychiatric (rather than theatrical) applications of psychodrama. In each case, the focus of the various exercises was to foster a deep understanding of the social processes at work within their (or their character's) lives through the presentation of alternative perspectives, and also to encourage an accurate psychological understanding of a character by the actor involved in the performance whilst purposefully creating an objective awareness of performance techniques and character by having other figures double, mimic or comment upon that performance.[3] Although these tactics are primarily associated with therapeutic practice, they were developed out of the Moreno's theatrical experiment at the Stegreiftheater and therefore enable an insight (albeit a limited one) into the types of training available to Lorre during this period.

Whilst Moreno's backstage techniques appear closely regimented in order to maintain both a subjective and objective mode of performance on the part of his actors, the onstage performances were much less rigidly monitored. Taking their cues from improvization and suggestion allowed the shows to live up to the troupe's prescribed 'spontaneous' image, and it was in this liberating atmosphere that Lorre flourished. The few recorded examples of Lorre's roles and performances reveal that the actor relished the challenge posed by the remit of the theatre which sought to combine the therapeutic value of acting out conflicts in a public sphere with entertaining characterizations and sketches. Moreno (1946: 4) outlined one such conflict, which Youngkin (2005: 17–19) has since recorded as involving Lorre, whereby the personal psychological fears of one actress were aided by the performance of a scenario in which an 'apache' (Lorre) attacked and murdered the actress, allowing her to confront her problems onstage.

This scene was specifically suggested and directed by Moreno, but there are less psychologically-motivated (and less brutal) examples which involved Lorre taking more responsibility for the direction of his own performance. It should be noted that this independence was a tactic employed by Lorre throughout his career in Hollywood, and many established directors, including John Huston, Frank Capra, Jean Negulesco and Roger Corman, have explicitly stated that they did not influence the actor's performance during their collaborations.[4] As Capra described, in relation to Lorre's work on *Arsenic and Old Lace* (1944): '[Lorre] was a remarkable innovator … a man who built his part. You're so grateful to him that his part just grows because he is making it into a real character. That is acting before your eyes!' (Youngkin 2005: 200).

During his time at the Stegreiftheater, two instances reveal how Lorre took control over his own performances, partly in the way he developed his sketches in order to offer his performance as a spectacle that was expressly designed to 'entertain' rather than 'heal'. In addition, they also illustrate that he strove to create a certain relationship between himself (as an 'actor' rather than as a 'character') and his audience by stepping outside of a particular narrative context to facilitate a certain form of engagement with his audience.

> One of [Lorre's] best roles was that of a wealthy miser who lived, however, in abject poverty and whose sole reason for living was to count his money, neatly stacking his coins and from time to time letting them run through his hands as if they were water. His delight in this was captivatingly infectious. (Youngkin 2005: 17)

> Peter Lorre performed in an act of his own, soon to become a favourite of the audience – 'How to catch a Louse'. This sketch, in addition to allowing Peter Lorre to make fun of people in the audience may have had a direct relationship to his original name, Ladislaus Löwenstein. (Marineau 1989: 72)

Even in these brief examples, a performance style that has been influenced by both subjective and objective perspective training can be discerned. There is an attempt to present a meaningful and colourful characterization (particularly in the first example), but there is also evidence that the relationship Lorre maintained with his audience seemed to occur through the acknowledgement of his status as a 'performer' as well as through the presentation of his 'character'. He appeared to use a self-reflexive mode of performance; commenting on his own circumstances through the pun on his name or signalling that the 'entertainment' should be found in how he constructed the role (such as his use of the coins as a prop) rather than in the character itself. It is not known to what extent these limited examples are indicative of all of Lorre's performances for the Stegreiftheater, but it remains significant that these are suggested to be the most memorable or popular, and that they clearly demonstrate a performance style that is repeated throughout Lorre's later screen work.

Lorre's time in Moreno's experimental theatre group was also profitable because it enabled him to become a professional actor and to establish himself as a visible presence within the Viennese theatrical environment. More than this, his popularity allowed him to continue his career plans and to expand his horizons. Lorre left the Stegreiftheater in 1924, along with many of the other members of the troupe. René Marineau discusses the break-up of the Stegreiftheater in relation to Moreno's own career as, by 1924, the psychodramatist had decided to return his focus to that of psychological therapy instead of theatrical innovation (Marineau 1989: 76). This shift jarred with many of his actors who were unwilling to use their own lives as psychiatric 'props' for Moreno's continuing exploration of social psychological relations, and many resigned soon after the changes were implemented.

Whilst it would be fitting to believe that Lorre shared this artistic stance regarding a necessary level of objectivity within performance, especially given the characteristics of his own acting style, the explanation offered by Youngkin (2005: 19) as to why he left the Stegreiftheater is far more likely: that a combination of ambition and the need to earn more money inspired Lorre to seek new employment. Between 1924 and 1926, Lorre worked in repertory theatre in Breslau and Zurich, before returning to Vienna between 1926 and 1929. In doing so, he gained vast experience and met with varying degrees of success. In March 1929, Lorre made a permanent move to Berlin, where, almost immediately, he auditioned at the Theater am Schiffbauerdamm for Bertolt Brecht.

Bertolt Brecht, the Theater am Schiffbauerdamm and 'Epic Theatre': 1929–1931

The particular relationship that Lorre had with Brecht (both on a professional and personal basis) is a complex one: Lorre starred in a number of theatrical productions at Brecht's Theater am Schiffbauerdamm in the early 1930s, and they remained close friends during their exile in the United States until Brecht returned to Germany in the late 1940s. My focus here is restricted to only one aspect of their lives together: the early theories of 'epic theatre' which were put into practice during the most widely discussed of their theatrical collaborations, the 'epic' production of *Mann ist Mann* in 1931.

In 1928, Brecht had made a spectacular impact on the theatre of Berlin with his production of *Die Dreigroschenoper* (The Threepenny Opera), and was subsequently seen as a revolutionary theatrical force. One of the ways in which he strove to achieve this potential for revolution was to favour a style and technique which sought to politicize the theatre. This coincided with a general resurgence of politics within the German theatre due to the increasingly precarious political and economic state of the country. Brecht moved towards a Marxist/Communist perspective regarding both subject matter and modes of representation. In direct contrast to Moreno, Brecht wanted to communicate a viewpoint that confronted social or historical conditions rather than psychological conditions, and it was in accordance with this agenda that he developed his theories of epic theatre between the late 1920s and early 1930s.

Despite these very different objectives, it is possible to see certain parallels between the theatrical practices of Brecht and Moreno. They both perceived their theatrical experiments to be a challenge to the dominant mainstream theatrical form: Moreno sought to restore vitality to the staid Viennese theatre, and many of Brecht's theories were intended to be an antithesis to Aristotelian drama or Stanislavskian performance which aimed to create an illusion of reality for the audience.[5] Both innovators attempted to construct an alternative type of relationship between performer and audience that rejected the passivity of conventional realist performance. Both men perceived that the theatre could be revealed as a site for potential social change through an increasingly interactive relationship between actor and spectator (although in very different ways). In addition to this, both of them attempted to develop a performance style which combined subjective and objective elements regarding methods of characterization.

Lorre successfully auditioned for Brecht at the Theater am Schiffbauerdamm for a role in the play *Pioniere in Ingolstadt* (Engineers in Ingolstadt), written by Marieluise Fleisser and directed by Jakob Geis, in 1929. During the following three years, Lorre was not exclusively employed by Brecht's company, and he worked for, amongst others, Karl Heinz Martin in his Volksbühne (People's Theatre) company. It was here that the actor achieved his most notable critical and commercial successes, including performances in Büchner's *Dantons Tod* (Danton's Death) and Wedekind's *Frühlings Erwachen* (Spring's Awakening) – the role that led to Fritz Lang casting him in *M*.

Despite his increasing fame away from the Theater am Schiffbauerdamm, Lorre remained closely associated with Brecht's work from this period. This was partly due to the amount of critical literature written about *Mann ist Mann* (both contemporaneous with and subsequent to the play's opening), and to the collaborative nature of Brecht's interaction with the actors and artists he particularly rated. Brecht (1968: 102) generally described the relationship he fostered with his performers as 'uninterrupted collaboration', whereby the playwright 'could influence and be influenced' during the rehearsal process. Both John Willett and Robert Gordon make an explicit link between Brecht's development of epic theatre and the interactive relationship created between playwright and performer. Willett (1988: 155) terms this 'collective' interaction, and Gordon (2006: 251) describes the group of actors who worked with Brecht during these years (including Lorre, Helene Weigel, Lotte Lenya and Oscar Homolka) as 'collaborators in the creation of a new mode of acting'. Eric Bentley (Youngkin 2005: 45) and Christopher McCullough (2004: 167) both cite Lorre as having an individual and often empirical influence on Brecht's performative theories at this time in terms of helping the playwright focus his ideas about the particular acting style and techniques required for epic theatre to be successful in its political objectives.

Brecht's theories of epic theatre and epic performance were put into practice in 1931 at the Theater am Schiffbauerdamm with *Mann ist Mann* – a play written by Brecht which had first been performed during the 1920s. The production was directed by Brecht and starred Lorre in the lead role of Galy Gay. (Lorre would have begun rehearsing the role at the same time as he was shooting *M*.) The plot concerned the attempts of a group of soldiers in British-occupied India to trick an Irish porter, Galy Gay, into becoming a replacement for a missing member of their company, Jeriah Jip. In order to convince Galy Gay that he is Jip, the soldiers involve him in the auction of a fake elephant, have him arrested for selling army property and sentence him to death. They stage a mock execution and on finding himself 'alive', Galy Gay happily assumes the identity of Jip; and the harmless little man is transformed into a ruthless fighting machine.

From a theoretical and practical perspective, Lorre was a performer who was especially suited to the concept of epic acting. Certain features of the epic style are reminiscent of Lorre's work with Moreno and with his later achievements on-screen. According to Brecht's theories, the primary function of epic theatre was to offer a critique of capitalist society through dramatic practice. This would be achieved by working against the creation of an illusion of reality (which was central to Aristotelian, realist and naturalist drama) by promoting a sense of distance between what was being presented and the spectator, often described as 'Verfremdung', 'Entfremdung' or an 'alienation effect'. This relationship was seen to encourage critical awareness rather than impassive consumption on the part of the viewer, as it would demonstrate that social conditions and actions were not natural or inevitable and therefore could be changed. As described by Brecht's contemporary, Walter Benjamin (1973: 2–4), epic theatre attempted to transform the audience from 'a collection of hypnotized test subjects' into a 'theatre full of experts'. Whilst this could be conveyed through the script or *mise-en-scène* of the play (for example, the use of audio-visual technology), central to the success of epic theatre was a carefully rehearsed form of non-naturalistic performance.

Epic acting required actors to employ a complex performance style which utilized different techniques in order to achieve certain effects at specific moments throughout the play. An ideal epic actor would possess a strong personality and distinct physicality which would remain visible throughout their performance as the character. They would use a demonstrative style whereby they presented themselves as an actor onstage who 'showed' the character to the audience, rather than attempting to 'become' the character at the expense of their own identity. Actors would move between subjective and objective representations, therefore maintaining both a sense of empathy and distance in relation to their character. This multi-layered perspective allowed the actor to step away from the role at various moments in order to comment upon the unfolding social or political conditions and choices being shown onstage. In turn, this would create a three-way relationship between the actor, the character and the spectator, that rejected (what, in the early 1930s, Brecht believed to be) Stanislavskian notions of identification in favour of an explicit Marxist agenda.

In order for the actor to avoid being identified with their character, epic actors were instructed to use self-reflexive and often contradictory techniques which broke up otherwise coherent (and realistic) performances to create the alienation effect desired by Brecht. One of the most effective of these techniques (and one which Brecht continued to employ throughout his career even after he moved away from the somewhat limiting concepts of epic theatre) was that of 'gestus'. Gestus is a piece of physical action that conveys social meaning; a gesture performed in conjunction with an understanding of the social and historical contexts which formed that gesture. An actor's use of gestus externalized the emotions of the characters and explicitly communicated the unconscious social attitudes that the characters adopted towards each other. Conventions of realism and coherent individual psychological representation were further compromised through the way that the action was split up into various episodes or 'moments' in order to emphasize the inherent contradictions of a character throughout a specific narrative trajectory. This allowed the actor to illustrate behaviour rather than to speculate about or reveal internal psychological motivations.

The stylized acting techniques of gestus and episodic acting were not the only elements that contributed to the construction of an epic performance, but they were one way of ensuring that the performance was not based upon emotional or psychological theories and that the alienation effect was achieved. More important than a rigid performative technique was how the relationship between actor and spectator was managed within an epic performance. By briefly isolating key performative features of this methodological style (away from its more political agenda), one can identify certain characteristics that link directly to Lorre's own acting experiences, both during this period (in his appearance in *Mann ist Mann*), and in a number of his subsequent screen performances.

Epic acting is inherently self-reflexive – a phrase that can also be used to describe particular aspects of Lorre's own work. Epic performance explicitly foregrounds the medium that is being used: the success of the performance relies upon the audience realizing that they are watching an actor in a theatre demonstrating a character. This level of awareness must also serve a purpose, and the performer must also be seen to communicate something within their performance other than mere reflexivity. For Brecht, this communication was a political one. In the instance of Lorre's self-reflexive screen performances, the communication can be interpreted (amongst other things) as a commentary on exilic status or on his position within industrial filmmaking hierarchies. This exchange ensures that a tacit dialogue is created between the performer and the spectator, where the audience identifies with the actor, not the role.

A relationship based upon self-reflexive communication and consumption within epic acting suggests notions of 'entertainment' and 'pleasure' that are removed from the more passive relationship created by the illusion of reality, central to realist or naturalistic representation, in which the performer is effectively 'hidden'. Brecht recognized that a political agenda could be communicated and the potential for subversion was increased when the audience was actively engaged in a way that provided a sense of 'pleasure' and 'fun' as in the use of parody. *Mann ist Mann* was described by Brecht as a comedy, and as McCullough (2004: 170) argues, much of the action can be seen as a series of pratfalls reminiscent of Charlie Chaplin's film performances. Brecht himself outlined his view that the pleasure of epic performance should lie in the dual process of showing and recognizing, and in the creation of a particular form of communication between audience and actor (quoted in Benjamin 1973: 12–13).

The potential for this knowingly reflexive and purposefully playful type of exchange between performer and viewer about the conditions in which a performance was constructed can be seen in many examples of Lorre's screen work, albeit with a much less explicit politicized agenda than Brecht's, and perhaps can most obviously be observed in the films Lorre made for Warner Bros. in the 1940s and American International Pictures in the 1960s.

After a lengthy rehearsal period, during which many of the potentially revolutionary theories discussed above were worked out in direct relation to the staging of the play, *Mann ist Mann* opened in February 1931. However, the new staging tactics met with much bemusement and a disastrous reception, closing after only five performances. Much of the criticism was directed at the performers and the unusual acting style, which prompted Brecht to publish a detailed response to his critics in the *Berliner Börsen Courier* on 8 March 1931 in an article entitled 'The Question of Criteria for Judging Acting'. This written response informs much of the academic discussion about the play itself and on Brecht's theories of epic theatre in general.

The staging and performances were highly original and controversial. In order to make the soldiers appear grotesque and unfamiliar, the actors were placed on high stilts and wore padded clothes, and their faces obscured with partial masks. The acting was also uniformly stylized, but most explicitly in the way that Lorre's central performance as Galy Gay was constructed using 'gestic' techniques and episodic acting. The character's development was split into four distinct episodes which all employed different 'masks', described by Brecht as: '[T]he packer's face, up to the trial; the "natural" face, up to his awakening after being shot; the "blank page", up to his reassembly after the funeral speech; [and] finally the soldier's face.' (Brecht 1931 in Willet and Manheim 1979b).

To emphasize the progression of these stages, Lorre delivered his words in a stilted and virtually monotone manner that attempted to illustrate the contradictory nature of Galy Gay/Jeriah Jip throughout the play. During the third phase, Lorre turned from the audience to dip his hands in chalk and whiten his face. He then dramatically confronted the audience with

Figure 1.1 Peter Lorre (second from left) in *Mann ist Mann* (1931). Photo: akg-images.

this new identity. This physically demonstrated both his fear of the situation and his new 'blank' identity, without the use of a psychologically-motivated transformation. The change from Galy Gay to Jeriah Jip was further emphasized by re-costuming Galy Gay in military garb and arming him (literally) to the teeth, and the repetition of a roll-call sequence where the differences in Lorre's two performances as 'Jip' became gestic, as in the latter sequence the character took on the identity of a soldier, rather than that of a packer pretending to be a soldier.

Despite the closeness with which the onstage performance, particularly Lorre's, followed Brecht's early theories of epic theatre, the experiment was not a popular one with Berlin's theatregoers. Critics bemoaned the lack of engagement and the emotionally restrained and contradictory performances. Two major complaints were directed at Lorre that Brecht directly responded to in his article: namely, '[Lorre's] habit of not speaking his meaning clearly, and the suggestion that he acted in nothing but episodes' (ibid.: 104). Brecht wrote that Lorre correctly and 'magnificently' conveyed the theories behind epic theatre in a practical setting; he was purposefully presenting the character in an episodic and incoherent manner in order to emphasize the changing nature of social relations, and the use of a monotonous delivery style resisted the creation of an empathetic relationship between character and spectator.

In addition to this contemporary response to the 1931 staging of *Mann ist Mann*, there has been a trend in more modern critical literature on Brecht to account for the failure of the experimental production through the presence of conflicting performative techniques preferred by Brecht and Lorre, where Brecht's theoretical objectives proved too difficult for an actor with Lorre's particular performative traits to effectively transcribe into dramatic form. Margaret Eddershaw (1996: 26) writes that Lorre's 'instinctive way of performing was more realistic [and] more emotional' than was required by the production, but that this 'realist' technique quickly led to Lorre's success within the medium of cinema. Michael Patterson cites Brecht's later success in the United States and post-war Berlin as evidence that the theories of epic theatre could be used in performance to great effect, but that Lorre did not have the skill or acumen to achieve this in 1931. More suited to this practice was Brecht's long-time collaborator (and wife) Helene Weigel, and Patterson compares the two actors, writing that 'Weigel knew better [than Lorre] how to maintain the interest of the audience without resorting to an acting display, and her cool, intelligent and sensitive style was to help Brecht ... to go beyond the failed experiment of *Mann ist Mann*' (Patterson 1981: 181).

Arguments such as these construct Lorre as an actor who was naturalistic in style, emotional in motivation and engagement, and relatively unskilled – at least in regard to performances based upon contrivance or artifice. By defining Lorre according to notions of naturalism or realism he is aligned with the dominant style of Hollywood filmmaking and performance. Whilst Lorre's screen work had a foundation in naturalistic practice, it is also important to recognize that it would have been necessary for Lorre to conform to a certain degree to this mode in order for him to maintain his employability within a Hollywood system that was reliant upon this aesthetic, regardless of his own preferred performative style.

In contrast, it is my contention that Lorre utilized naturalistic and non-naturalistic elements within his screen performances. Acknowledging this can alter readings of specific performative decisions in evidence within the actor's work. For the moment, it is only relevant to state that it is inaccurate to characterize Lorre merely as a naturalistic or instinctive actor, either before his employment at the Theater am Schiffbauerdamm or after his collaborations with Brecht. Indeed many of the performative principles developed for the production of *Mann ist Mann* were adapted within his later roles.[6]

Theatrical Training and Pluralistic Performance Style in Mainstream Hollywood: *The Beast with Five Fingers* (1946)

Lorre's theatrical past and his work within studio era Hollywood cinema can be usefully contrasted in order to highlight the ways in which the actor's screen performances can be read as experiments that made use of his non-naturalistic training within a naturalistic system. My example here is *The Beast with Five Fingers* (1946). McCullough (2004: 172) has dismissed the film as 'a horror film … of little note', but nonetheless it remains a film that contains a purposely complex and self-reflexive series of representations that pertain to Peter Lorre, both as a working performer and as a persona constructed in relation to that actor.

Superficially, *The Beast with Five Fingers* perhaps conforms most readily to the prescribed image associated with Peter Lorre: a 'horror icon' associated with psychotic or monstrous behaviour, often with murderous consequences. The film's narrative is constructed from conventional horror tropes: the sudden death of Francis Ingram (Victor Francen), a temperamental pianist, throws a gothic Italian household into chaos as the house guests and relatives convene to squabble over his fortune. Soon it becomes apparent that the house is being haunted by the dead pianist as ghostly music is heard during the nights, amid sightings of a disembodied hand on the piano. Strange deaths occur, the superstitious peasant staff abandon the house, and it seems likely that a malevolent and supernatural force is threatening the safety of the remaining house guests. As the story progresses, it is revealed that Lorre's character, Hilary, is the real danger. In fear of his financial security, he has descended into pathological insanity and has convinced the house of the mysterious hand's existence. He dismembered Ingram's body, rigged the piano to play by itself, killed one house guest and violently attacked another. In the end, Hilary is so consumed by this fantastical situation that he himself dies, convinced that the hand is strangling him.

Given the resonance between the narrative and characterization present in this film and the corresponding extra-filmic persona of Lorre, it seems surprising that *The Beast with Five Fingers* is not one of Lorre's most iconographic films, especially considering the absence of conventional horror motifs from the majority of Lorre's Hollywood films. One possible reason for this is down to the performative choices made by Lorre as Hilary, in collaboration with the director, Robert Florey.[7] Lorre's performance appears to be simplistic in the way his character is revealed to be a tormented and insane man, but when considered within the context of his career – including his early theatrical experiences – it lends itself to a more pluralistic definition which further complicates the way that the film seeks to engage with its perceived audience.

It is possible to read Lorre's performance as Hilary in a number of different ways. Raymond Valinoti Jr (2005: 85) considers it to be a particularly successful appropriation of naturalistic and psychologically-motivated techniques within a melodramatic genre, writing that 'Lorre imbues his role with an intensity and a haunting vulnerability … Thanks to Lorre's acting skill and magnetism, his character's descent into madness is completely believable'. However, in comparison with many of Lorre's other performances and in relation to his public image, the psychological 'believability' of Hilary is compromised to a large degree.

Instead, the performance can be defined as an amalgamation of Lorre's non-naturalistic performative techniques. Here, Lorre repeats certain performative mannerisms that he developed throughout his career, such as vocal stylization and a deliberate pacing, in combination with a style that seems to directly reference either characteristics of his own extra-filmic persona or his identity as an actor, rather than focusing on a method that supports one coherent characterization. Lorre uses a dualistic, often histrionic, acting style whereby a superficially calm exterior suddenly gives way to violence; and he juxtaposes soft speech patterns with explosive outbursts. Additionally, Lorre's physical representation of Hilary appears to have much in common with his own negative description of acting as 'face-making', as he relies upon increasingly extreme facial contortions, and on the movement between an impassively blank, virtually mask-like, countenance and grotesque expressions, in order to signal Hilary's madness.

Throughout, Lorre is aided by the equally referential modes of formal representation used by Florey. The director revels in depicting Hilary's increasingly psychotic behaviour through stylistic techniques which disrupt the otherwise naturalistic aesthetic. Lorre is often isolated from the main group within shot compositions, or is shown in unmotivated cut-away shots which jar with the way the on-screen action is developed linearly. As it progresses, the style of the film becomes more explicitly expressionistic, and the representation of Hilary increasingly uses techniques associated with Weimar cinema, such as the presence of low-key lighting and the use of low or unusual camera angles to photograph the character. Additionally,

Hilary's modernistic black costume serves to highlight the unnatural bright white countenance of his face in certain sequences, visually cueing the viewer to his more 'monstrous' characteristics. The formal methods used by Florey act as alienating techniques similar to those used within Brecht's theatre, and the decision to costume and photograph Lorre in a certain way could seen as a reference to the actor's performance in *Mann ist Mann*. In certain sequences, Hilary's blank white face corresponds to the white mask used by Lorre in Brecht's play.

The combination of these non-naturalistic performative and formal techniques lend themselves to a reading of Lorre's acting as self-reflexive in a number of ways. It can be discussed in terms of an apathetic performance by the actor, whereby he merely repeated certain performative tricks that he had come to rely upon (and that signified a typical 'Peter Lorre' performance), such as pulling faces and the sudden juxtaposition between a soft voice and a raised voice, rather than taking any particular care over the individual characterization of Hilary. Lorre's performance can be seen as a form of parody, which makes reference to his extra-filmic persona and performative style in order to either, on the one hand, subvert and therefore ridicule the more melodramatic genre conventions of the film itself, or on the other, to ensure that the film maintained his marketability as an actor by conforming to public associations of Peter Lorre: a stereotypical image of the actor.

Either way, this level of self-reflexivity creates a particularly incoherent characterization as the realistic development of Hilary is interrupted by the sudden stylized shifts in performance which make explicit references to the actor's work and/or his extra-filmic persona. For example, during a scene where Hilary tells Ingram that the musician's beloved nurse is in love with another man, Hilary widens his eyes as he reveals the couple's whereabouts – a physical tactic the actor often employed when his character revealed important information. Additionally, Hilary swiftly descends into a violent and hysterical state as he describes how he saw the couple kissing, which is in keeping with the sexual inadequacy or immaturity that formed a key component of his persona (usually characterized as a perversion of some kind).

In addition to these potential means of analysing Lorre's performance as Hilary, it is also possible to view it in the context of his theatrical histories, especially in relation to his work with Brecht and epic theatre. Lorre's acting is reliant upon the repetition of a series of alternating mannerisms or expressions throughout the film, often at the expense of a psychological exploration of Hilary's motivations. As such, rather than merely 'making faces', Lorre characterizes Hilary through an episodic structure which purposefully uses a juxtapositional style to depict the contradictory nature of the character. In doing this, Lorre creates a sense of distance between the spectator and the character, and this technique has its foundations in the theories of epic theatre. Despite the emotional journey that Hilary undergoes, he remains a deliberately unengaging character because of the overly-demonstrative and disjointed method that Lorre uses to present him. This is supported by Florey's formal methods of alienation which reference techniques used in both expressionist cinema and epic theatre.

Whilst it is possible to see *The Beast with Five Fingers* as an epic production in some ways, it would be incorrect to characterize the text, or Lorre's performance within it, as wholly conforming to 'Brechtian' theories per se. Although Lorre's performance makes reference to epic practices, the way in which Lorre uses these techniques means that the explicit Marxist agenda associated with the narrative, style and staging of a number of Brecht's plays is not a prevalent feature. Nevertheless, an implicit political focus to the actor's performance can be discussed. Instead of foregrounding a wider sense of ideological agency for the spectator, Lorre's performance serves to foreground the individual agency of the actor. By implication, this subtle emphasis on the position of the actor rather than the character can also be interpreted as having a political consequence, because in doing so it highlights performance as a labour process and therefore the actor's place within the capitalist system of production in which that process occurs (Hollywood).

In addition to this, Lorre's performance as Hilary can be characterized as a pluralistic rather than a specifically Brechtian performance. His performance contains elements of experimental theatrical practice, parodical or self-reflexive strategies pertaining to Lorre as an individual performer, and even includes moments of exaggerated melodrama which prioritize action and narrative over character or actor (such as the scene where Hilary literally fights with the disembodied hand, in spite of the impossibility of this situation through the subsequent revelation that this is an imagined moment). As well as these more purposefully playful examples of performative choices, it also contains elements of realist performance, partly in order to conform to the naturalistic practices of Hollywood filmmaking in general, which explains why Valinoti Jr can describe Lorre's acting as 'believable'. In this film, and throughout his career, Lorre constructed his performances from a variety of naturalistic and non-naturalistic acting methodologies. Whilst he certainly used Brechtian practices at various moments, it is problematic to wholly define him as a Brechtian actor working in Hollywood.

Lorre's use of a pluralistic performance style, whilst indicative of the complex nature of his screen acting, is not always a successful strategy. In *The Beast with Five Fingers*, the presence of these various performative styles and strategies results in an incoherent and inconsistent performance which seeks to prevent an emotional engagement with the character for various reasons. Therefore, whilst at a superficial level the character of Hilary appears to conform closely to the prescribed public image of Peter Lorre, the incoherencies at the level of performance mean that the role has never been considered emblematically metonymic of Lorre's film career. Instead of being *the* representative or iconographic role of Lorre's career in terms of the way it closely adheres to the actor's extra-filmic persona, the role becomes most significant because it reveals issues, that are central to this book, such as the way in which Lorre was able to use experimental theatrical techniques within his cinematic roles, the complex decision-making processes that existed behind his individual screen performances, and the often misconstrued association between his screen labour and his extra-filmic persona.

Notes

1. 'Der Sumpf' was a poem written by Brecht that described the slow drowning of a figure in a swamp as witnessed by a close friend who was unable to save him. Since a German version of the poem was found amidst the personal papers of Lorre after his death in 1964, it is widely assumed to be an allegorical poem about how Brecht thought Lorre was slowly corrupted by the world of Hollywood.
2. Youngkin suggests that 'Peter' came from either a friend of Moreno's (Peter Altenberg) or from a perceived resemblance the actor had to the character from German children's literature, 'Struwwelpeter', and that 'Lorre' came from a German term for either 'parrot' or 'role'. NB: Lorre's original name is also sometimes spelled Ladislaus or Ladislav Löwenstein.
3. See Adam Blatner 1997 and Paul Wilkins 1999.
4. Huston, Capra and Negulesco quoted in Youngkin 2005: 181–82, 199–200, 218, 227. Corman quoted in the director's autobiography: Roger Corman (with Jim Jerome) 1990: 86. All four directors also comment that in many scenes they did not realize the effectiveness of Lorre's acting until they viewed the performance away from the set and on a screen.
5. Brecht later revised his ideas about Stanislavskian acting methodology once he gained wider access to the actor's own writings.
6. The relationship between Lorre's time with Brecht and his film work subsequent to this collaboration has been explored by Christopher McCullough (2004), who also suggests that the embryonic nature of Brecht's own theories may have contributed to Lorre's ultimately unsuccessful epic performance as Galy Gay.
7. Robert Florey had already worked with Lorre on *The Face Behind the Mask* (Columbia, 1941). This film is discussed in Chapter 3.

Chapter 2

M, FRITZ LANG AND HANS BECKERT (1931)

When studying the career of Peter Lorre, particular prominence must be given to Lorre's first major screen role: Hans Beckert, the serial killer at the centre of Fritz Lang's 1931 film, *M* (Nero-Film). More than any other role, Beckert has come to be seen as the character which had the biggest impact on Lorre's life – both in terms of his continued employment in the film industry and also in the way that this character contributed to the development of Lorre's otherwise extra-filmic persona.

Throughout Lorre's internationally successful career, and up to the present day, attitudes towards the actor found in a variety of sources, ranging from Hollywood promotional material to scholarly and journalistic retrospectives, recurrently frame the status of Lorre's fame and reputation in accordance to his memorable appearance in *M*. In particular, a significant number of the retrospective essays which purport to analyse Lorre's career repeat a similar three-step template: (a) they present *M* as a significant artistic achievement, (b) they praise Lorre's performance within it, and (c) they then describe the ways in which his later career either failed to live up to this promise or suffered from typecasting as a result of the association between the actor and the character of the deranged serial killer.

Gerd Gemünden (2003: 89) makes the link between Lorre's typecasting and his role in *M* in the most explicit terms, choosing to read Lorre's Hollywood career as 'an extended quotation, re-writing and mimicking that of the paedophile and killer, Hans Beckert'. He defines the remainder of Lorre's screen work as highly limited, and argued that Hollywood either cast Lorre as a pervert, a serial killer, a sexual threat or an outsider. Pronouncements such as these construct a direct correlation between the character of Beckert and Lorre's later Hollywood roles, and in turn, posit that the similarities between his film roles were seen to directly inform Lorre's famous but restrictive persona, whereby the actor was too closely associated with the very marketable image of a dangerous killer or a sadistic pervert.

The common accusation that Hollywood did not employ Lorre to the best of his abilities has its genesis in the reception of *M*. *M* is seen to be an anomaly within Lorre's career: a widely acclaimed performance in a major European art film that was both commercially and critically successful. As Beckert, Lorre demonstrated immense potential but his Hollywood work promised much yet – for many – delivered too little, too often. Lorre's career has repeatedly been read in terms of diminishing returns. The commentary on *M* in *The Films of Peter Lorre* illustrates this as the authors rather unfairly present the supposition that 'had Peter Lorre retired from the screen after making *M*, his importance in film history would in no way be diminished. In fact, it could be argued that his reputation would be greater had *M* been his only contribution to motion pictures' (Youngkin, Bigwood and Cabana Jr. 1981: 63). Attitudes like this have had a detrimental effect on the critical reputation of Lorre as, increasingly, the spectre of *M* and the character of Beckert are seen to have cast an inescapable and sombre shadow over the actor and the trajectory of his Hollywood screen career.

Such reflections upon Lorre's life encourage the perception that the actor can be defined through a tragic narrative in which his potential artistic achievements were cut short as a result of his exile from Germany and his arrival in Hollywood in 1934. An underlying pessimistic and mournful tone typifies many retrospective accounts about Lorre's emigration. Speculative questions are often raised about what Lorre could have achieved 'if only' he had been able to remain working in Europe – the implication being that his artistry was quickly corrupted by the Hollywood filmmaking industry. These perspectives rely upon the notion that Beckert was an exceptional role and that *M* was virtually unique, enabled by the presence of both the directorial skill of Fritz Lang, and the remarkable skill of Lorre's own performance.

One of the flaws of this argument is that it is reliant upon a binary division between person/persona, at the expense of an accurate consideration of the labour of the actor and the circumstances under which he operated, because it emphasizes the problematic relationship between the ambitions of Lorre as an 'artist' and the limitations of Lorre's extra-filmic persona. In keeping with this, there has been little discussion about the work that Lorre put into his performance as Beckert, other than to vaguely praise it or to state that it led to typecasting. As such, when *M* is reviewed in relation to the rest of Lorre's career, it primarily analyses how Beckert contributed to the persona of the actor. This neglects direct comparisons between performative contexts, conditions of employment and specific technical strategies in evidence throughout Lorre's screen, stage and broadcasting work in an international arena, or even in terms of the actor's own agency within the role. This has led to a situation whereby the significance of *M*, in relation to Lorre's career, has been overstated and misunderstood.

The Production of *M*:
The Creative 'Partnership' between Lang and Lorre

A detailed analysis of Lorre's performance of Beckert allows for a more balanced view of how this film fits within the wider context of Lorre's film career. Doing so also suggests possible reasons as to why critiques of this performance have proved elusive. This is partly due to the complex relationship that existed between Lorre and his director/screenwriter, Fritz Lang, during the filming process, and also retrospectively, because of Lang's presence as a figure who was redefined as an auteur during the 1950s and 1960s and Lorre's more lowly critical position during the same time period. The apparent downward trajectory of Lorre's career post-*M* has meant that, in many ways, the presence of Lorre as an active agent has been exorcised from analyses of the film itself, in favour of a more detailed discussion of what Lang achieved on-screen.

Despite this, *M* contains a complex and 'star-making' performance from Lorre which undoubtedly furthered the actor's career. It enabled him to gain employment with both Gaumont-British film studios in the UK, where Lorre made two films directed by Alfred Hitchcock: *The Man Who Knew Too Much* (1934) and *Secret Agent* (1936), and Harry Cohn's Columbia Pictures in Hollywood after his exile from Germany. For the first five years of his screen career, Lorre was perceived as a highly skilled artist as a result of *M* and other film roles; a position which mirrored the reputation he had already been developing prior to 1931 in his work on the European stage. As discussed in the next chapter, after 1937, perceptions regarding Lorre began to change significantly as a result of how the actor was presented to the public by marketing discourse, and it is around this period that interpretations of the creative agencies within *M* also began to shift dramatically.

This shift was aided, first by Lang's increasing commercial success during the 1940s and 1950s in Hollywood, and secondly by his critical 'reappraisal' during the 1960s. During the early years in which Lorre's critical reputation was on the rise (1928–1930), Lang had already attained privileged status as a director within German silent cinema, but had suffered a series of critical and commercial failures, and had undertaken the project of *M* as an attempt to rectify his downturn in fortunes – a strategy which proved successful. In light of Lang's wider achievements as a director and Lorre's own supposed career troubles from the mid-1930s, the latter's apparent failure to match his performance in the screen appearances that followed the film (in both Europe and Hollywood) has suggested an underlying assumption that, despite the talent of the actor, his success in the role could be attributed more to Lang's skilled direction than to Lorre's own creative input.

Stephen D. Youngkin uses a comparison between the trial sequence in Lang's film and its French version that was (in keeping with established filmmaking practices of the time) filmed concurrently, and also starred

Lorre as the killer, to claim that the success of Lorre's performance was primarily down to Lang's control. Youngkin (2005: 62–63) argues that in the French film, when left to his own devices, Lorre took his performance to 'where he felt it belonged: … [Lorre] stands instead of crouches, wildly flipping his head and shaking his body. He directs himself outward rather than inward in a portrayal that is more personified than personal.' The English version of the same film, recently uncovered in its entirety, features a similar situation: a somewhat static *mise-en-scène* devoid of Lang's expertise, coupled with an overbearing and blustering performance from Lorre.

However, between the various versions that exist and the changes within Lorre's acting, there are other factors to take into account. In the English version, Lorre himself speaks the dialogue, but given that he did not become fluent in English until around 1934, the lack of nuance is understandable. In the French version, a French actor redubbed the lines for Lorre and this may explain the increased attention that Lorre paid to the physical, gestural aspects of his performance – effectively this is what he was solely responsible for. The implied mimetic characteristics of the performances which followed Lorre's original German performance may be present precisely because it was a moment of mimicry: Lorre was imitating what he had already placed on film.

During the filming of the trial sequence, Lang reportedly subjected Lorre to excessive physical brutality in order to create the hysterical countenance of the imprisoned Beckert (enough to supposedly irrevocably taint Lorre's view of the director). Youngkin notes that the changes in Lorre's performance in the other language versions were not only due to being 'left to his own devices' but also indicative of being 'freed from Lang's notorious sadism', although he does not draw further conclusion from this. Lang's treatment may have helped engender the fragile emotional state of the character, but Lorre may have also relished the opportunity to act in opposition to his previous direction – regardless of whether it was appropriate or not. The differences in the performance could as easily be the culmination of a battle of wills between two artists (one, an established cinematic force, and the other, an up-and-coming star of the Berlin stage) as an indication of skilled practice and control.

These are all deliberately hypothetical observations about Lorre's performance in the three versions. What they highlight is the difficulty in making absolute or conclusive statements about on-screen performance. Rather than aiming to definitively 'prove' Lang's power (or Lorre's skill – or even lack of it), the films and my readings of them emphasize the intangible and mutable nature of screen performance and interpretation. Creative authorial agency can be suggested and argued but very rarely proved, despite stories which persist around the extent of Lang's control, such as Henry Fonda's claims that the director would literally place actors within the frame with his own hands.[1]

The dismissal of Lorre's significance in favour of the mythicizing of Lang's creative authority was a view that Lang himself was more than happy to supplement via anecdotal evidence in interviews, particularly during the period of intense critical interest in his work towards the end of his career from the mid-1950s to the 1970s, and in stories which were subsequently repeated in Patrick McGilligan's 1997 biography of the director.[2] Two specific stories repeated by Lang work towards diminishing Lorre's political economy and creative agency in his work on the film. Firstly, on employing Lorre, it was reported that Lang refused to reveal the nature of the character of Beckert to the actor until he felt it was appropriate to do so, and the director stipulated in the conditions of employment that Lorre must not appear in any other film role until *M* was finished. By fulfilling these terms, Lorre would remain relatively powerless and unknown to the mass cinema-going audience and could therefore be introduced as Lang's 'discovery': the product of the director's autonomous creative power.[3] Secondly, there is the story that Lang was himself responsible for the most famous element of Beckert's characterization: the whistling of a melody from Grieg's *Peer Gynt* ('In the Hall of the Mountain King') which signifies the presence of the killer. Lang frequently claimed that he had to provide the whistle because Lorre was unable to do so. This is untrue as Lorre whistles in many of his other films, but in retelling the story so that he *had* to do the whistling, rather than because he chose to (because Lorre could not achieve the particular off-key pitch required by Lang), Lang shifts part of the creative agency for determining the physicality of the character away from Lorre and onto himself.

However, Lorre's own creative history and performative skills played a far more central role in Lang's casting of *M* than these stories acknowledge. Lorre's practical theatrical training, in experimental productions and as part of avant-garde companies around Europe, had encouraged the development of a multi-layered acting style that could be described as 'dualistic' or even 'pluralistic' through tone, character or engagement, self-reflexive, and either stylized or naturalistic dependent on what was perceived to be most appropriate. Lang first saw Lorre in the Volksbühne (People's Theatre) production of Wedekind's *Frühlings Erwachen* (Spring's Awakening) in Berlin in 1929, playing – to great critical appreciation – a role which required the actor to present a character that was highly distasteful and yet sympathetic to the audience.

This proved to be the perfect audition for *M* as Lang perceived that his killer had to invoke a similar response in the film's audience, and had to appear harmless to those around him within the film whilst simultaneously hinting at the horror beneath the benign surface. Lorre's experience demonstrated that he could represent a character's internal conflicts in a way that provoked a conflicted sense of sympathy and engagement with that character on the part of the audience. In addition to his skills as an actor, Lang also believed that Lorre's particular physical appearance would add a further layer to the characterization of Beckert. The actor's youthful and chubby physicality would suggest an ironic element as Lorre's own appearance, which resembled an overgrown schoolboy, would align

Beckert much more closely with his intended victims than with the adults who were intent on pursuing the killer.

Within critical writing about the film, the importance of Lorre's portrayal has always been recognized. However, the degree to which the impact of Beckert has been credited to Lorre's performative agency has changed since 1931, as has the understanding of the particular creative relationship between director and actor. Earlier critical opinion tended to emphasize Lorre's central creative force within the film, often placing the actor and the director on equal footing regarding accountability. This perspective can be observed in a review of the 1937 re-release of *M* by the *New York Herald-Tribune* (27 June 1937) which stated that 'Peter Lorre can take almost equal responsibility with Mr Lang for the creation of a masterpiece', and in one of the later pieces to subscribe to this viewpoint by Siegfried Kracauer (1947: 220), who calls the performance the 'true centre of the film'. From the 1950s and 1960s onwards, it became more common to prioritize the figure of the director, and as such, focus on the role of the actor diminished and discussions concerning the methods that Lorre employed in his portrayal were sidelined in favour of analyses of Lang's directorial techniques.

The apparent imbalance that this critical approach engendered has been highlighted by Anton Kaes, who moved beyond a consideration of the creative influence of Lang in order to pose a tantalizing question about creative agency within the film: 'If *M* made Lorre a film star, Lorre also made *M* what it is. For many critics then and now, the film's centre of gravity lies in Lorre's unique dramatic persona. In the final analysis, is *M* as much a Peter Lorre film as it is a Fritz Lang film?' (Kaes 2000: 26). Kaes's suggestion that both Lorre and Lang played different but equally significant creative roles requires further development, and this can be discerned within the film through an analysis of how both chose to represent the character of Beckert.

Both Lang and Lorre refuse to present Beckert in wholly 'black and white' terms, leaving the audience to contemplate a killer who is shown to be all too human rather than simply a monstrous incarnation of evil, despite the opinions of the other characters within the film's narrative. One of the most important formal strategies employed by Lang was the choice to make *M* a film of two distinct halves: in each half particular techniques are used to create a different tone or focus. In the first, Lang relies upon a series of distancing techniques as he sets up the premise that the killer is a shadowy presence who permeates the lives of the inhabitants of the unnamed German city. Despite his central importance in *M*, Beckert appears in only nine scenes or sequences in the entire film. In the first half of the film he is only seen briefly and has virtually no dialogue. The viewer sees him perpetrate his crimes before his face or his name is revealed. The sense of disconnection created between Beckert and the viewer occurs primarily because of Lang's decision to film Beckert in long shots with little dialogue when he is occupying the position of the 'hunter', and through Lorre's use of non-naturalistic performance and exaggerated gesture. By contrast, the second half aims to draw a certain emotional response from the viewer, as the net tightens around the murderer who is reconstructed as a 'hunted' character, especially during the trial sequence. However in terms of Lorre's representation, there is more to Beckert than a simplistic performance of two halves, and even within the first half of the film he uses both non-naturalistic and naturalistic acting. It is this careful manipulation of acting techniques throughout Beckert's scenes which reveals the extent of Lorre's creativity and his understanding of how to present the character most effectively in line with Lang's own remit.

In his early scenes, Beckert is closely associated with the idea of the 'monster' through a series of interlinking stylistic and performative devices and thematic motifs that introduce and then juxtapose imagery of 'Beckert as a monster' with imagery of 'Beckert as a man'. One of these devices is the repeated visualization of Beckert through the use of virtual images, such as shadows and reflections. This effect denies Beckert any physical substance and encourages the perception of him as a mythical intangible being that is always just out of reach. Beckert's first scene in the film is announced only by the appearance of his shadow which falls across a poster that details a reward for the killer's capture. Against this setting, Beckert's black profile speaks to his latest victim, Elsie, before (it is assumed) abducting, abusing and killing her.

The visual strategy of depicting Beckert as a shadow is often used to signal his presence when the viewer may not otherwise be aware of it, and contributes to the pervading sense of paranoia within the first part of the film. In a later sequence in which Beckert is stalking another young girl, Lang cuts to a blind beggar (Georg John), who is the key to identifying the killer as he sold Elsie a balloon whilst she was in the company of Beckert. The beggar hears a man whistling the same melody he heard during Elsie's abduction and strains to hear where it is coming from. Lang's choice of framing for this scene means that he places the camera in between the beggar and Beckert so that the only clue to Beckert's whereabouts is the shadow that falls across the beggar's face. Even at this moment of hope – that he might be recognized and apprehended – the killer remains as elusive as ever, both for the characters in the narrative and for the audience watching it unfold.

Although in this first half Beckert is mostly represented as a shadowy unseen figure, an early sequence somewhat surprisingly reveals the face of the murderer to the viewer. This enables Lorre's performative techniques to be foregrounded more substantially. The image remains in the context of the impersonal 'police procedural' that characterizes the first half of the film, since it is accompanied by the voiceover of a graphologist outlining the possible psychological profile of the killer, but it also offers an audience-only insight into the killer as Beckert stares into his dressing-table mirror trying to 'see' the psychopath that is being described aurally within his own seemingly benevolent face. Beckert is presented as a man whose indistinct physicality allows him to pass unnoticed by potential witnesses and evade capture. (Although in later years Lorre was often described as physically unusual, in *M* his physical appearance was predominantly used to signify youth and conventionality.) Although the audience is apparently privileged with this point of view that recognizes the 'abnormality' beneath the surface, the sequence relies upon the distancing techniques of both Lang's framing and Lorre's performance. In doing so, its apparent status as a moment of psychological connection is purposefully undermined as the use of the reflection constructs a barrier between the audience and Beckert that belies the apparent closeness of the image.

In addition to the mirror image which dominates the frame, Lang includes Beckert's actual face in the right-hand side of the frame. Due to the position of the camera and the angle of the shot, only a partial view of the face's left side is visible. Therefore, whilst Beckert is contorting his features into the increasingly disturbing mask-like faces in his reflection, his actual face (as visible to the viewer) barely changes expression. This sequence becomes a way of successfully conveying an interior process: Beckert is outwardly 'normal' and does not actually change into an obviously visually monstrous character when his murderous desires are aroused. It remains an internal transformation, but through the use of a reflected image rather than a 'real' image this can still be presented in a visual and physical sense without destroying the reality of the situation.

Within the sequence, Beckert's capacity for murder is demonstrated through Lorre's physical performance. Lorre utilizes a technique which is highly reminiscent of those practised in his own experimental stage experi-

Figure 2.1 Lorre as Hans Beckert in *M* (1931). Photo: Nero-Film AG/Foremco Pictures Co.

ences, such as the development of epic theatrical strategies with Bertolt Brecht. Using an epic mode of performance which attempts to create a distancing or 'alienating' effect between actor, character and audience, Lorre demonstrates the character to the viewer rather than trying to create an illusion of reality by 'becoming' the character. Rather than conveying the transformation via one seamless facial movement, Lorre uses a series of disjointed and increasingly shocking expressions which resemble a number of 'masks' being put on by the character. This objective technique is reinforced because the visuals effectively mimic the emotionless voiceover of the graphologist's report into the possible psychological make-up of the killer (a visual and aural juxtaposition which is, in itself, also an explicit commentary on the performative aspects being used throughout the sequence), despite both Beckert and the graphologist occupying different physical and possibly temporal spaces within the narrative. In this brief moment Lang and Lorre are able to demonstrate the internal struggles of Beckert, and Lorre's alienating performance coheres with Lang's equally distancing visual representation.

Lang's use of this technique occurs throughout the first half of the film where Beckert remains a threatening presence. The psychological 'insights' offered are conveyed through the use of reflected images, and this illustrates an attempt on the part of Lang to effectively prevent the viewer from making an emotional connection with Beckert. The most notable example of this is the moment when Beckert realizes he has been discovered and branded with the letter 'M'. He becomes aware of this by turning and looking at his reflection in a darkened shop window. This is the last scene in which Lang uses the reflection motif. The chalk mark signals the killer's identity to all: he is no longer able to hide behind a façade of 'normality', and the articulation of his hidden abnormality does not have to be communicated via the technique of the virtual image.

However, whilst Lang effectively relies upon two distinct approaches over the first and second halves of the film, Lorre's performance is not as easily split into these oppositional techniques. Throughout the film, his acting juxtaposes non-naturalistic and jarring representations with more naturalistic and coherent moments of characterization. The same visual transformation from 'man' to 'monster' that is being performed in front of Beckert's bedroom mirror is repeated in the later sequence where Beckert is entranced by the reflection of a young girl in a shop window and slowly begins to stalk her, but this time Lorre performs it without the literal 'face-making' required by Lang's alienating distancing effect (although the director continues to use the motif of the reflected image). The viewer no longer merely sees a demonstration of, and commentary upon, the stages of 'evil', but, through Lorre's performance, is presented with a clearer insight into the psychological process of Beckert's mental struggle. In effect, the same transformation occurs in both sequences, but there are purposeful differences within the specifics of Lorre's performance. Even if one takes into account claims that Lang physically manipulated actors within the frame, these two scenes reveal that there was still space for the actor's own agency, either in terms of the specific gestures used by Lorre or in the way he chose to structure and pace his movements between each separate directed action.

Within this silent sequence, Lorre carefully uses facial and bodily movements, with props, to externalize Beckert's thoughts. He begins by showing Beckert as 'normal' – smiling and happily eating some fruit. As he spots the girl all signifiers of normality disappear: his hands drop heavily down to his side and his smiling face becomes expressionless. By wiping the fruit juice off his mouth with his left hand, Lorre is symbolically removing the last trace of 'normality' from Beckert.[4] The way his fingers pull down the corner of his mouth is reminiscent of the last 'mask' he contorts his face into from the earlier scene in front of his bedroom mirror. Here, unlike that previous sequence, Lorre demonstrates that this is not a straightforward transformation into evil: there is a struggle for control within Beckert between the sane and the insane elements of his mind. This internal conflict is represented physically through Lorre's use of his hands: his right hand, which still holds the fruit, is connected to Beckert's 'normal' persona, whereas the left hand still hovering at his mouth is linked with the perverted desire within.

The ambiguity of this scene – as to whether Beckert will act upon his murderous desires – is reflected in the positioning of Lorre's hands. Whilst he is struggling with himself he brings them both down to the handrail where they rest inactively as he considers the situation. Once he decides that his impulses cannot be ignored, his left hand malevolently moves slowly to grasp the air as if to pull the girl towards him, but then falls to his side and reluctantly repeats the gesture. Despite this moment of resistance, the 'monster' within finally gains supremacy, and with the course of action decided, Lorre's hands are thrust firmly inside his coat pockets out of sight. This sequential movement will become more significant as Beckert argues in his defence that he is a vulnerable 'victim' who is compelled by forces within him to act out horrific fantasies that spiral way out of his control.

Within the second half of the film, Lang dramatically reversed the structure and style that he had so far used. Instead of being a predominantly unseen catalyst for the unfolding narrative, Beckert is now placed centre stage and the viewer is positioned to bear witness to his loss of control over the unfolding events: namely his pursuit and capture by the underworld forces. Lang also chooses to replace the episodic, impersonal style employed in the first half of the film with a more linear, personal one. This encourages a sense of forward momentum within the story that was lacking in the pseudo-documentary style used to outline the growing mass hysteria and the various police procedures being employed. Additionally, the combination of this style with the structure of the first half tends to distance the viewer from any particular character, resulting in a noticeable absence of identification figures. Anton Kaes (2000: 52–53) has discussed the way in which the traditional 'hero figure' of the investigating officer, Inspector Lohmann (Otto Wernicke) is undermined by Lang. A similar interpretation can be taken towards the alternative protagonist, the underworld boss Schränker (Gustaf Gründgens), whose physicality, costuming and dialogue convey a close association with terror and oppression, and whose moral obligation to catch the killer stems from the desire to continue with his business free from police interruption, rather than from a superior moral position.

Lang's decision to undermine the 'heroic' characteristics of both Lohmann and Schränker prompts the audience to look elsewhere for an empathetic character. This remains a somewhat problematic decision since it creates a space which encourages an emotional connection between the viewer and Beckert. This connection contributes to the source of the film's main ambiguity: that despite the danger posed to society by Beckert, the viewer is not necessarily encouraged to wholly condemn him. This ambiguity would be difficult to support if the film had offered the viewer an acceptable alternative hero figure. The change in tone and tempo of the film also directs the audience's attention towards Beckert and succeeds in reducing the impact of the pursuit narrative as the dramatic changes subvert the significance of Lohmann's and Schränker's goal to capture one man. Therefore the formal construction of the other main protagonists promotes a particular perception of Beckert by the audience. Lang uses the structure of the film as an aid to develop the representation of Beckert as a troubled human being rather than an anonymous force of evil.

The decision to make Beckert a continuously visible presence throughout the second half of the film allows Lorre's performance to humanize the killer and develop him as a rounded character, and as such his presence dominates the film, despite his relatively short screen time. Much of this power is generated from the final sequence in which Beckert is put on trial and Lorre delivers his extended monologue. However, the strength of Lorre's performance does not come from this impassioned speech alone or from his position only within the film's second act. Looking at Lorre's scenes throughout the film, a carefully considered performative strategy can be determined which aims to foreshadow the objectives of the trial sequence, in the way that the sequence offers a challenge to the viewer's supposed attitudes towards Beckert, the monstrous child killer. Throughout the film, Lorre works in conjunction with Lang's formal techniques to conduct the process of humanizing a monster. This is achieved by utilizing alternating performance styles throughout the action: moving between a performance that encourages distance from the character and a performance that draws the viewer into an emotional connection with the killer.

When considered alongside a detailed analysis of his acting techniques in other scenes, Lorre's performance in the final trial sequence is not as shocking a departure as we might first believe. Although it is explored most fully in this sequence, the idea that Beckert is more than an incarnation of 'evil' is present throughout Lorre's performance as a whole and he clearly demonstrates the ongoing process of humanizing an abstract hate figure. However, because of the formal choices made by Lang that place certain restrictions on Lorre's acting, it is in the trial scene that the full extent of Lorre's construction of Beckert is revealed, despite Youngkin's insistence that Lang remained the dominant creative force during this sequence. Rather than being carefully manipulated by the director, Lorre is set free from the technical constraints and visual trickery employed by Lang, and the long sequence is played very much as a theatrical sketch, with minimal camera movements or cuts as Beckert begins his defence.

The sequence begins by directing the audience to question the legitimacy of a 'trial' run by the criminal underworld, most notably in the brutal way Beckert is physically treated and in the shrieking laughter directed at him when he says in surprise, 'But you can't just murder me!'. Throughout this, the viewer is encouraged to form an emotional connection with Beckert that deepens as he speaks, through formal and performative means. The position of the camera holds Lorre's face in a medium shot throughout most of the sequence and is the most detailed visual presentation of the actor (and character) experienced so far in the film. Beckert turns towards the camera, but does not look directly at it, as direct address would have a self-reflexive and confrontational effect, drawing attention to the moment as one of a 'performance' by an actor and breaking the possible empathetic connection with the viewer. Instead of occupying a position which distances the viewer from the character, Lorre's performance figures the moment as one which strives towards conveying the psychological 'truth' of Beckert. He demonstrates Beckert's confused state of mind by focusing on nothing. This stance also positions Beckert's words as an authentic confession rather than a calculated speech which seeks a particular response from the diegetic audience. In addition to this, Lorre uses quiet words and small controlled movements which make Beckert appear much less animalistic than his wild entrance into the 'court' (a motif also used in the previous sequence, where the pursuit and capture of the killer resembled the hunt for a wild animal).

The pacing of both Lorre's verbal performance of Beckert's speech and the specific choices the actor makes about when to employ different physical performative modes during the speech are also significant in demonstrating how the scenes work towards (and at times, against) creating the level of empathy in the viewer needed by Lang in order for the film's conclusion to be successful. On the whole, Lorre uses a naturalistic style based around revealing the psychological motivations of Beckert, but at times he chooses to revert momentarily to a contrasting non-naturalistic physical performance. One such instance occurs early in the sequence as the 'prosecutor', Schränker, shows Beckert photographs of the murdered children. In response, Lorre melodramatically jerks backwards and clasps his fists into his mouth. Lorre's movement illustrates that the moment is a turning point in the trial, as it identifies Beckert as the killer that held the city in a grip of terror. In keeping with this, Lorre adopts a stance which parallels the earlier representation used by himself and Lang, briefly demonstrating the 'monster' within through a symbolic series of expressionistic gestures rather than using more naturalistic techniques.

In contrast to this moment, which briefly attempts to break the realistic and emotionally engaging representation of Beckert through physical means, the way that Lorre's performance is verbally structured seeks to maintain this connection between character and viewer. As Beckert pleads with the court, saying 'I can't help myself', he is accused by one of the jeering crowd of using the old trick of pleading madness. To counter this accusation, Lorre reverts back to a mode of representation based around the performance of Beckert as a 'normal' sane figure (briefly seen elsewhere in the film when Beckert buys fruit from a street vendor). He intelligently and articulately accuses the court of being merely career criminals unqualified to judge his own mental state. The moment aligns Beckert with the audience, who have been encouraged to formulate a similar viewpoint through the brutal treatment of Beckert in the sequence and through the overall representation of Schränker. Furthermore, the positioning of this brief moment of sense and lucidity is crucial because it occurs just before Beckert launches into an intense and detailed description of his crimes. An immediate movement from the animal-like hysteria which characterized his entrance into the room, to the frightening world of Beckert's compulsion to kill, would have destroyed the necessary emotional connection between the character and viewer. This convincing moment of sanity serves to reinforce the notion that Beckert is more 'man' than 'monster', and as such could be received as a possible figure of identification or sympathy.

As Beckert begins to explain himself, Lorre allows the intensity to return to his voice and stance. His brief words describing 'the fire, the voice, the torment' inside him build up the tension and uneasiness around the character that is wholly constructed through this more naturalistic performance. There are few symbolic, mythic or distancing aspects to this part of the performance, and every gesture used by Lorre can be seen less as a Brechtian-style commentary on the character's behaviour, and more in keeping with realistic or even Stanislavskian modes of performance which attempt to convey a sense of 'psychological truth'. In keeping with this agenda, which was derived from realist approaches to theatrical performance, Lang minimizes cinematic 'distractions' and uses no editing, dramatic music or lighting changes to embellish the struggles of the character. Only once, after Beckert says 'And I shadow myself', does Lang momentarily relieve the tension by cutting to the courtroom. In contrast to earlier, the 'jury' are now silent and a few have begun to nod in confused empathy. Over these shots, Beckert's voice continues, growing louder and higher. Lang cuts back to him in order to visualize the internal battle of the character. As he breathes, every part of Lorre's body moves in and out to illustrate physically the capture and release of Beckert's two personalities. As Beckert continues, Lorre increasingly keeps his movements to a minimum. Instead he shifts the struggle between his personalities back towards an internal one, conveying this via changes in his voice rather than through changing facial expressions or physical gestures. He uses a high pitched shriek to describe his emotions, followed by a muted emotionless voice to describe the ghosts that haunt him (implying that it is his capacity to kill rather than the consequences of his actions which terrifies him the most).

This part of the performance works towards allowing the viewer to have some sympathy for Beckert by gaining an understanding of the mental processes that drive him through Lorre's first physical, and then verbal, performances. However, this film has a more complex agenda than merely reconstructing Beckert as a sympathetic killer. Having revealed Beckert as a damaged human being, the film refuses to ignore the horrific nature of his crimes. Again this is demonstrated through elements of Lorre's performance which juxtapose naturalistic with non-naturalistic modes, and move swiftly between moments which engage or alienate the viewer. During his heartfelt confession, Beckert also continues to repulse the audience by recounting the pleasure he feels whilst killing. As with the earlier example of seeing the photographs of his victims, at this moment, Lorre's acting ensures that Beckert is once more visually represented as a 'monster': as he says the words 'Except when I'm doing it', the actor suddenly returns to a grotesque and mask-like facial expression and allows a malevolent lustful smile to fill his face. This briefly severs the empathetic connection created between him and the audience, as the actor objectively reminds them who they pity. This commentary only surfaces for the briefest interlude, and in the next instant the mask is gone and the childlike bewilderment returns, along with the less reflexive performance style.

Through his tension-filled and skilled performance, Lorre successfully demonstrates that Beckert's psychological struggle is one which can only continue indefinitely. Repeated phrases, such as 'Don't want to! Must!', which vary only in the way Lorre delivers them using different volume, speed and intensity, emphasizes Beckert's loss of control over his conscious behaviour and emotions as he describes his desperate existence that condemns him to repeat his actions over and over with no hope of ending the struggle. The overall cyclical structure of the speech increases the tension as it makes it difficult to anticipate when and how it will end. Lorre's continually shifting performance style echoes the ongoing internal fight of the character, and the formal techniques used by Lang illustrate an unwillingness to either interrupt Lorre's acting with cinematic 'distractions' via editing, or allow the other characters into Beckert's temporal space in order to stop the confession.

Given the general objective of constructing an ambiguous position regarding the punishment of Beckert, the sequence must end in a way which encourages neither condemnation nor support for the killer. Lang and Lorre carefully manage a conclusion which conforms to this by continuing the theme of repetition which has been central to characterizing Beckert's speech. To finish, Lorre repeats one line four times: 'I can't!'. The repetition illustrates the lack of forward momentum and Beckert's mental and physical exhaustion. With each reading, Lorre slows his delivery and lowers his voice, so that it moves from a terrified scream to an exhausted sob, winding down the performance and moving the focus back to 'political/social' concerns (the legitimacy of the trial and treatment of the killer), rather than to the 'psychological' (Beckert's emotional experiences). In accordance with this, Lorre's acting again moves from a style which encourages emotional engagement to one that constructs a sense of distance between viewer and character, as he reacts non-naturalistically to the steadying hold of the unseen policeman by ignoring it.

The Impact of *M* on Lorre's Career and Screen Performances

As previously outlined, there is an assumed close association between Lorre's appearance in *M* and the remainder of the actor's international career. The remainder of Lorre's characters may have elements in common with Beckert at some level, but the direct correlation with the other roles is not strong enough to describe it accurately as typecasting. Even in the immediate aftermath of *M*, and the keenness of the German film industry to capitalize on the impact made by the actor by offering him the same types of roles, Lorre resisted this particular employment strategy. Instead, he played a range of characters in a variety of different genres and worked mainly as a supporting actor for the rest of his European film career, including: musical performances in *Was Frauen Trämen* (What Women Dream) (1933); comic or romantic roles in farcical films such as *Die Koffer des Herrn O.F* (The Trunks of Mr. O.F) (1931); as support to the popular star Hans Albers in *Bomben auf Monte Carlo* (Bombs over Monte Carlo) (1931), *FP1 Antwortet Nicht* (FP1 Doesn't Answer) (1932), and *Der Weisse Dämon* (The White Demon) (1932); and unsympathetic criminal roles in popular thrillers like *Unsichtbare Gegner* (Invisible Opponent) (1933). This template is equally applicable to his Hollywood career, during which Lorre played a wide variety of roles from comic sidekicks, quirky eccentrics, dangerous criminals, fatalistic anti-heroes and cynical mercenaries, rather than being restricted only to roles which could be described in limiting terms as either serial killers or psychopaths.

Within the context of Lorre's overall screen career, *M* can be seen be an especially atypical performance. I have described how Lorre shifts from a non-naturalistic, almost Brechtian, style to one which actively courts a particular emotional engagement from the viewer, using a combination of his own earlier theatrical training and realist conventions of early sound screen acting. Although Lorre often utilizes a similarly dualistic acting style in many of his following films, there are differences which have a significant effect upon characterization and the potential for engagement with his audience. The biggest difference between *M* and the other films in which Lorre juxtaposes a non-naturalistic distancing style with realist or naturalistic acting is that in the latter category, through Lorre's use of either self-reflexive or distancing techniques, the juxtaposition serves as political or industrial commentary on his employment within a mass media industry which favoured a realist aesthetic. In each film, Lorre's acting choices carefully ensure that his position as a performer is continually highlighted in addition to (or at times, at the expense of) the characterization of his role. In many of his Hollywood films made between 1935 and 1964, the spectacle of Lorre's performance is often presented as the potential point of engagement with the viewer, instead of through the presentation of a psychologically-realistic character.

With regards to *M*, Lorre's agenda for using a non-naturalistic acting style at certain moments is first to create a barrier between the audience and Beckert. Gradually, this barrier is then eroded by the more naturalistic elements of his performance as the film progresses, culminating in the trial sequence. By contrast, many of his later performances attempt to achieve the opposite effect in terms of identification. This shift is a calculated strategy on the part of Lorre and can be recognized even at the smallest gestural level, and as such these expressions should be considered as complex articulations of character rather than as evidence of the actor's tendency to simply 'make faces'. As Beckert, Lorre repeats certain intended movements, such as holding his eyes wide open or raising his brow line, the aim of which is to have a humanizing effect by conveying the vulnerability of the character to the viewer. Lorre uses the same gestures throughout his career, but in his later films they are used as a specific distancing effect rather than a moment of engagement. For example, in *All Through the Night*, Lorre raises his brow line to signify that his character, Pepi, has changed from a comically harmless figure to one who is dangerous and unpredictable. The gesture is contained within a close-up of Lorre's face (and is therefore not included for the benefit of other characters) and is intended to create a moment of disquiet and tension in the mind of the viewer, rather than being used to signify a moment of empathy.

Although Lorre uses contrasting performative techniques throughout *M*, the naturalistic style remains the dominant style of acting. This is mainly due to the way it is appropriated within the trial sequence. For the most part, this crucial scene conforms to concepts of realistic performance that were influenced by Stanislavsky's approach to characterization in its aim to convey the psychological 'truth' of the character. As such, the impact of the scene is created by the way in which the emotionally engaging acting style allows for a challenge to conventional perceptions surrounding the killer's motivations and actions to be mounted, which have otherwise been communicated through excessively expressionistic representations. Furthermore, naturalistic practices – rather than more experimental or self-reflexive techniques – have historically been very compatible with the principles of mainstream film acting (and many mainstream appraisals of what constitutes 'good' acting). This may help to explain why Lorre's performance as Beckert is seen in a more favourable light than any of his other more obviously self-reflexive or non-naturalistic performances.

Looking at *M* from the wider perspective of a consideration of Lorre's international career, it is difficult to pigeonhole Lorre's performance style, screen roles and extra-filmic persona on the basis of this film alone. *M* occupies a significant place within the career of Peter Lorre, but it is simplistic merely to define Peter Lorre according to his appearance as Beckert or to analyse his later work in Hollywood and Germany solely around its relation to this film. Much of the special significance that can be identified in *M* with specific regard to Lorre comes from one of the most overlooked elements of the film: the labour that the actor puts into his performance. Lorre's performance as Beckert is a carefully constructed exercise in characterization and audience engagement which demonstrates how the actor appropriated his own professional experiences to bring authorial agency to the character rather than just relying on his natural attributes and appearance, unconscious personal gestures or directorial instruction. However, *M* cannot be seen as the one and only significant work in Lorre's international career – from either a perspective that prioritizes the actor's labour and performances or one which prioritizes Lorre's persona. The film is a very precise example of Lorre's skill as an actor, but it is not the only example.

Additionally, an analysis of the way Lorre constructs Beckert – particularly within the context of his whole career – challenges the assumption that Lorre spent his entire professional life playing echoes of this one character or that he was incapable of playing characters too far removed from the image of the serial killer, because it reveals the differences between Beckert and other characters at both the level of Lorre's deliberate performative choices and also the industrial and artistic decisions behind the employment of the actor. Although he uses techniques and gestures in this film that can be found throughout his other films, there is little sense of cohesion between this role and the roles that Lorre subsequently played in both Europe and Hollywood. Despite the insistence that *M* cast a long shadow over Lorre's career, especially in the way that the Hollywood industry used him, there is little evidence that his American employment – at least on the cinema screen – was conditional upon a repeated association with his character from *M*.

Linked to Lorre's employment within the American filmmaking industry is the central role played by the American mass audience within the career of Peter Lorre. The major consumers of Lorre's labour and image were the American public, and he worked almost exclusively within the United States between 1935 and 1964. Just as it is impossible to describe Lorre's cinematic employment by Hollywood as predominantly indebted to his role in *M*, it is also difficult to view the reception of Lorre by the American public as a whole as dependent upon an explicit association with Hans Beckert. It is highly unlikely that the average American picturegoer would have had frequent or prolonged access to *M* on-screen. Therefore, they would also be unlikely to have derived a perception of the actor based upon his role or performance in the film – these perceptions came from other sources. Those who were able to see Lorre in *M* would have done so on only a few occasions in selected cinemas (on its initial release, at a New York re-release in 1937, and in 1959 when a shortened version was re-released first in Germany and then worldwide).[5] Therefore, for the majority of his Hollywood career, his performance as Beckert would have been at best a distant memory to Lorre's largest potential audience. The public association of Lorre's image with a particular type of unsavoury character was aided by promotional material which continually made reference to *M*, although publicity departments had specific agendas for making this connection, and were not always accurate in their representations of the actor's relationship to the film.

The close relationship between *M* and Lorre has been overplayed partly because his appearance as Beckert appears to support and explain the actor's nefarious extra-filmic persona in the United States. Whilst there are obvious connections between the role and the image, this is also a more complex relationship than may otherwise be assumed for a number of reasons: firstly, because so few other screen roles contribute meaningfully to the construction of Lorre's extra-filmic persona (in spite of their frequent notoriety); secondly, despite being linked to the German film, *M*, Lorre's extra-filmic persona remains a construct of a variety of American media industries; and thirdly, the extra-filmic persona which most coherently signified 'Peter Lorre' only came into existence circa 1937 – six years and fifteen films after Lorre's appearance as Beckert. Lorre's persona may have its origins in *M*, but its creation was not necessarily a direct progression from that film.

Notes

1. Henry Fonda (1966) commented at the height of Lang's redefinition as an 'auteur' that '[Lang] is the master puppeteer, and he is happiest only when he can manipulate the blank puppets. He would actually manipulate you with his hands.'
2. Interviews in Barry Keith Grant 2003; Henry Hart 1956: 13–15; Gretchen Berg 1965: 50–80; Gene D. Phillips 1975: 175–87; Patrick McGilligan 1997.
3. This was stipulated despite Lorre's growing reputation within theatrical circles circa 1930 (see Chapter 1) and despite his brief appearances in two films prior to the release of *M* – *Die Verschewunde Frau* (The Missing Wife) (Karl Leiter, Österreichisches Filmindustrie, 1929) and a short recording of *Mann ist Mann* (Man Equals Man) directed by Brecht in 1931.
4. It remains ambiguous as to whether this 'wiping' action is Lorre's invention or Lang's own direction. Stephen D. Youngkin cites the moment as being present within the script (and therefore not credited to Lorre), but the script to which he refers to is not the shooting script written by Thea von Harbou, but a version published in 1968 and subtitled an 'English translation and description of action' by Nicholas Garnham. Garnham's script makes no mention of von Harbou and constructs its text from a direct description of the film itself. Nicholas Garnham 1968: 58.
5. The limited release of *M* in English-speaking countries was noted in a 1937 British article about Lorre, which stated that 'Although comparatively few English-speaking people saw *M*, [Lorre] has never been able to get away from that grim murderer': John K. Newham, *Film Weekly*, 3 July: 14. The paradoxical nature of this type of statement has rarely been explored in critical appraisals of the actor's career.

Chapter 3

THE HOLLYWOOD LEADING ROLES (1935–1941)

Peter Lorre moved to Hollywood in 1934, having accepted a long-term contract with Columbia Pictures that same year. He had left central Europe the year before, leaving Vienna after completing the Austrian film, *Unsichtbare Gegner* (Invisible Opponent), as the threat to Jewish personnel from the Nazi regime increased. Lorre went first to Paris, where he had a cameo in G.W. Pabst's film, *Du Haut en Bas* (From Top to Bottom) (1933). He then moved on to London, where he appeared in *The Man Who Knew Too Much* (1934), directed by Alfred Hitchcock.

Although *M* is seen as an early defining moment within Lorre's career, his work with Hitchcock played a significant part in drawing the attention of Hollywood. *The Man Who Knew Too Much* was Lorre's first original performance in the English language (after his mimetic performance in the English version of *M*). Lorre played Abbott, the leader of a terrorist group who are planning to assassinate a diplomat at the Albert Hall in London. A British couple, Bob and Jill Lawrence (Leslie Banks and Edna Best), stumble upon the plot, and to ensure their silence, Abbot has their daughter Betty (Nova Pilbeam) kidnapped. As Bob searches for her, he and Jill become further intertwined in the assassination plot and eventual defeat of the gang. It was a key film for Lorre, not only in terms of what he achieved on-screen in his nuanced portrayal of a villainous anarchist terrorist, but also because his widely celebrated performance in Hitchcock's film demonstrated that Lorre could be employed in English-language films: a skill that made him highly valuable to the American market.

Lorre's English skills were reportedly virtually non-existent and he learnt his lines phonetically during filming, only becoming fluent upon his arrival in the United States. This has become a popular story, often recalled, about the actor and his early relationship with Hitchcock – based on Lorre's ability to say only 'yes' or 'no' to the director, and to sense the appropriate moment to laugh at Hitchcock's jokes. However, a comparison between Lorre's performance here and in the English version of *M* problematizes this myth somewhat. Whilst his acting in the alternative version of *M* was overplayed and simplistic, his delivery in *The Man Who Knew Too Much* is far more practised and subtle, suggesting a more comprehensive familiarity with the nuances of the English language than Lorre possessed in 1931.

Carefully staged tonal shifts within Lorre's performance as the terrorist mastermind can be observed which develop the character despite the brevity of his appearances on-screen. A review in *The Times* (12 December 1934: 12) described him as one of the film's strongest elements, observing that 'there is real subtlety in the acting of Mr Peter Lorre' which contrasted usefully with the straightforwardness of Banks' and Best's portrayal of Bob and Jill. Comical touches introduce the villain and fool the viewer (including a line which addresses Lorre's apparent unskilful use of English), and yet, this humour remains even after the true nature of Abbott is revealed. He is a hardened and unsentimental murderer who takes pleasure in the anguish of Bob – the ordinary man thrust into an extraordinary situation – by dryly taunting him with threats of his daughter's death. This brutal temperament is reflected in the character's scarred face. But a convincing level of easy charm and humour are also integral aspects to Abbott's success as a terrorist, and Lorre manages to achieve this duality within his performance, particularly when Abbott prevents the police from searching the gang's premises by calling into question the sobriety of the man who has summoned the officers – Bob's sidekick, Clive. This sequence illustrates Lorre's skill at combining humour and menace, and his increasing comfort with the new language in order to embellish what could have been a one-dimensional villain reliant on phonetically reciting lines of written dialogue – a charge that could be made towards his performance in the English version of *M*.

Hollywood had long been aware of developments within German cinema and had been actively importing talent from Europe throughout the 1920s. Owing to his work in *M* and the increasing proliferation of European émigrés within Hollywood, Lorre would have been known by the industry. However, since *M*, Lorre had mainly played minor parts in German-language films, ostensibly to escape typecasting. Prior to *The Man Who Knew Too Much*, he had not proved himself to be a viable long-term commercial commodity. This relatively high-risk and unstable star status altered upon the release and subsequent international success of Hitchcock's film. Not only did Lorre's performance garner much attention, but extra-textual discourses also focused upon him when discussing the film, thus increasing public perceptions of the actor as a more conventional 'star' figure. He was central to the film's marketing strategy: the dominant image on the poster depicted a large close-up of his face fully made up as the scarred Abbott, and listings in *The Times* from the UK second-run used Lorre's name to publicize the film rather than Leslie Banks. Additionally, Lorre's potential audience grew immeasurably due to his new English skills. These factors, in addition to his work on *M*, prompted the offer of a contract from Harry Cohn at Columbia, who saw Lorre's potential to be Hollywood's newest European star (Youngkin 2005: 92).

Lorre was primarily employed at two Hollywood studios between 1934 and 1941: he was under contract at Columbia between 1934 and 1936, and in 1936 he signed to Twentieth Century-Fox, where he remained until 1940. Throughout this period, Lorre mostly played leading roles (although towards the end of the 1930s he also made an increasing number of appearances in secondary roles, which will be discussed in the following chapter). The majority of the leading performances that Lorre gave throughout his career occurred between 1935 and 1941: *Mad Love* (1935); *Crime and Punishment* (1935); the Mr Moto series – *Think Fast Mr Moto* (1937), *Thank You Mr Moto* (1937), *Mr Moto's Gamble* (1938), *Mr Moto Takes a Chance* (1938), *Mysterious Mr Moto* (1938), *Mr Moto's Last Warning* (1939), *Danger Island* (1939) and *Mr Moto Takes a Vacation* (1939); and finally *Island of Doomed Men* (1940) and *The Face Behind the Mask* (1941). Only Lorre's first two American leading roles were in major 'A' productions, whilst the remainder were smaller-scale 'B' films that were shot quickly and cheaply. This divergent nature of Lorre's employment has helped to construct certain perceptions about the European actor's Hollywood career during this period.

Despite the proliferation of Lorre's leading roles between 1935 and early 1941, there is a tendency to prescribe to the view that after the initial fanfare of his arrival in Hollywood, circumstances quickly soured for the actor and did not recover until 1941 and Lorre's 'reinvention' as a supporting actor in Warner Bros.' production of *The Maltese Falcon* (1941). Lorre's early Hollywood career is constructed as an intense period of rapid marginalization, whereby the celebrated European 'star' was quickly relegated to performing in lowly 'B' pictures, employed within the confines of a limiting persona, and played roles that can be characterized as having 'foreign' or 'othered' statures. Evidence which supports this perception has traditionally been found in events such as the delay in finding a suitable project for Lorre's American debut, his extended tenure as the Japanese detective, Mr Moto, and the apparent reliance of his 'B' picture roles upon the endless recycling of his extra-filmic persona.

Three distinct stages which can be easily discerned within Lorre's employment during this period are: his 'A' movies (1934–1936); the Mr Moto 'B' series (1937–1939); and his other 'B' movies (1940–1941). Although this categorization suggests a downward trajectory, the conventional explanation that Lorre's talents were misused by an industry that was quick to typecast the actor becomes a questionable stance when one separates the actor's screen roles from his extra-filmic persona. It is more productive to consider Lorre's career from 1934 to 1941 by making a distinction between Lorre's labour and the various marketing strategies that were used to promote him away from the cinema screen, and exploring the relationship between the two factors.

Two promotional strategies which define Lorre as either an 'artist' or as 'typecast' are conspicuously prominent within these years. The way in which one definition developed into the other is significant because the close relationship between marketing methods and critical assessments of Lorre's work demonstrates the ease with which various promotional schemes (often with conflicting agendas) can supersede considerations of a screen actor's on-screen labour, in the way they are taken to be accurate assessments of a performer's career. As such, a close re-evaluation of Lorre's work during these years reveals that dominant discourses, which encouraged the perception that the industry did not know how best to employ the actor, have effectively obscured a more complex and purposeful pattern of employment conducted almost independently on two fronts: screen labour and promotional techniques. Therefore, the concepts of 'artistry' and 'typecasting' are as much deliberate industrial marketing strategies which aim to give a sense of coherence to an otherwise disparate career, as they are evaluative critiques of a performer's work.

Columbia Pictures and Peter Lorre, the 'International Artist': 1934–1936

Lorre signed to Columbia Pictures in 1934, but did not make his Hollywood debut until the following year with *Mad Love*. This extended period of inactivity was unusual in the fast-paced Hollywood industry of the 1930s and 1940s, especially for male leading actors. This somewhat atypical term of employment was further compounded by the fact that when Lorre did make his first film, he was loaned out to MGM rather than finding a suitable vehicle for his talents at Columbia. In fact, Lorre only made one film for Columbia under the contract of 1934: *Crime and Punishment* (1935). The initial delay and subsequent protracted work for Columbia has been interpreted as a sign that, despite Lorre's apparent value as a leading performer, the studio was undecided as to how employ the actor in the most appropriate way (Youngkin 2005: 141). However, these unusual circumstances can be explained through an acknowledgement of Lorre's commodity value in 1934, and the motivations behind Harry Cohn's decision – as chief of Columbia Pictures – to sign Lorre in the first instance.

Cohn had been eager to employ the young European actor as early as 1933, but only acted after the success of *The Man Who Knew Too Much*. Lorre signed a five-year contract that paid him US$500 per week, and whose terms stipulated that it was to be reviewed and renewed every six months (Youngkin 2005: 92). The agreement between Lorre and Columbia was as unconventional as the conditions of his early employment since Cohn usually preferred actors to be kept on short-term contracts, as this minimized the potential risks and expenditures associated with leading performers. The presence of Lorre was a central part of Cohn's wider strategy for Columbia during this period and one which reflected Hollywood's attitudes towards German cinema over the past decade. During the early-to-mid 1930s, Cohn was in the process of supervising the transformation of the studio from one of the lesser 'poverty-row' studios into a more stable and financially profitable venture. Although it was still not considered one of the major studios because this transformation did not include the purchase of real estate or means of exhibition, Cohn was keen to present Columbia as a viable competitor within 1930s Hollywood. This meant constructing Columbia as a studio that was capable of handling the accoutrements associated with the major studios, especially after the transition to sound: big budgets, theatrically trained actors, and internationally reputable stars who appealed to both domestic and foreign markets and had the potential to produce prestigious films.[1]

Central to the success of this reinvention of Columbia was the presence of international talent. The prevailing view within Hollywood from the late 1920s onwards was that European cinema, most notably German expressionist cinema, had elevated film into a 'high art'. Therefore, signing key practitioners associated with German cinema was seen to be potentially fortuitous to legitimizing Hollywood cinema in general. An additional and more economically significant benefit was the international status of European star performers. During the 1920s and 1930s, Hollywood pursued a 'voracious program of acquisition' of European star talent as one means of strengthening Hollywood's hold on foreign markets: American films with established European stars sold well to European audiences (Vasey 1997: 163). Any move that would benefit sales of the American films in overseas markets was important, especially the important and profitable German market, at a time when foreign markets were attempting to challenge Hollywood's 'imperialism' by imposing quotas on the import of American films during the late 1920s and early 1930s (Saunders 1999; Gomery 1980). Aware of Lorre's reputation following *M* (even though it had not been widely released in the United States), and spurred on by the commercial success of *The Man Who Knew Too Much*, Cohn pursued Lorre because the actor was already positioned as a highly skilled screen 'artist' and 'star' of German cinema. Cohn aimed to capitalize on this status in order to benefit Columbia's own reputation and economic standing.

Cohn's view of the direction that Lorre's career should take in Hollywood reflected the strategy he had for his own studio. The studio supported Lorre's desire to pursue roles and projects that were distanced from the psychotic, the horrific or the murderous. Initially, this approach appeared to benefit both parties, and the projects that Lorre actively pursued during this period bore the hallmarks of literary and historical prestige, in keeping with Cohn's overall aims. Lorre was instrumental in ensuring that *Crime and Punishment* reached the production stage. He was also involved in potential stage and screen versions of Ferdinand Bruckner's *Napoleon the First* (Youngkin 2005: 143–45);[2] and he had long harboured a desire to film the stories of Kaspar Hauser – something he had been in the process of pursuing when he left Europe in 1933 – along with Jaroslav Hašek's novel, *The Good Soldier Schweik* (*New York Times*, 3 November 1935: 5).

Lorre was given extra time to develop these culturally desirable projects. For the first eight months of his contract, Lorre was effectively employed to research rather than to make films. Cohn did not take the option of cancelling the contract after the initial six months. Instead, the actor remained a fixture at Columbia, until Lorre secured his own release in 1936. Although there were problems in finding Lorre screen work that was suitable to both actor and studio, Columbia persisted with their investment. However, in spite of these 'noble' intentions it soon became apparent that the studio could offer Lorre nothing apart from 'a featured role in a Jack Hart melodrama' (ibid.). This finally forced Lorre to take charge of his own development, and he resolved to approach studio executives with his own idea for a prestigious picture: an adaptation of Dostoevsky's *Crime and Punishment*.

Cohn agreed to make the film, but before production commenced on the adaptation, he temporarily loaned Lorre out to MGM to make *Mad Love* (possibly in order to recoup the investment of having employing the actor without casting him in any films). *Mad Love* was an adaptation of Maurice Renard's novel *Les Mains d'Orlac* (The Hands of Orlac), which had already been filmed in Austria in 1924 with Conrad Veidt in the title role. In the 1935 version, the focus shifted away from the eponymous character, Stephen Orlac (Colin Clive), a noted pianist whose hands are crushed in a train wreck, to the more peripheral character of Dr Gogol (Lorre), the surgeon who is obsessed with Orlac's wife, Yvonne (Frances Drake). Gogol's obsession leads him to replace Orlac's damaged hands with those of a recently executed killer, in the hope of framing the pianist for murder so that the doctor may pursue his deranged infatuation with Yvonne. Despite the grand intentions of Columbia for their European 'star', not only did Lorre make his Hollywood debut for another studio, but he played the type of psychotically murderous character that he had been keen to distance himself from. In a move that seemingly typecast him for the rest of his career, Lorre's role as the 'mad doctor' fuelled the argument that Hollywood was only able to perceive the actor as valuable in terms of his associations with specific genres and disturbed roles. However, the significance of *Mad Love* in relation to Lorre's career is more complex than this overview suggests.

First and foremost, Lorre's debut in a horror film should be seen as a temporary matter of convenience rather than a coherent industry-wide employment strategy. For Columbia, loaning Lorre to MGM was a means of quickly and pragmatically promoting their acquisition without having to deviate from their own prestigious aims, which the studio still hoped to achieve with the production of *Crime and Punishment*. Since MGM was a much larger studio, and one already connected with notions of prestige, it could be argued that the association between the two studios (through

Lorre) would benefit the smaller studio to a large degree. Additionally, MGM had no long-term goals concerning the management of Lorre's career, either as a horror star or otherwise. Therefore, Lorre fitted into their existing scheme for producing *Mad Love* in some other way.

Mad Love was an obvious attempt by MGM to capitalize on the success of the Universal horror cycle of the early 1930s which included *Dracula* (1931) and *Frankenstein* (1931), and turned Boris Karloff and Bela Lugosi into icons of horror cinema. The film conformed to many conventional aspects of horror cinema and iconography from this period, such as narrative patterns and visual imagery, including the interruption of sexual and social stability by a grotesque and monstrous antagonist, who forms, along with the central couple, a perverse love triangle which must be broken in order for normality to resume and the narrative to end satisfactorily.

The Hollywood horror films of this period also shared a certain cinematic coherence which may explain the reasons MGM chose to hire Lorre; a resonance with the same well-regarded German expressionist cinema that had prompted Harry Cohn to approach Lorre in the first instance. MGM had already hired the German émigré, Karl Freund, to direct the remake of *Orlacs Hände*, and it may have been a question of attempting to maintain a certain overall consistency by employing a German (or more accurately in the case of Lorre, 'Germanic') star. To this end, Lorre suited the interim needs of the studio regarding the maintenance of an appropriately 'European' atmosphere within their remake. *Mad Love* is inherently connected to traditions within European Art Cinema through Lorre himself, Freund, and the original 1924 film, and is typical of an alignment between a 'low-brow' Hollywood genre and a 'high-brow' European cinema, and Hollywood's targeting of German markets through the employment of German émigré personnel that took place during the decade. It is also through wider associations such as this one that the definition of Lorre as a 'horror' actor from the onset of his Hollywood career can be seen as a simplistic appraisal of the terms of his employment.

In a process which is almost unique within Lorre's whole career, the character he played conformed far more closely to (what would become) the conventional public image of the actor, than the extra-filmic publicity discourses which promoted him during the film's release. The film text itself adhered to established practices within horror cinema, and the way in which Lorre was used and represented (although not necessarily in his performance) within *Mad Love* is equally in keeping with this strategy.

This can be illustrated at a most basic level by the decision to deviate from the story of both the source novel and the Austrian film version by making Gogol, not Orlac, the leading character. It is not clear when in the production process this decision was taken, but the casting of Lorre may have been a motivating factor in the move to concentrate on Gogol. Orlac is a tragic hero, a happily married man who becomes an innocent victim of circumstances beyond his control. Gogol is a villainous manipulator who uses his skills to harm others in the pursuit of his own goals. In his first Hollywood role, Lorre is presented as a performer who plays the 'abnormal' rather than the 'normal' figure – a representation which may have taken its cue from the cinematic heritage of Lorre, through his appearance in films such as *M* and *The Man Who Knew Too Much* (the trailer for *Mad Love* makes reference to both these films). Changing the focus towards Lorre/Gogol demonstrates a particular decision regarding perceptions and representations of the actor in relation to mainstream American cinema. This implicit distinction between what roles Lorre should (or should not) be given is further compounded by the representations of the character and the actor within the film.

Mad Love presents the actor as a cinematic spectacle, and the spectacular nature of Lorre as Gogol is linked to notions of the unconventional, the bizarre and the perverted. From the outset, both Gogol and Lorre are presented as 'othered' figures. Gogol's head is completely bald (Lorre shaved his head for the role), which over-emphasizes Lorre's already distinctive facial features, as does the surgeon's costume that Gogol wears in later scenes. Many of Gogol's scenes frame Lorre's face in isolation and are carefully photographed using expressionist low-key lighting, forcing the viewer to peruse the image of Lorre's face and also suggesting an element of the grotesque. He is explicitly characterized as 'foreign', although as would be the case in a great many of Lorre's subsequent Hollywood roles, it is not stated precisely where he is from. Gogol is first seen in the 'Theatre des Horreurs', wearing an elaborate fur-trimmed coat, where he has come to see Yvonne 'perform' onstage; he appears to derive sexual pleasure from an act which sees her being tortured. The extreme and horrific nature of the role is continually emphasized through formal means such as costume, *mise-en-scène*, and narrative.

In spite of the ways in which *Mad Love* can be characterized as mainstream low-brow genre filmmaking and the potential of the film to help typecast Lorre as a horror icon, intertextual connotations and publicity campaigns served to undermine these perceptions. First, the twin notions of prestige filmmaking and 'artistry' through performance ran throughout the film's production and reception. This was partly created by the implicit link to the 'artistic' German cinema. In addition to the cinematic heritage alluded to by the film, certain literary references also formed an integral part of the narrative and characterization within *Mad Love*. This was by no means unusual in horror films from this period, many of which had literary sources, but *Mad Love* builds upon the literary horror of Renard's original novel by depicting Gogol (and by association, Lorre) as a cultured man who quotes extensively from the myth of Pygmalion and Galatea, Oscar Wilde's 'Ballad of Reading Gaol' and Robert Browning's 'Porphyria's Lover'.

The most explicit method by which *Mad Love* was associated with prestige and artistry was through extra-textual discourses that pertained to the figure of Lorre. This is most apparent in the trailer for the film which, although produced by MGM to advertise its own production, served a dual purpose in the way it promoted both the film and the 'new star' who was making his American debut. Again, it is unclear as to precisely why MGM took this approach, which seemed to mirror Harry Cohn's perceptions of how his star and his studio should be presented, although there is no record of any such agreement being made in the terms of Lorre's loan-out. It is perhaps in keeping with publicity discourses favoured by MGM which emphasized the role (and skill) of the star-actor over the position of a film within

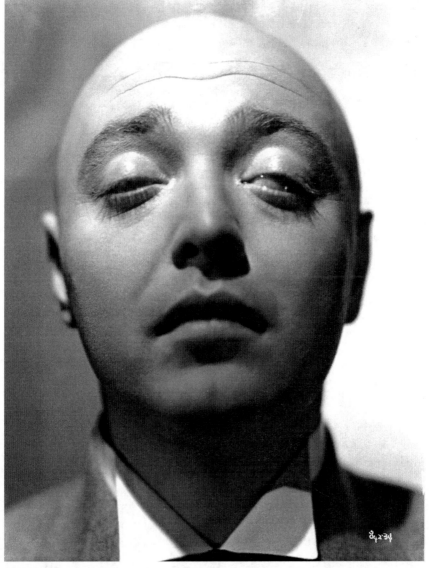

Figure 3.1 Lorre as Dr Gogol in *Mad Love* (1935). Photo: MGM/Photofest.

Figure 3.2 The trailer for *Mad Love* (1935).

an established genre, or presented him as a recognizably conventional star identity, in keeping with other major international stars of the era.

The trailer for *Mad Love* by no means disguised the horror aspects of the film, but primarily promoted it with a clear indication that Lorre was a highly trained actor. To do this, it used a framing device around the main advertisement (which showed extracts from the film itself). This framing section introduced the viewer to Lorre, by quoting words attributed to Charlie Chaplin which described Lorre as 'the greatest living actor'. This emphasis was extended through a sequence in which the actor has a telephone conversation with an attractive female fan, whose excitement at talking to Lorre appears to cause him much amusement. This scene makes reference to Lorre's history as a successful screen actor who appeared in the internationally noteworthy films, *M* and *The Man Who Knew Too Much*.

In direct contrast to the film itself, the trailer also presents Lorre in recognizably conventional terms, as a 'normal' man. Significantly, this mode of representing the 'real' Peter Lorre would rarely be used in this way throughout the rest of his career. Unlike the bizarre spectacle of the bald Dr Gogol, Lorre is shown with a full head of hair, he is dressed casually in a lounge suit, and he is charming, relaxed and modest in conversation as he reclines in private domestic space (complete with pet). The short sequence aims to explicitly present Lorre as ordinary. In contrast to extra-filmic representations, such as many of his appearances on American radio or in interviews, here there is never any suggestion that the 'real' Peter Lorre is similar to the psychotic killer that he portrays on-screen. In fact, the opposite is emphasized, as the skill involved in creating a screen performance is made explicit. The trailer highlights the process of acting, not the presence of horror; and that through his screen work, Peter Lorre has acquired the status of an 'artist', not a potential horror icon.

Mad Love enhanced Lorre's professional reputation as an actor, rather than his public image as a horror star. In commercial terms, the film was a box office failure that suffered from being released at the end of the 1930s horror cycle; according to Steven Thornton (1999: 57), 'It experienced dismal returns in both the domestic and foreign markets ... and was con-signed to the film vaults [where] it languished until the early 1970s'. Whereas one might assume that the role of Dr Gogol played a vital role in shaping how the American public came to perceive Peter Lorre, since Gogol's insane, perverted and murderous personality has much in common with Lorre's extra-filmic persona that was established in the years that followed the film's release, it appears that mass audiences had little access to the film until the beginnings of cult horror fandom in the 1960s and 1970s. The unique appearance of Gogol may have aimed towards an iconographic status similar to that of Karloff's Monster or Lugosi's Dracula, but the striking visual image of a bald-headed Lorre never achieved this iconic position. Indeed in the most recognizable image from the film, Lorre's identity is obscured, as Gogol wears a gruesome mechanical dis-guise and speaks in a low-hissing whisper. A crucial point to register here is the fact that the film did not lead to Lorre's 'typecasting'. Since it was a commercial failure, it made little economic sense to repeatedly cast Lorre within the genre (either by Columbia or other studios) and he did not make another horror film for another five years (and eighteen films).

Mad Love is more indicative of how Lorre was perceived at this early stage in his Hollywood career in its critical, rather than commercial, re-ception. This is again linked specifically to the decisions made within Hollywood publicity discourses, which preferred to emphasize the status that Lorre enjoyed as an internationally reputable actor. At the time of its release, critical reviews of the film in the American press were mixed; however, many articles were dominated by almost universal praise for Lorre's performance. Both the *Hollywood Reporter* (27 June 1935) and the *Motion Picture Herald* (29 June 1935) described Lorre's performance as one which signalled the discovery of a new star of the American box office. There were also a number of established critics in both the United States and in the UK who used *Mad Love* as a means of championing the actor as one of the most talented performers of that particular period in Hollywood. A notable example was the praise of the British writer, Graham Greene, who first reviewed the film for *The Spectator* in 1935, arguing that:

> Mr Lorre, with every physical handicap, can convince you of the goodness, the starved tenderness, of his vice-entangled souls. Those marbly pupils in the pasty spherical face are like the eye-pieces of a microscope through which you can see laid flat on the slide the entangled mind of a man: love and lust, nobility and perversity, hatred of itself and despair jumping out at you from the jelly. (reprinted in Parkinson 1995: 16)

Greene followed this review with an article entitled 'The Genius of Peter Lorre' (July 1936), and this celebratory attitude towards the actor was shared by other prominent figures writing in the United States. Prior to his ap-pearance in *Mad Love*, and as used within the film's trailer, Charlie Chaplin had apparently been impressed enough with Lorre's talents to call him 'one of the greatest character actors' (Sumelian, June 1936: 51) and 'Europe's greatest actor' (Youngkin 2005: 99); and after Lorre's Hollywood debut, these words were again recycled within press reports. The *New York Times* journalist, Andre Sennwald, described Lorre as 'among the great screen actors' in his review of the film (5 August 1935: 12), and also wrote a piece devoted to Lorre entitled 'Peter Lorre: Poet of the Damned' (31 March 1935: 3). Otis Ferguson's film reviews and articles from the mid-1930s often hailed Lorre as an exceptional screen artist. He wrote that 'Lorre is above all the actors I can think of in using the best resources of the screen' (Chamberlain and Wilson 1997: 149). Ferguson is typical of a number of critics and cultural commentators who chose to focus on the artistry of Lorre's screen performances between 1935 and 1937 (beginning with *M* and *The Man Who Knew Too Much*, but continuing with *Mad Love* and others), regardless of what films he was appearing in or what roles he was playing.

This individual or independent critical response to Lorre's screen work worked in harmony with the overall aims of Columbia and Harry Cohn, and this perception of Lorre as an 'artist' was mirrored within studio-produced or studio-monitored publicity discourses, such as biographies or interviews, that were released between 1935 and 1937 (this also includes the early stages of his work at Twentieth Century-Fox). Although, as will be outlined in Chapter 7, promotional material was a key factor in the eventual definition and delineation of Lorre's nefarious public image (along with other non-cinematic media contexts), during this period an alternative 'version' of Peter Lorre existed within publicity rhetoric: 'The Actor as Artist'. Lorre's performative talents, his artistic temperament, and the intense labour that went into a particular performance were continually emphasized. Rather than being presented as having inherent continuities with the characters he plays on-screen, Lorre was described as a craftsman who carefully constructed his performances, who took pleasure in the challenge of 'acting', and in the differences that existed between himself and his roles.

According to *Modern Screen*, Lorre would 'rather act than eat'. Furthermore, the article includes a rather poetic statement from an executive source at Columbia which purposefully fuels this notion of acting as a challenging form of artistic labour: 'Lorre haunted the studio like a sick kitten during all those months of waiting for the right role to turn up', one of Columbia's executives commented. 'He's miserable unless he's acting 14 hours a day. I believe it nourishes his body as well as his soul' (Lynn, January 1936).

During these years, Lorre described acting as 'the only thing I am really serious about' (Sumelian, June 1936: 51) and that 'there must be some higher motive [than money]' (*New York Times*, 3 November 1935). When asked about being 'typed', the actor replied that he 'finds the [Hollywood] roles broad enough to handle all the acting technique I can summon together' (*Detroit Free Press*, 4 January 1937). This form of promotion which prioritized Lorre's position as an actor of artistic merit continued even when Lorre completed his new contract with Twentieth Century-Fox. Harry Brand, the studio's publicity director, made this most explicit when he compiled the studio's first biography of their new acquisition using the following terms: '[Lorre] understands the innermost feelings of the characters he portrays so instinctively that he is never actually Peter Lorre but his current part ... And his dramatic power is so great that he has become the most feared actor in the world ... So Lorre remains the Man whom nobody in Hollywood knows' (Brand 1936).

Even when, from 1937 onwards, shifts within media representations of Lorre began to refer to him primarily via his monstrous and murderous extra-filmic persona, the actor's publicity still briefly included moments where his performative practices were discussed – from his professional disdain for make-up, to the very different personality revealed by the actor when he was not acting (Hall, 2 October 1937; and Tildersley, 25 April 1937). In these examples, much is made of Lorre's 'horror' roles and associated public image, but in doing so, there is a clear understanding of the actor's 'artistry' in the construction of his performances. Up to and including 1937, there can be discerned an underlying objective within Lorre's promotional discourses which impacted upon both employer (Columbia and Twentieth Century-Fox) and employee (Lorre): that cinematic prestige could be achieved through an actor's screen performance.

The apex of this strategy which foregrounded notions of prestige occurred with Lorre's leading role in *Crime and Punishment* in 1935. That the film conforms to the studio's early mode of representation, which sought to publicize Lorre as an 'artist', is most obvious in the actor's unusual on-screen title credit from *Crime and Punishment*, which explicitly defined the actor as 'the celebrated European star'. However, the impetus, at least in the pre-production stages, remained Lorre's. Although it was a prestigious literary adaptation, there is some evidence to suggest the executive powers at Columbia were not wholly convinced that the film was suitable material. A contemporary newspaper report interpreted Lorre's loan to MGM as evidence that Cohn had been outmanoeuvred by the actor because the deal forced Cohn into producing *Crime and Punishment* with Josef von Sternberg in place as director: 'The Hungarian Napoleon had outsmarted the Hollywood Wellingtons' (*New York Times*, 3 November 1935). Lorre himself recorded how he passed a simplistic two-page synopsis to Cohn, in order to persuade him to make the film, but also reports that there were moments of conflict, not least the attempt to shorten Raskolnikov's name to the more audience-friendly 'Rasky' (Lorre, undated).

Lorre's creative input was central to the film; in addition to supplying the synopsis, there were rumours that Lorre contributed extensively to the script – although it was credited to S.K. Lauren and Joseph Anthony (Smith 1999). Not only did he see the project as a major opportunity to star in a defining role, but he had an especially deferential attitude towards the source novel itself. This can be observed in an essay written by Lorre entitled 'The Role I Liked Best'. Although a short version of this was published in 1946, an earlier and longer draft exists which reveals the author's tone to be more literary and grandiloquent. In it, Lorre describes the novel as 'one of the great classics of literature', and initially outlines Raskolnikov as 'the quintessence of tragedy because he was the quintessence of isolation' (Lorre, undated).

This retrospective essay demonstrates Lorre's interest in the complex psychology of the character and the ramifications of his actions, and this informed his performance. The dominant performative style used to portray Raskolnikov is naturalistic striving towards realism and psychological verisimilitude. Unlike many of Lorre's other performances (both pre- and post-*Crime and Punishment*), this is a character-driven performance that is singular rather than pluralistic in tone and style. The illusion of psychological coherence is maintained throughout: Lorre uses no non-naturalistic or self-reflexive techniques here which attempt to break the 'fourth wall'. Indeed, his performance conforms to Stanislavskian conventions through the prevention of a dialogue between actor and spectator. The relationship is firmly constructed between character and spectator, whereby the actor generates no obvious 'spectacle' of performance. There are no moments where Lorre draws attention to himself as a performer, and throughout the film his performance works towards maintaining the illusion that Lorre 'is' Raskolnikov.

The atypical naturalism of Lorre's performance can be illustrated by a comparison of two humorous sequences in *Crime and Punishment* and *Mad Love* (two films which are not comic texts, although *Mad Love* contains elements of dark humour). Within the former film there is a scene in which Raskolnikov mocks his prospective brother-in-law, Mr Lushen (Gene Lockheart). To achieve this, Lorre uses physical and verbal methods (breaking Lushen's top hat and describing him as holding anything up to 'fifteen' government positions). It is a singularly unambiguous performance in a broadly comic episode that has one purpose; to foster a clear understanding of both Raskolnikov's emotional and social positions – he is powerless to prevent his sister's marriage for money, and therefore these moments are isolated petty victories on his part. Through the way the two significant characters (Raskolnikov and Lushen) interact, the viewer is encouraged to support Raskolnikov's small victories rather than to question their validity. Lushen is created as a ridiculous and grotesque figure through Lockheart's decision to represent him as excessively prim, overbearing and officious. Lorre's performance is momentarily comic, but it remains in line with the character's state of mind and it temporarily releases the frustration and tension surrounding Raskolnikov in an engaging and believable manner, partly through Lorre's appropriately small-scale acts of destruction.

By comparison, the comic sequence from *Mad Love* is more pluralistic in tone and performance, aiming as it does to dramatize the underlying irreconcilability of Gogol's attitudes to the welfare of his patients and the achievements of his own personal desires. Gogol sits by the bedside of a sick child that he has been treating, who has just managed 'her first natural sleep in weeks', when he receives a telephone call informing him that a guillotining is about to take place (spectating at the public event is a hobby of the doctor's). His subsequent excitement at this news wakes the child who begins to cry. The potential farcical impact of the comedy is undermined somewhat by how Lorre plays the scene. His technique combines excessive physical gesture with a verbal underplaying of his dialogue. The performative element of Lorre's acting is reinforced because the scene is framed in mid-shot throughout; a choice which prevents the child's crying being seen merely as a punch-line to the set-up. In addition to the formal methods employed, the actor's multi-layered and ambiguous performance heightens the scene as a moment of black comedy (rather than farce), as Gogol's genuine concern for his patient first introduces an extra dimension to his own characterization as well as allowing the juxtaposition to work humorously, rather than being a singular mode of representation that has the primary objective of making the character's actions psychologically appropriate, as Lorre does in *Crime and Punishment*.

Lorre's verisimilar and somewhat restrained performance as Raskolnikov demonstrates the closeness of the actor to the source material. This also explains many of the film's (and Lorre's) faults. Whilst Lorre gives a confident and mature performance of a complex character, the film was not a wholly successful one – something Lorre himself commented on in 'The Role I Liked Best' – and on release it received a poor critical and commercial response. Lorre's attempt to portray Raskolnikov using naturalistic practices drew mixed reviews. Many critics derided the simplicity of the film as a whole (drawing unfavourable comparisons with both the novel and a French adaptation, *Crime et Châtiment*, that had been released only a few months previously), although a few singled Lorre out for praise. Others were more disdainful of Lorre's acting, believing it to be an ineffective and often incoherent portrayal that failed in its attempts to reveal Raskolnikov's psychological journey. One commented that the focus upon Raskolnikov, 'as the only characterisation allowed to retain any subtlety', had an unbalancing effect as other characters became mere ciphers for him to act against (Levin 1971: 102).

Andre Sennwald, the earlier champion of Lorre's work, was equally critical of the representation of Raskolnikov in an article that revisited his original review in order to focus upon the role of Josef von Sternberg. In it, he laid the blame firmly with the director, stating that 'Von Sternberg's Raskolnikov is erratic and unconvincing ... Having a vast regard for Mr Lorre's talents, I refuse to charge him with failure to create a full-length portrait of a character who is psychologically meaningless in the very writing of the American script' (24 November 1935: 5). In many contemporary reviews which shared this view of the film's artistic failings, that failure is often characterized as Sternberg's rather than Lorre's. This perspective, which underlined the place of the film within the context of the director's career, soon came to define perceptions: in its immediate reception, it was seen as the continuation of Sternberg's failing career (his contract with Paramount had recently been terminated); and with hindsight, as a minor and forgettable entry in the director's canon. Whether positive or negative in nature, the emphasis on Sternberg in the film's reception is somewhat surprising given the central and publicly acknowledged role that Lorre played in the pre-production of *Crime and Punishment*. Although most critical responses did not specifically censure Lorre – in fact the majority continued to promote him using the same 'artistic' discourses – the disappointing response towards *Crime and Punishment* marked a turning point in Lorre's career regarding the terms of his employment within Hollywood, the roles he was offered, and the way that the actor was perceived and publicized. The effect that these dramatic changes had on Lorre's place in Hollywood was fully established by the end of 1937.

The Transitory Period: 1937 and the 'Mr Moto' Series

The failure of *Crime and Punishment* to achieve the necessary prestigious reception caused concern for Cohn and Columbia, and frustration for Lorre. After investing in the actor for over two years, in 1936 the studio relented and Lorre won a release from his five-year contract. In November of the same year he entered into another long-term contract with Twentieth Century-Fox in a move masterminded by the vice president in charge of production, Darryl F. Zanuck, who, according to Lorre's biographer, promised to showcase the actor's versatility (Youngkin 2005: 141). In addition to his executive position, Zanuck was also heavily and directly involved in day-to-day filmmaking decisions at Twentieth Century-Fox. He was credited as producer on all of the 'A' pictures that Lorre made for the studio under the 1936 contract (with the exception of the actor's first film *Crack-Up* in 1936), including *I Was an Adventuress* in 1940 which was made during Lorre's period as a freelance contractor. Throughout his long career in Hollywood, Zanuck had a significant impact on casting choices, role allocation and the management and development of the careers of Twentieth Century-Fox's major stars. Despite not being directly involved in Lorre's first film for the studio, in the same year Zanuck also allowed his new star's image to be used in the Sonja Henie vehicle, *One in a Million*.[3] Following Lorre's engagement as Mr Moto, it was Zanuck who was specifically reprimanded in an article by Jimmie Fidler in the *Chicago Sunday Times* in 1938 for failing to make the best use of the actor and wasting his talents on mediocre roles (10 July 1938).

To begin with, the labour strategy of Lorre's new employer was to cast him in a series of supporting roles rather than leads: *Crack Up* (1936), *Nancy Steele is Missing* (1937) and *Lancer Spy* (1937). Most relevant to an exploration of Lorre's Hollywood leading roles is the decision taken during 1937 by Zanuck to alter Twentieth Century-Fox's primary employment strategy which had hitherto defined Lorre exclusively as a supporting player. Lorre made only one more supporting appearance under the contract of 1936: as an affable hobo whose fortunes dramatically change when he meets a disillusioned millionaire in *I'll Give a Million* (1938). Stephen D. Youngkin (2005: 162) describes how the actor was initially cast in a further supporting role in *Four Men and a Prayer* (1938), only for Zanuck to substantially redraft, cut and recast the role before production without proper explanation for the removal of Lorre from the supporting cast. Instead, the actor's status as a leading actor was re-established in 1937. However this was through a series of 'B' movies which contrasted greatly with the big-budget 'A' picture adaptations that had characterized his screen work as a Hollywood lead so far. Management of Lorre's career was effectively passed to Sol Wurtzel, head of Twentieth Century-Fox's 'B' department (although as the *Chicago Sunday Times* article suggests, Zanuck still maintained full and final control), when Lorre was cast as the eponymous character in a new series Wurtzel was producing based on the 'Mr Moto' detective stories by J.P. Marquand.

Mr Moto was Japanese and since he was played on-screen by Lorre – a white European actor – it is impossible to discuss the series without acknowledging the issue of what has come to be termed 'yellowface' performance: portrayals of Asian characters by white actors. These portrayals often used generic methods of representation, whereby what was invoked was vaguely 'oriental' rather than specifically Chinese or Japanese. I am not aiming to provide a full exploration of yellowface discourses here; instead I will highlight some of the issues that are most relevant to an analysis of Lorre's career as a whole and to his portrayal of Moto. Histories of yellowface firstly outline how certain representations of Asian characters became prominent during various periods. This included a move from the negative 'bad Asian other' of the 'Yellow Peril' in the 1920s to the superficially 'good Asian other' figure of the Oriental Detective in the 1930s, where Lorre's Mr Moto existed alongside Mr Wong (Boris Karloff) and Charlie Chan (Warner Oland).[4]

Examinations of the representation of oriental characters in Hollywood critique the performative methods used to portray these characters: namely the use of white actors made up to 'appear' oriental. The employment of, in particular, Europeans in oriental roles was common practice throughout Hollywood's history, and this strategy helped to perpetuate inaccurate and often explicitly racist stereotypes of Asian figures through the way that portrayals bastardized certain aspects of Asian cultures. This was especially true regarding the methods used to represent physical appearance, voice or accent, and mannerisms or behavioural qualities. These critiques are equally applicable to Twentieth Century-Fox's Mr Moto series, which is as guilty as any example cited by critics of yellowface in the way that the films suggest that the Mitteleuropean actor could unquestioningly pass as Japanese. The inherent ridiculousness of this mode of representation was compounded by the repeated use of actors of Asian heritage in supporting roles, which only drew attention to Lorre's lack of authentic oriental identity. Notable examples included Keye Luke (repeating his role as Charlie Chan's 'No.1 Son', Lee from the Chan films) in *Mr Moto's Gamble*; Lotus Long ('Karen Sorrell') in *Think Fast Mr Moto* and *Mysterious Mr Moto*; and Philip Ahn in *Thank You Mr Moto*.

Within the context of Lorre's transnational career, it is important to consider the specifics of Lorre's individual performance as Mr Moto in relative isolation from the negative associations of yellowface. It is true that aspects of the films conform to oriental stereotypes, such as the use of aphorisms ('A beautiful girl is only confusing to a man'), which support Thi Thanh Nga's (1995: 39) description of the dialogue as 'fortune-cookie one-liners'. However, to reduce any analysis of Lorre's performance as Moto merely in terms of its generic oriental 'ah-so' qualities is a misreading of the many issues raised by the casting of Lorre, particularly when considered within the context of the direction Lorre's career was taking and the public discourses surrounding the actor during the late 1930s. As such, I want to reconsider what the role of Mr Moto reveals about Peter Lorre rather than vice versa: to prioritize the position of the individual actor over the ethnic identity of the character.

Indicative of this alternative perspective towards the relationship between actor and character is the concept of 'otherness'. The role of Mr Moto has been interpreted as one of many types of roles that cast Lorre as explicitly foreign, thus helping to construct an image around the actor which served to reinforce Lorre's own position as an 'outsider' within Hollywood filmmaking and American society. Again, this casting of actors (usually Europeans) who were widely identified by the American public as 'foreigners' in Asian roles in American films has been read as an industrial compromise in the representation of oriental characters. Although Asian actors were rarely cast in leading heroic roles (such as those of the oriental detectives), certain European actors were seen to be able to convey a generic 'foreignness' or 'otherness', whilst their 'real' European/Caucasian identity was also seen to allow the American viewer to identify with the Asian character.

This relationship is somewhat complicated with regards to the 'outsider' status of both Lorre and Mr Moto. A number of the conventional readings of the roles played by Lorre, or his own personal circumstances and national/cultural identities which construct the actor as occupying this position, can be questioned. Secondly, certain changes were made in adapting the Mr Moto stories for the cinema. Within the Twentieth Century-Fox films, the character of Mr Moto is significantly Americanized. Rather than being presented as wholly foreign, Moto is partly constructed through various means that imply that he is Japanese-American and is familiar with American customs and institutions: for example, he speaks perfect English (a move which also worked to differentiate Moto from Charlie Chan, whose idiosyncratic grasp of English was used to create 'comedic' moments) and identifies himself in *Think Fast Mr Moto* as a graduate of Stanford University ('Class of '21'). In this respect, Mr Moto, and by implication, Lorre himself, is allowed to possess a somewhat fluid cultural and national identity, rather than being constructed as a marginalized figure. In turn, this reflects the more complex position of many other roles played by Lorre that have otherwise been read as rigidly 'foreign' or 'othered', including his appearances in horror films and the patriotic war dramas of the 1940s.

To some degree, aspects of Lorre's performance as Moto seek to distance him from certain extreme conventions of yellowface. Whilst the overall objectives of the performance and presentation of the actor remain concerned with 'appearing' oriental, in comparison to many of the other representations of Asian characters the techniques chosen by Lorre are particularly minimal. Unlike other white actors who were cast in oriental roles, Lorre did not wear facial prosthetics in order to obscure his own (already distinctive) Caucasian features in order to affect a supposedly more Asian physiognomy. Traditionally, cross-ethnic make-up techniques were outlined in instruction manuals and included eyepieces that went over eyelids, rubber bands and facial colouring. These methods transformed the appearance of the actors, but the results looked neither convincingly Asian nor recognizably white.

In his portrayals of Moto, Lorre wore a slightly darker base make-up (something he also used in *The Maltese Falcon*) and a pair of circular wire-rimmed glasses. These glasses barely disguised one of his key identifying features – his large eyes; and the way in which his bespectacled face was photographed in many sequences actually emphasized these features, effectively destroying any pretence to an illusion of oriental identity. Again, in contrast to more traditional yellowface performances, Lorre did not attempt an oriental accent in his characterization of Moto. Instead he used a higher and softer tone for the detective's everyday voice. He only adopted a more stereotypical representation (such as staccato accents and broken dialect) when Moto was in disguise. Since Moto's work often relied upon concealing his identity, despite Lorre's measured performance as the detective, a number of sequences within the films comply with the more obviously excessive (and therefore, racist) overtones of yellowface practice, although these do not dominate Lorre's portrayal.

Since Moto was a (mostly) calm and impassive character who rarely revealed his emotions or motives, the core of Lorre's performance had to be based around more minimalist techniques of gesture and expression. The actor came to rely upon a carefully constructed interaction with props, coupled with a slow and deliberate use of his eyes (helpfully framed by his spectacles) as a means of expressing character and creating tension within the mystery stories.

Elements of Lorre's performance, especially his apparent refusal to use conventional make-up, played an important role in early publicity strategies employed by Twentieth Century-Fox. In both studio-released biographies and studio-monitored interviews (circa 1937) conducted with Lorre, the actor is credited with the creation of the character through psychological means rather than physical transformation. Lorre is seen to be employing a Stanislavskian-style realistic performance (again, as opposed to a method that could be described as merely 'face-making'), and is quoted as saying that 'Character comes from inside the player – and is not something that can be applied as paint or putty' (Brand 1937) and 'For the time being, Peter Lorre ceases to exist' (*The Family Circle*, 8 July 1938: 12). This mode of marketing clearly continued the strategy begun by Columbia, which sought to emphasize Lorre's artistry as an actor, and his apparent preference for recognizably naturalistic performative styles which strove towards psychological realism, rather than defining Lorre's work as Moto in line with the more obviously experimental or demonstrative forms of impersonation that the actor had used in the past, both on-screen and onstage.

Whilst Lorre's decision to eschew make-up and accent may have led to his performances being reported as 'naturalistic', it also implicitly prioritized the position of the actor over the character; a perspective that was central to more experimental performative techniques. Throughout his employment as the oriental detective – and despite his own words to the contrary – Lorre's own identity was never fully submerged in the role, and he remained highly recognizable as the actor Peter Lorre. The Moto films illustrate that Lorre continued to use a style that employed many non-naturalistic elements within a system of production and exchange (Hollywood) which was constructed around concepts of naturalism and realism – a practice which heavily contradicted the various forms of advertising discourses which attempted to characterize Lorre as a naturalistic dramatic artist.

This performative style, which attempted to maintain the distance between actor and role, also had an effect on Lorre's public reception. The Mr Moto series was a very popular and successful series with the American mass public – as was grudgingly acknowledged by the critic, Bosley Crowther, who wrote in the *New York Times* in his review of *Mysterious Mr Moto*: '[T]he long run of Mr Moto adventures ... are of the kind that breeds a soft tolerance in a reviewer: what is to be gained, after all, from swimming against a trend apparently as well established as the Gulf Stream' (19 September 1938: 16). The role of the Japanese detective generated a level of fame for Lorre among American audiences that none of his previous roles had managed. In many ways it can be described as the role that made Lorre a star, albeit as the 'star' of a series of 'B' movies that made up the second half of a double-bill feature. Significantly, the image of the 'oriental' did not play a major factor in informing how the American public perceived Lorre's extra-filmic persona during the years that the series was produced (1937 to 1939). Instead, his extra-filmic persona remained fixed around notions of horror or menace.[5]

As the Mr Moto series progressed, the way in which Lorre was marketed began to shift further away from the pattern first established by Columbia. Initially, publicity continued to present Lorre's career in wholly positive terms through discourses which made a link between the detective films and notions of a skilled performance (as discussed above in the way they outlined the processes of performing and the construction of character). This maintained the perspective of Lorre as an actor of considerable artistic merit. Biographies and articles chose to focus on Lorre's talents by describing the role of Mr Moto as a new 'challenge' (Brand 1938) for the actor to increase his popularity at the box office and to play a 'likeable, sympathetic characterisation' (*The Family Circle*, 8 July 1938: 12). This was in spite of the lowly status that the Moto films had within the industry. However, as will be explored in the next section, between 1938 and 1941, descriptions of Lorre's 'artistry' become less prominent as he became more associated with low-budget studio filmmaking. In keeping with this perceived drop in status, the overall tone of Lorre's publicity material also changed, and it can be characterized as making both negative judgements on Lorre's past career and more positive pronouncements concerning the potential of his future roles. Furthermore, an alternative phrase was increasingly being introduced in order to define Lorre's position as an actor: he moved from being an 'artist' to being 'typecast'.

A 'Victim of Typecasting': Promoting Lorre from 1938 to 1941

Scholarly discourses which emphasize the commercial value of actors explicitly situate performers within systems of production and exchange which seek to create and then manage or promote performances. These perspectives can be very useful in understanding why specific promotional strategies were applied to Lorre. Pamela Robertson Wojcik (2003: 224) observes that marketability, coherence and familiarity – 'the necessity for known commodities' – are all key components of film acting, the star system, and the determination of individual economic value. Barry King (1985) foregrounds the role played by the actors themselves in the creation of a central defining image with which they can be marketed (and therefore employed), describing the development of a 'valid personality' on the part of the performer through which they interact with employers, press and audience. Whilst the lack of continuity between Lorre's screen roles and his extra-filmic persona problematize aspects of this theory, the level of agency that King attributes to the actor in the creation of this image is significant as it suggests complicity between public pronouncements attributed to the actor (about his own career) and the perceived value of that actor by the industry, or more specifically his employers. One can see the shift in Lorre's own increasingly pessimistic definitions of acting – a vocation he described in 1936 as, 'the only thing I am serious about', but in later years characterized by a far more disparaging attitude, as evidenced in phrases such as 'face-making' and in the statements he made about his inability to escape 'typecasting'. They were as much about a need to publicly maintain continuity with his changing commodity value, as they were indicative of his own disillusionment with his profession and his performative style.

Throughout the late 1930s and early 1940s, value judgements of Lorre's screen work were unduly influenced by the way that he was publicized by his employers, and also by comments from the actor himself. His public perception originated from an extra-filmic marketing strategy constructed in line with a specific industrial purpose rather than an accurate description of his work. This is implicitly highlighted within *Variety*'s review of *Island of Doomed Men* (1940), which attempts to be critical of the film itself, but only does so in terms which illustrate the inherent commodification of the actor. It summarizes the film as little more than 'Lorre [doing] his standard horror tricks' and 'The Peter Lorre name and its sinister selling angle of sinister evil-doing will be an aid' (27 May 1940). Recent retrospectives of Lorre's career, which perpetuate the myth that Lorre was typecast in certain roles, also reveal the continuing influence that this promotional scheme has had. The question remains as to why the subject of typecasting is invoked in such a conspicuous and deliberate manner in promotional material pertaining to Peter Lorre, when it did not characterize the specific conditions of the actor's employment or performances.

A close analysis of the series of Twentieth Century-Fox biographies of Lorre, taken from his early contracted years at the studio (1936–1937) and from his first freelance engagement for the same studio in 1940, illustrates how definitions of the actor subtly encouraged a shift in the way Lorre was constructed, first as an 'artist' and then as 'typecast', often using the same roles as evidence of their pronouncements. These 'biographies' were short paragraphs outlining the actor's life and career that were produced by the studio's publicity department and circulated to the press upon the release of a new film. This stance was subsequently repeated within more independent printed media (including interviews, reviews, and career overviews) from 1938 onwards.

As quoted above, the Twentieth Century-Fox biography produced in 1936 makes explicit reference to Lorre's 'dramatic genius' as an actor (Brand 1936). It comprised descriptions of his instinctive naturalistic skill and range as a performer, able to work in drama and comedy, and onstage or on-screen. Central to the text is the notion of Lorre's flexibility: there is no mention of a repeated style or role that characterizes his work. The 1937 biography (in which Lorre discusses his appointment as Mr Moto) is equally focused upon the specifics of Lorre's craft, and exhaustively details the research into Japanese culture that Lorre undertook in California (Brand

1937). However, it also implicitly changes the terms of the debate concerning Lorre's artistic status: whereas the 1936 version used excessive hyperbole ('greatest' and 'genius') to position Lorre high up within the Hollywood hierarchy, the 1937 version describes Lorre in more subdued terms, as the 'master of *character* roles' (my emphasis). Its opening statement that 'You can't fool the camera', also foregrounds the industrial context of Lorre's work; as an actor whose portrayals are reliant upon the presence of cameras, props and equipment, rather than being created solely from an instinctive internal performance.

By 1940, the tone had shifted dramatically, and the subtle foregrounding of business and industrial contexts over artistic endeavours that was implicit in the 1937 biography is made explicit in the version from 1940. This was written to publicize Lorre's freelance contracted role in *I Was an Adventuress*. In this biography, Lorre was defined as 'typecast' as a result of his film roles: his career is described as nothing more than 'four years of being typed by Hollywood' (Brand 1940). However, this direct reference to the issue of typecasting is really describing Lorre's extra-filmic persona rather than his screen roles, and the inherent inaccuracy of the term is made apparent when Lorre is quoted as including Mr Moto within this mode of typecasting: [the actor says] 'I've been the sinister menace constantly. Even in the Mr Moto films, where I was a detective, I was a horror man.'

This wholly negative, and highly questionable, view of Lorre's career by the Twentieth Century-Fox publicity department (including a number of films made by that studio) was presented in order to publicize Lorre's one-off engagement in a role which did not correlate with Lorre's extra-filmic persona. Because of the short-term nature of Lorre's employment, the emphasis was on how the actor's 'unique selling point' (his extra-filmic persona) could be seen to relate to his role, and the apparent opportunity to escape from being typecast served as the main focus of the biography. Therefore, it seems likely that invoking discourses on typecasting served a wider purpose. It was a specific strategy that sought to manage the disparity between roles and extra-filmic persona, and the fact that Lorre rarely conformed to the expectations of his public image, by insisting the opposite to be true: that Lorre remained a 'known commodity' and that this was an isolated diversion from an otherwise coherent film career.

Even in the period between the late 1930s and the early 1940s, when discourses surrounding Lorre began explicitly to characterize the actor as 'typecast', a survey of Lorre's roles reveals this to be an oversimplification. Despite Lorre's own statements, the Mr Moto films have very little association with 'horror': they are adventure stories in which Lorre's detective is heroic, acutely intelligent and acting in the interest of American patriotic causes. The roles that Lorre played both prior to and after his appointment as Moto often shifted between the sympathetic and the unsympathetic. Furthermore, Lorre's performances in the twelve films made between 1937 and the beginning of his association with Warner Bros. in 1941 can be described using a wide range of terms. He created characters who were, at various times, charming and engaging (Louie in *I'll Give a Million* and Polo in *I Was an Adventuress*), smugly professional and mercenary (Baron Taggart in *Crack Up*, Major Grunning in *Lancer Spy* and Captain Chang in *They Met in Bombay*), cruelly manipulative and sinister (Danel in *Island of Doomed Men*, Fenninger in *You'll Find Out*, and My Hyde in *Mr District Attorney*), or pathetic and submissive (Cochon in *Strange Cargo*), as well as including characters who do not easily fit into any one singular categorization (Sturm in *Nancy Steele is Missing*, The Stranger in *Stranger on the Third Floor* and Janos/Johnny in *The Face Behind the Mask*).

A few of these roles make direct reference to Lorre's extra-filmic persona (The Stranger and Fenninger); however the majority cannot be seen as contributing greatly to the overall image of menacing or psychotic horror. Additionally, whilst some continuities can be discerned throughout Lorre's performances, the sheer difference in scale of the parts which ranged from primary lead, singular support and ensemble support, and even cameo appearances (*Mr District Attorney*), demanded a variety of performative techniques and methods.

Much of Lorre's screen work from this period contains performances that are more complex and subtly executed than the 'artistry' on display in either *Mad Love* or *Crime and Punishment*. One of his remaining leading performances, Janos/Johnny Sazbo in *The Face Behind the Mask*, demonstrates the quality that Lorre was still producing during these apparently lean years. The irony of Lorre's situation was compounded to a certain degree because the film was produced by Columbia – the scene of Lorre's initial bid for artistry – which employed him on a twelve-day freelance basis (the schedule permitted for the film) in their 'B' department. In spite of these inauspicious circumstances, *The Face Behind The Mask* is a complex text in its own right, and is also noteworthy because of the central role played by Lorre – partly in the way that Lorre is used in a reflexive manner by the director, Robert Florey (in a similar way to their later collaboration, *The Beast With Five Fingers*) and through the actor's own performative choices.

Critiques of *The Face Behind The Mask* emphasize how the narrative appears to reference Lorre's own life, turning the story into an allegorical reflection upon the way that Hollywood perceived the actor (Youngkin 2005: 174; and Gemünden 2003: 100). Janos is a poor but hopeful and skilled immigrant who arrives in New York seeking work as a watchmaker. His face is irreparably scarred in a horrific accident when his hotel burns down. Owing to his grotesque appearance, society shuns him and he is forced to turn to a life of crime in order to survive – which he does to great success. Fully Americanized as 'Johnny', the criminal mastermind, the increasingly bitter man finds salvation through his relationship with a blind girl, Helen. After a misunderstanding leads to her death at the hands of Johnny's former gang, he swears revenge and kidnaps the perpetrators, stranding them (and himself) in the desert to die. Whilst there are reflexive elements used by Florey and Lorre in the film, conclusive readings which seek to link Janos's fate with Lorre's own fate as a skilled actor, whose unconventional appearance and outsider status limited his own fortunes, are undermined to a certain degree when one becomes aware of the variety and level of success that Lorre achieved on-screen, both up to 1941 and beyond.

The film is notable in the way that Lorre combines a number of performative styles within his singular portrayal in order to suggest different aspects of Janos's characterization. In and of itself, this fractured method of representation is highly reminiscent of the episodic acting that was central to Brecht's practices of epic theatre in the early 1930s (although the overall performance does not conform precisely to 'epic theory'). There are four distinct stages which are used to represent Janos – all of which consist of individually crafted performances on the part of Lorre: the 'immigrant', the 'freak', the 'gangster' and the 'lover'.

Out of all four performances, the most significant one is the 'immigrant' stage, as it establishes the character against which the remaining stages will be judged. It also constructs Janos as a heroic character who attempts to command both audience sympathy and identification. In keeping with this requirement, Lorre's performance as the 'immigrant' is wholly in keeping with realist or naturalist styles that prioritize the importance of the character over the actor, and give an awareness that the actor is 'performing'. Lorre's adherence to this technique is much more successful than that of his portrayal of Raskolnikov, as the 'immigrant' is deftly created at the expense of the actor's own identity, although this may also be due to the relatively short screen time given to this stage. In order to present Janos the immigrant, Lorre utilizes a soft-toned and high-pitched voice, coupled with a wide-eyed stare and a slightly hunched stance (emphasizing his short height). This works in conjunction with the dialogue, which also presents the character as vulnerable, innocent and naive.[6] Janos's humorous malapropisms ('I am gangstered!') are underplayed by Lorre in order to make Janos's behaviour seem psychologically believable rather than present him as a broadly comic character. Additionally, Janos is physically expressive, but not excessively so, as this would draw attention to the performative elements used by Lorre.

By contrast, the second stage (the 'freak') – which chronicles Janos's disfigurement until his procurement of the titular mask – explicitly foregrounds the notion of 'performance' and makes specific reference to certain non-naturalistic cinematic conventions. This is partly due to the formal restrictions of the sequence: Janos's scarred face is revealed only once, meaning that Lorre is primarily photographed using high-key lighting with his back to camera or in shadow. In this section, Lorre's physical performance becomes far more expressive: sitting in the doctor's chair with his back to the camera waiting for the bandages to be removed from his face, Lorre waves his arms around as Janos describes his watch-making talents. This technique serves a purpose in addition to working within the visual restrictions, because the wild expressionistic gestures used mark a split from the naturalistic and empathetic hero of the earlier section. This 'dehumanizing' process is continued through Lorre's verbalizations. As the bandages come off, a nurse is barely able to stifle a scream. Janos asks, 'Why did she scream? What have you done to my face?'; but his soft voice is replaced by one that incorporates a growling and guttural quality. This underlying tone continues to make an appearance throughout the section to signal Janos's lowest moments. The formal and performative elements conspire to construct Janos as 'animalistic', or even 'monstrous' – and use visual tactics more reminiscent of horror cinema than crime drama. On seeing his reflection, Janos becomes violent and has to be sedated. The ensuing struggle, where the brightly lit doctors attempt to subdue the faceless, wild threat, is filmed as a moment of horror – an effect heightened by a dramatically charged orchestral accompaniment.

The movement away from naturalist techniques continues in the third section (the 'gangster'). Lorre's performance in this extended sequence makes specific reference to his previous stage work with Brecht in *Mann ist Mann* – albeit without Brecht's explicit political agenda. It also builds upon the minimalist performance style that Lorre had begun to use in the Mr Moto films. Janos – now 'Johnny' – has stolen enough money to buy a mask to cover his burnt face. Significantly, the viewer is not shown Johnny's steady rise to power (it is depicted through the befuddled reactions of the police); instead it shifts abruptly from the tormented 'monster' to the 'mask', mirroring, to some degree, the purposefully fractured characterization of Galy Gay in *Mann ist Mann*. In both examples, the objective is to deny an empathetic connection between character and audience.

The visual appearance of the mask seems to be making a reference to an aspect of the earlier controversial performance. In Florey's film, there is no literal mask, but the effect of a mask-like visage is constructed by brightly whitening Lorre's face, just as Lorre chose to reveal Galy Gay's new identity by covering his face in chalk dust. In keeping with Johnny's new identity as a ruthless crime lord, Lorre's minimalist performance emphasizes the blank and immovable nature of the 'mask', and greatly contrasts with the charmingly expressive characterization of the 'immigrant'. As the 'gangster', Lorre's eyes are kept half closed and his voice is quiet, but a hard quality comes through because of his careful annunciation, and his humour is dryly ironic. Every aspect of Lorre's performance depicts Johnny as being in complete control of his environment, and mirrors the doctor's final pronouncement of Johnny's injuries: that 'the nerves are dead'.

The final sequence (the 'lover'), in which Janos/Johnny meets, marries and avenges Helen (Evelyn Keyes), combines elements of the three preceding performative strategies, as the different identities struggle for ascendancy. Even during the course of short sequences (such as when Janos meets Helen or when he reveals the truth to her) Lorre is able to move convincingly between naturalistic and non-naturalistic styles through a swift juxtaposition of verbal and physical techniques (from a change in his tone of voice, to the sudden explosive expression), without disrupting the overall development of both narrative and character. Lorre's 'face-making' reveals the precise structure of his characterization rather than suggesting a mode of careless or lazy performance. As Janos tells Helen about his past, Lorre's physical performance literally represents the four 'faces' of Janos: the wide-eyed hopeful immigrant, the hardened blank-faced crime boss, the shunned freak that no one looks at, and the grotesque monster that he has become as a result of both his disfigurement and criminal activity.

Lorre's highly complex performance, in spite of the many restrictions (such as time, budget, photographic decisions and make-up), includes a series of self-contained and carefully prepared strategies that work in isolation from each other, whilst also maintaining an overall sense of coherence. It is a very clear demonstration of the 'artistry' that can be found in Lorre's period of employment in 'B' pictures. And yet it was widely depicted as conforming to the notion that Lorre was 'typecast' in mediocre menacing roles which merely repeated aspects of his extra-filmic persona in order to maximize the economic potential of the actor. As described

Figure 3.3a The 'immigrant' in *The Face Behind the Mask* (1941).

Figure 3.3b The 'freak' in *The Face Behind the Mask*.

Figure 3.3c The 'gangster' in *The Face Behind the Mask*.

Figure 3.3d The 'monster' in *The Face Behind the Mask*.

(somewhat wearily) in a review in *Motion Picture Herald*: 'Continuing in the roles that have typed him with audiences throughout the country, Peter Lorre returns to the screen in a vehicle that gives him ample opportunity to render another horror characterisation' (15 February 1941).

Discussions which implicitly or explicitly advertised the craft and skill of the screen actor were absent from promotional discourses that pertained to this minor Columbia release.[7] Ironically, given the studio's initial reluctance to promote their 'renowned' new star as a horror star, Columbia actively billed *The Face Behind the Mask* as a horror film. The tagline on the film's poster asked 'What weird madness turned an ordinary man into a monstrous cold-blooded killer?'. The trailer went further and emphasized the link between the film, the horror genre and Peter Lorre, although the terms used are wholly inaccurate when one considers the film itself: 'Peter Lorre ... man turned monster. The underworld's PHANTOM TERROR.' Lorre's specific commodity value is clearly delineated as originating from the close coherence that is suggested to exist between the actor and specific types of film roles and film genres. However, analyses of his film work reveal that, in reality, the unity within Lorre's career came away from the cinema screen in the way publicity strategies continually referenced typecasting via the actor's extra-filmic persona in the marketing of his films.

The publicity rhetoric of typecasting followed Lorre throughout the remainder of his career. However, its continued presence within pressbooks, biographies and other printed material demonstrates – albeit obliquely – that although the actor was presented as such in extra-textual discourses, he was not repeatedly typecast on-screen. This label was often used in released statements by studios advertising films in which Lorre's 'new' roles signalled a release from the typecasting which had hitherto limited the variety within his screen work. Examples of this dichotomy exist throughout Lorre's promotional material, but to give an indication of the frequency with which it occurred beyond the 1930s (and the first appearance of the term 'typecasting'), the following three excerpts were written between 1942 and 1943 by the Warner Bros. publicity department, and included in pressbooks to advertise *Arsenic and Old Lace*, *The Constant Nymph* and *Background to Danger*. The three pressbooks credit three different films for enabling Lorre's 'new' direction: (a) in advertising of *Arsenic and Old Lace*: 'Peter Lorre says film reform is a great relief' (1942: 11); (b) 'Peter Lorre Does Reverse for *Constant Nymph*' (1943: 15); and (c) 'Even Peter Lorre, long established as one of the screen's arch fiends, is having a chance to do his work for liberty and justice in the new Warner Bros. picture, *Background to Danger*' (1943). What remains important to recognize here is that the definition of Lorre's career as one constrained by typecasting is partly due to the tone and language of the promotional material used to (inaccurately) advertise Lorre's screen work.

On many levels, Lorre's career, especially in his earliest period in Hollywood between 1935 and 1941, can be described as having disparate qualities. There is little sense of homogeneity within the terms of Lorre's employment, either in the roles he was given, the performance styles he used, or even in the position he held within the industry at specific studios (for example, star or supporting status, or the association with one particular studio). However, actors who are hard to define are also hard to sell within an industry that was (and is) reliant upon 'known commodities'. As such, the promotional discourses that were used to market Lorre can be seen as a means of establishing a sense of continuity to the otherwise divergent career of a leading (and sometimes supporting) actor.

Notes

1. For further information, see Douglas Gomery 2005; Bernard F. Dick 1992b; Joseph Garncarz 2006: 110.
2. The 'Napoleon' project faltered early on, but not before Lorre had been photographed in costume and Cohn had announced to the press that Josef von Sternberg was to direct the film. *Napoleon* Production File (1935), Warner Brothers Archives, University of Southern California, Los Angeles, USA.
3. This version of 'Peter Lorre' is discussed in Chapter 7.
4. Warner Oland played Charlie Chan at the height of the oriental detective genre's popularity between 1931 and 1938, but the character made appearances throughout the 1940s, played by Sidney Toler (1938–46) and Roland Winters (1947–49).
5. The only lasting resonances of Lorre's specific association with an Asian character lay in the fact that he was occasionally drawn on as an actor with the requisite skill to perform such roles effectively – he played a Chinese boat captain (with the use of facial prosthetics) in *They Met in Bombay* (Clarence Brown, MGM, 1941); a Japanese Axis agent in *Invisible Agent* (Edwin L. Marin, Universal, 1942); and his cameo as a Japanese steward in *Around the World in Eighty Days* (Michael Anderson, Michael Todd Productions, 1956) somewhat surprisingly, given the notoriety of Lorre's 'horror' image during the 1950s, also made reference to his oriental roles.
6. This specific physical and verbal combination was one that was often used for sympathetic characters, including Polo in *I Was an Adventuress* and Dr Einstein in *Arsenic and Old Lace* (Frank Capra, Warner Brothers, 1944). By contrast, his portrayal of more 'schizophrenic' characters would often combine the soft vocalization with a stretched-out physicality (standing straight and firm, raised eyebrows, etc.) in order to suggest another layer underneath the initial presentation (Pepi in *All Through the Night*).
7. One of the few positive reviews of the film from 1941 was prompted by 'Lorre's stunning performance' to call it an 'unsung' film, and posed the question of why Hollywood did not do more to promote it as a quality picture. *Hollywood Reporter*, 24 April 1941.

Chapter 4

THE SUPPORTING ACTOR (1941–1946)

Lorre spent five years at Warner Bros. between 1941 and 1946.[1] During this time he made twenty films: fifteen produced by Warner Bros. and five with other major studios or independent companies. This period coinciding with the Second World War was a time of sustained employment for Lorre. It was also the period that Lorre attained his greatest level of celebrity, as the popularity of his on-screen roles was matched by his off-screen presence on radio and in the press, and in the increasing appropriation of his likeness in cartoons and caricatures. In contrast to the level of his fame, Lorre's employment during these years was predominantly as a supporting actor performing opposite established stars such as Humphrey Bogart, Charles Boyer and George Raft, rather than as a leading actor in his own right. The exception to this was his on-screen 'partnership' with Sydney Greenstreet, where both actors shared a complex leading status.

This period raises issues concerning Lorre that have come to define very precisely how the actor's work has been considered. His role as Ugarte in *Casablanca* (1942) – Lorre's most iconic appearance in a Warner Bros. film – crystallizes certain key arguments about how to read Lorre's career. Firstly there is the association between Lorre and the type of character suggested by Ugarte, which has been taken as indicative of the limited choice of roles available to him at this time and of his own already established murderous extra-filmic persona. Secondly, it was a role that emphasized Lorre's European identity within a film that remains heavily associated with the position of the exile actor within Hollywood. Lorre's status as a European émigré was seen to be a major contributing factor to his successful employment by Warner Bros. during the Second World War. Thirdly, it was little more than a cameo appearance, albeit one which contains some of Lorre's best known utterances. Ugarte/Lorre arrives at 'Rick's', trades cynical banter with Rick/Bogart (Ugarte: 'You despise me, don't you'; Rick: 'If I gave you any thought, I probably would'), and gives Rick the letters of transit to hide. Following this, he is apprehended by, and runs from, the authorities, pleading with Rick to help him ('Rick, Rick! Do something! You must help me!'). Lorre's screen time is minimal but his presence lingers nonetheless, as described by the *Hollywood Reporter*: 'Lorre is in and out of the picture in the first reel, yet the impression he makes is remembered' (12 August 1942).

Lorre's association with Warner Bros. remains a determined but ambivalent one. The perception is that in becoming a notable addition to Warner Bros.' stock of character actors, Lorre's career and star status was also 'saved' to some degree by the success of the studio's output during this period. The repositioning of Lorre as a support to popular stars, and his appearances in a number of enduring 'classic' or 'quality' films like *Casablanca*, may have been a setback in terms of hierarchical status, but they also afforded Lorre the opportunity to maintain an important and central level of visibility. The studio may have been typically restrictive in how it used him, but it also allowed the actor more freedom to perform in these supporting roles than those produced elsewhere. Lorre's achievements in his Warner Bros. films are perceived to be markedly more refined than the supporting performances that had immediately preceded them.

The actor's time under contract at Warner Bros. can be seen not only as a vital aspect of Lorre's own development, but also as an indicative example of the ways in which actors in general (especially non-leading actors) were perceived, employed and marketed by the studios who invested in them. In addition to this, the years which immediately preceded his steady employment at Warner Bros. should also be recognized as highly significant. Although closely associated with Warner Bros. during this decade, Lorre was not exclusively tied to the studio. Therefore, it becomes problematic to assign sole creative control over his career and image to one studio or even one producer. Lorre's complex transitory labour status, which shifted between 'lead' and 'support' throughout the 1930s and 1940s, makes explicit the notion that actors do not necessarily occupy a fixed commodity status that can easily be defined as 'star' or 'supporting actor' for the extent of their whole career. The supporting roles from this period also offer an indication of Lorre's abilities as a screen actor and an awareness of his changing status within the industry. Through some of his key performances, Lorre is able to reveal the laborious processes of screen acting and to articulate how his position as a supporting actor came to impact upon his performative strategies.

Lorre's Supporting Roles Prior to Warner Bros.: 1937–1940

The redefinition of Lorre as 'merely' a supporting player, rather than a profitable leading performer in his own right, was not an immediate demotion that occurred in 1941 upon the actor's first contract for Warner Bros. The change in status had been a gradual process in the mid-1930s. Whilst Lorre's status as a leading performer has been discussed in the previous chapter, it is also pertinent to consider some of his supporting roles from the same period in order to contextualize his position and work as a supporting actor at Warner Bros.

From 1937 onwards, Lorre's work as a leading actor was offset with supporting parts, both during his early work for Twentieth Century-Fox and within his freelance appointments. What distinguished Lorre's earlier supporting status from his appearances for Warner Bros. was the nature of his on-screen billing. In *Crack Up* (1937), *Nancy Steele is Missing* (1937) and *Stranger on the Third Floor* (1940), Lorre is given an inflated credit (often first or second billing), yet his screen time rarely matches this billing. These types of appearances, both in terms of their formal construction and within Lorre's performances, encouraged the gradual erosion of his tenure as a leading performer and allowed for the dramatic change in his professional status.

In these three films, Lorre was employed as the primary villain: the antagonist whose crimes motivated the narrative of the more 'heroic' protagonist(s). Although Lorre was not engaged as the leading actor in the two Twentieth Century-Fox films, *Crack Up* and *Nancy Steele is Missing*, the publicity campaigns which accompanied these films over-emphasized the actor's identity and, consequently, his position within the film itself. The over-publicizing of Lorre's role can be seen to serve two purposes. Firstly, it demonstrated that Lorre was perceived to possess a higher commodity value than many of the other performers, despite their more prominent roles, and that this existing level of fame could be used as a convenient marketing tool. Secondly, it illustrated a long-term investment strategy on the part of the studio executives, in which the over-billing of Lorre also worked towards building upon the actor's already established position within the public sphere (despite his employment in minor roles) as the continued high-profile promotion enabled Darryl F. Zanuck to protect his investment in the actor through extra-filmic means without necessarily having to source potential leading roles for Lorre.

Lorre was the best known of the actors who appeared in *Stranger on the Third Floor*. However, the billing strategy used by RKO can be seen as different to that of Twentieth Century-Fox because of both the nature of narrative and the terms of Lorre's employment at that studio. *Stranger on the Third Floor* was produced as part of Lorre's short-term two-picture contract with RKO in 1940.[2] Unlike Twentieth Century-Fox, RKO had no long-term investment in the freelance actor's career. Lorre's established level of celebrity was what motivated his employment and determined the way the film was marketed. The specific commodity value of Lorre was further emphasized through the film's formal composition. Although he appears in only a few scenes, the film's narrative is structured almost entirely around the actions of his character, The Stranger. Furthermore, the actual characterization of his role is heavily associated with a vague appropriation of Lorre's extra-filmic persona (a grotesque mysterious figure capable of murder). Given the importance of his persona to the film as a whole, Lorre's top billing is justified to a certain degree, despite his relative on-screen absence.

Lorre's characters in the three films – Colonel Gimpy/Baron Taggart (*Crack Up*), Professor Sturm (*Nancy Steele is Missing*) and The Stranger

(*Stranger on the Third Floor*) – are identified as cold-blooded murderers almost as soon as they appear in the narrative: personal qualities which easily lend themselves to charges of typecasting. However, this is a somewhat superficial engagement with the texts which over-emphasizes Lorre's image at the expense of his labour.

One of the major differences between the characters of Gimpy/Taggart, Professor Sturm and The Stranger, and Lorre's leading roles from the same period, is that the supporting roles are not developed into fully rounded characters by the script or by Lorre. They only appear in a few scenes because they remain defined as plot functions that direct the narrative in a specific direction, and disappear when this task has been fulfilled. There is also little interest in making them psychologically realistic – as evidenced by their names, which are certainly evocative, but also serve to reduce them merely to 'types'.

In his leading roles Lorre had the opportunity and freedom to imbue his characters with more depth than the script may have otherwise suggested. *Crack Up* necessitated a shift in Lorre's chosen performance style towards making an immediate and entertaining impact rather than subtle and considered characterization. In *Crack Up*, this is most obvious in the sequence where Lorre shows the transformation from imbecilic 'Colonel Gimpy' into the ruthless political activist 'Baron Taggart' through a series of economical gestures, including losing his limp and combing his hair into a different style.

In general terms, Lorre's acting became more overt – both through verbal and physical practices: his gestures were more pronounced and his words were deliberately emphasized. This mode of performance style has been highlighted by James Naremore as indicative of the performative techniques employed by the majority of supporting actors during the studio era. In comparison to the lead performers, supporting players – because they had limited screen time – tended to favour a more animated non-naturalistic style, because it was felt to make an immediate impact on the viewer (Naremore 1988: 43). This style of acting also emphasized the 'naturalism' or the 'ordinariness' of the leading performers by comparison, which was a necessary element of an audience's ability to identify with a star performer.

Lorre's new dual status meant that he employed a condensed style of performance in the films which employed him as a supporting actor rather than those in which he was used as leading actor. He chose to use certain performative elements in order to quickly convey meaning and character. Some of these elements had their origins in his previous work – from specific gestures such as a rolling of his eyes, to more complex techniques such as the swift juxtaposition between two opposing emotional positions. Some were only introduced during this period (and became more nuanced during the 1940s), such as a very deliberately structured vocal delivery. Lorre's reduced screen time meant that these techniques were used with concentrated frequency. Therefore, as they were repeated in this shorthand form, they soon came to be defined as performative 'tricks' that Lorre was presumed to rely upon in many of his subsequent screen roles (*New York Times*, 10 June 1940).

Lorre combined his use of performance mannerisms with a further performative strategy. He utilized a non-naturalistic style of 'overplaying' favoured by the supporting player in a self-reflexive way that effectively drew attention to the process of his own acting. This decision to adopt a 'knowing' performative style played an equally important part in the way that he came to be valued by his employers, especially by Warner Bros. post-1941. Until 1941, Lorre used this technique, not so much as an aid to complex characterization, but more to emphasize his position as an important supporting performer. *Crack Up* is a film which demonstrates the 'obviousness' of Lorre's performance through the juxtaposition of the very different ways that the actor plays the two characters of Gimpy and Taggart. In particular, the broadly farcical comedic performance of Lorre as Gimpy, which opens the film, immediately foregrounds the overtly performative aspects of the portrayal.

This self-reflexive technique is developed in a more subtle way in *Nancy Steele is Missing* and can be seen in the scene which introduces Professor Sturm to the nominal 'hero' Dannie (Victor McLaglen). Both characters share a cramped prison cell; Dannie, the new arrival, is a large brutish-looking man, whilst Sturm is a youngish and dainty man. Over the course of the night, Sturm explains to his new cellmate the reasons for his incarceration: 'The authorities call it manslaughter ... but really it was *murder*. What else was I to do? I am so little, and he was such a big man ... as big as you.' Lorre is positioned on his bunk and underplays these lines, delivering them with a distracted air. This gives the effect of disinterest – both from the character and from the actor – as if the lines are quite meaningless to both. However, the tone of the performance is dramatically reversed by Lorre in two moments. The first occurs when Lorre says the word 'murder', which he delivers in a contrasting 'purring' style that emphasizes the word through Lorre's rolling intonation. Secondly, before he says 'as big as you', Lorre slowly rolls his eyes to look up towards Dannie. In doing so, the speech changes immediately from a story about the past, to a direct threat about Dannie's present situation, as communicated through Lorre's use of a darkly playful (and, given the difference in physical size between the two, comedically inappropriate) gesture.

As well as operating as a low-level mode of characterization, these two moments forcibly depict the relish with which the actor reveals this information about his character. The careful pacing of the scene sets up an illusion of indifference on the part of the performer which is then completely destroyed in two moments of overly expressive acting. The palpable sense of enjoyment that Lorre conveys about the careful mechanics of a structured performance also provides moments of black humour for the audience to enjoy. In narrative terms, it is a moment of tension, but in performative terms, it is predominantly an entertaining moment. The successful management of the two tones was highlighted, and attributed to Lorre, by a 1937 review which wrote, 'Peter Lorre sustains a brilliantly whimsical sinisterness in his brief appearances' (*Film Weekly*, 10 July 1937: 29).

Lorre's new performative flexibility led to a shift in the way he was perceived, by both employers and consumers. Lorre began to prove his worth as a colourful support, and his reputation as an entertaining and engaging performer was developed. Descriptions in which Lorre is defined as an actor of 'great playfulness and perception' and an 'irrepressible scene stealer' are born from his successful redeployment as a supporting actor (Fujiwara 2004). Watching Lorre perform came to be seen as an experience that had the potential to combine 'pleasure' (through the spectacle of performance) with something more 'sinister' (the dominant narrative or characterization). A later interview from 1943 articulates this duality by suggesting that 'there was always something endearing about Lorre even in his most degenerate phase' (*New York Herald-Tribune*, 27 June 1943). In the context of the interview, that 'something endearing' remains somewhat intangible, but my suggestion is that this is created by the intersection between Lorre's lightly self-reflexive performance style and the darker nature of these characters. The style Lorre utilized as a supporting actor also had an implicit impact on his extra-filmic persona. Whilst the roles themselves remained disconnected to this public image, Lorre's 'abridged' performative mannerisms were referenced within other media forms, by the actor himself on the radio, and independently of Lorre through writers, impressionists and caricatures.

Without the potential to engage with the viewer at this level, it is unlikely that Lorre's extra-filmic persona would have been as indelible as it proved to be throughout his career (and after). Additionally, because this aspect of Lorre's persona (as an identity constructed primarily for its marketable value from the sense of cohesion it gave to Lorre's career) was created through the performance style of the actor, rather than through the script or the roles he played, it is also possible to argue that Lorre possessed a degree of control over aspects of his extra-filmic persona, apart from other factors (such as typecasting) that have traditionally been held responsible.

Lorre's supporting roles are significant because they demonstrate that during this period, despite the gradual change in his Hollywood status, he still maintained a level of cultural and economic value within the industry above many other conventional supporting actors. This is most evident in *Stranger on the Third Floor*, which is constructed around the cultural caché of Peter Lorre in various ways, from the dialogue which actively references Lorre's extra-filmic persona, to the *mise-en-scène* that playfully reveals the presence of the actor in sequences for different effects.

The Stranger is an emblematic character who possesses virtually no individual characterization other than that he is played by Lorre (and all the incumbent associations of that performer circa 1940). He is set up as a bizarre figure who may be a killer, or who may be a figment of the troubled imagination of the protagonist, Mike (John McGuire). The implication that the film encourages is that either option is possible because of the more fantastical qualities associated with Lorre and through references to the actor's own professional history. This self-reflexive position is further emphasized because the audience possess a privileged perspective to that of the characters on-screen – they are assumed to already have an awareness of 'Peter Lorre'. In this respect, Lorre not only performs The Stranger, but is an embodiment of his own extra-filmic persona. The complex relationship created between narrative, character, actor and audience is effectively demonstrated during a sequence where Mike's girlfriend, Jane (Margaret Tallichet) describes The Stranger to a minor character who responds somewhat incredulously: 'I never thought of somebody that'd look like that!'. Whilst the characters appear horrified by the idea of The Stranger, the audience is meant to derive a certain amount of pleasure from the knowledge that they are able to identify the one person who fits the description: Peter Lorre.[3]

The film continuously plays with the audience's awareness of Lorre's place within the hierarchical structure of Hollywood performers and with their own expectations of the associations conveyed by his public image. Through the formal treatment afforded to Lorre, *Stranger on the Third Floor* articulates his somewhat problematic status of being a well-known actor occupying a supporting role. The film also uses this unconventional status to manipulate the gaze of its audience. Lorre/The Stranger is first introduced sitting outside Mike's apartment block. The character receives no formal introduction but Lorre dazedly rises up, touches his hat and wryly smiles in greeting. The attention spent on this moment suggests that it serves a specific purpose, despite being unrelated to any scenes that immediately precede or follow it. The purpose appears to be to provide the audience with a moment of recognition – to become aware that Peter Lorre is on-screen. Once Lorre has been recognized, the scene takes on a much greater significance because of his particular cinematic and cultural identities. Because Lorre is associated with a specific extra-filmic persona, the audience is encouraged to think there is something 'sinister' in the relationship between these two characters (which is true – The Stranger commits a murder that Mike is arrested for).

In a later sequence, the privileged position of the audience is further referenced through the framing used by the director, Boris Ingster. He allows the audience to 'hear' Lorre before they 'see' The Stranger. This moment is the first time the character speaks, so Ingster relies upon the assumption that his audience can easily recognize the sound of Lorre's voice in order to create the dramatic irony that is central to the scene. Jane stands wearily at a café's counter-top, having failed in her attempts to find The Stranger; as she does so, an unseen distinctive voice makes the following bizarre order at the café: 'I'd like a couple of hamburgers and I'd like them raw.'

It is then revealed that the man she has been searching for is standing next to her, and the tension of the situation is intensified as Jane fails to notice The Stranger whilst the audience easily recognizes Lorre. The use of these formal techniques also emphasizes the film's reliance upon Lorre's already-established persona, rather than it being an example of a film which plays an active role in the construction of that persona. In the way that *Stranger on the Third Floor* makes highly self-reflexive references to Lorre's existing extra-filmic identity, it becomes more difficult to define the character of The Stranger as merely another instance of Lorre's apparent typecasting in cinematic roles that created a persona which subsequently limited the actor's employment opportunities within Hollywood.

Considering Lorre's early Hollywood supporting roles, one can begin to determine a series of repeated gestures and mannerisms, carefully practised management of pacing and structure, and a performance style that suggests attempts to balance characterization with self-reflexive or demonstrative acting. These changes within Lorre's screen performative techniques are both due to, and a reflection upon, the differing levels of his employment as a leading and supporting actor within the industry between 1937 and 1941. What is more difficult to determine is any sense of homogeneity between the characters that Lorre played during these years; and this is equally applicable to his casting in leading and supporting roles. Whilst Gimpy/Taggart, Sturm and The Stranger are all 'lead villains', their motivations and their crimes remain quite disconnected from each other and (with the exception of The Stranger) from Lorre's own extra-filmic persona.

My suggestion of typecasting through performance perhaps continues the conventional perception in which Lorre's career can be seen to suffer a significant downward turn through his compromised labour position as supporting actor. However, many of Lorre's most important films were made during or after 1941, and his association with Warner Bros. has come to characterize much that was positive about his Hollywood career. Not only did he continue to demonstrate his skill as a screen performer through a variety of performative methods, but the decade was very successful for him; as his extra-filmic persona became firmly established within American popular culture, he gained stable and financially profitable employment through his work for Warner Bros. Therefore, to dismiss Lorre's value simply because he was not a conventional leading actor becomes a problematic stance to perpetuate. It is more pertinent to ask what was different about his employment at Warner Bros. and why did he flourish in the way that he did at this particular studio, at this particular time.

Lorre, Warner Bros. and *The Maltese Falcon* (1941)

In his observations about typecasting during the Hollywood studio system, Ezra W. Zuckerman (2005) makes some useful claims about the individual example of Warner Bros. which might suggest why the studio had such a positive impact upon Lorre's career in the 1940s. Zuckerman recalls Warner Bros.' reputation for being the most penny-pinching of the major studios, and relates this to the studio's employment of contracted acting labour (offering a comparison with MGM). He quotes MGM casting director, Leonard Murphy, to illustrate that Warner Bros. worked towards achieving the most cost-effective use of its stock company of performers via a tendency to 'put their whole contract list in every picture whether they fit or not'. This money-saving enterprise led to a flexibility within studio casting processes and allowed certain performers (such as Bogart) to escape restrictive typecasting: given the studio's financial investment in them, it was more important that they worked regularly than to have each performer being encouraged to maintain a cohesive screen identity over a smaller number of suitable film roles.

According to Zuckerman, the desire to keep contract personnel fully utilized led to increased experimentation within the screen roles assigned to each actor under contract. Whilst Warner Bros.' economic policy might readily appear to explain Lorre's increased and wide-ranging film engagements during the 1940s, considering an actor whose career was as complicated and mutable as Lorre's also complicates Zuckerman's arguments about the basic differences between each Hollywood studio. Firstly, contrasting Warner Bros. with MGM, a studio that pursued a more obviously high-cost/high-quality strategy, polarizes perceptions of the studio system between the 'extravagant' and the 'restrained', and downplays other studios that followed a similarly cautious economic strategy, such as Lorre's old employers, Twentieth Century-Fox.

Secondly, it reduces discussions of the studios to a singular coherent identity ('Warner Bros.', 'MGM', etc.) without giving recourse to the individuals who were involved in implementing production and economic strategies, particularly the roles played by studio presidents, heads of production, or other individual producers and directors. Lorre's Hollywood career had already been shaped by Harry Cohn, Darryl F. Zanuck and Sol Wurtzel, and his tenure at Warner Bros. was equally dependent upon how he was perceived by men who ran the business of the studio and the production of his particular films. Studio Vice-President and Head of Production Jack Warner was heavily involved in day-to-day production decisions and there is administrative evidence of his role in decisions that directly relate to Lorre – but not in all of the actor's films; additionally a number of Lorre's films were produced by Hal B. Wallis, Jerry Wald or Henry Blanke, but by no means all of them. Stephen D. Youngkin (2005: 211) suggests that Wallis was a significant and influential figure who felt that Lorre was 'a unique and fine performer [who] added considerably to any picture he was in', but Wallis left Warner Bros. in 1944 to form his own production company whilst Lorre continued at the studio for another two years. Even with the input of high-ranking individuals such as Wallis and Warner, it remains problematic to credit one individual with overseeing a deliberately focused strategy of employment and publicity regarding Lorre, in spite of the coherence that can be observed within his work for the studio. Whilst it is tempting to explain the lack of recorded deliberation via Lorre's somewhat diminished status (as a supporting actor), much of Lorre's value during this period was derived from his individual star presence, even in supporting roles, and many of his Warner Bros. films were explicitly constructed to accommodate this individuality.

Much of the discourse surrounding acting labour within the studio era relies upon the existence and enforcement of long-term contracts by the studios. The management of actors' labour was at once highly restrictive and could result in suspension, but it also provided a secure work environment that a freelance career could not. Warner Bros. is often discussed in this regard, as a number of its most famous stars rebelled against the terms of their employment (James Cagney, Bette Davis, Olivia de Havilland and Humphrey Bogart). Lorre, however, was employed on a series of rolling single-picture contracts until 1943, when he signed a nominally five-year multiple-picture contract which was annually reviewed, revised and extended until 1946. During this period he was also continually employed elsewhere – firstly on a freelance basis and then through the 'outside' picture clause of his Warner Bros. contract. The secure working environment and sustained studio investment highlighted by Zuckerman does not necessarily describe Lorre's time at Warner Bros., despite being a period of relative freedom for the actor in terms of on-screen casting and performative space. This disparity is reflected in the often recondite relationship that was forged between Lorre, the studio's production personnel, the films he appeared in, and the way he was publicly perceived and marketed.

Lorre's first appearance in a Warner Bros. film, as Joel Cairo in *The Maltese Falcon*, remains one of his most recognizable screen performances. It had a significant impact on the direction of his subsequent employment and upon his preferred mode of on-screen performance. The film has often been credited as revitalizing Lorre's apparently flagging fortunes. Despite his extended period as a freelance actor it was his first engagement for the studio. According to Youngkin (2005: 178), Warner Bros. initially had little interest in welcoming the actor into their stock of supporting actors, and Lorre's casting is usually attributed to the insistence of first-time director, John Huston. However, Lorre's name was first on the list of twenty-four actors suggested by casting director Steve Trilling to play Cairo, so it may be more accurate to characterize the studio's perception as cautious rather than reluctant, as evidenced by Jack Warner's offer of a short-term freelancer's contract (*The Maltese Falcon* Production File, 1941). In effect, *The Maltese Falcon* was the first step in a prolonged screen test for Warner; an audition to test Lorre's economic value before further commitment and investment. This resulted in the actor occupying an unusual position within his Warner Bros. films: a star identity contained within a series of supporting roles.

As ever, there is a disparity between the character of Cairo himself and Lorre's extra-filmic persona, but it is a series of diluted adaptations of his performance as 'Joel Cairo' which served to create the iconic association between Lorre's screen performances and his employment as a supporting actor by Warner Bros. Unlike Lorre's psychotic public persona, Joel Cairo is defined as a rationally motivated and cynical individual. His actions pursue a purely financial goal – the Falcon. Nevertheless, Cairo does occupy the status of an 'outsider' as he is an exotic foreigner (in the novel he is explicitly from the Levant), with mercenary tendencies: an immoral thief who swaps accomplices according to who is most in control of the financial prize. He is also highly coded as a homosexual man who thinks nothing of using his sexuality to aid him in his pursuit of the Falcon, as revealed by the conversation between him and Brigid (Mary Astor) about 'the boy in Istanbul': an obstacle Brigid could not overcome, but Cairo could.

The way in which the two dominant elements of Cairo's character (his homosexuality and his mercenary loyalties) have affected perceptions of the actor is a useful way of highlighting how evaluations of Lorre's persona have come to supersede evaluations of his on-screen work. Cairo's sexuality has been seen as a justification that certain roles contributed to the limiting extra-filmic persona which emphasized the 'abnormal' qualities of the actor. However, in terms of his actual employment on-screen, this can easily be refuted. Lorre's extra-filmic persona is certainly associated with the idea of sexual perversion: indeed many contemporary descriptions of the actor reinforce this through the authors' decisions to repeatedly describe Lorre's roles using this terminology. The most obvious genesis for this association is both *M* and *The Maltese Falcon*. However, it is not accurate to describe Lorre as always cast in his Hollywood films as a 'pervert': during the course of Lorre's English-language career, only two films explicitly link his characters with 'abnormal' sexuality (*The Maltese Falcon* and *Mad Love*), whereas approximately 70 per cent of his films make no overt reference to sexual desire – conventionally heterosexual or otherwise.[4]

The disparity between persona and screen roles is reversed when one considers Cairo's 'mercenary' status in relation to Lorre's public image. The mercenary qualities seen in Cairo played a significant role in how Lorre was employed by Warner Bros. in the years after 1941. Despite this repetition, this type of character plays virtually no part in the make-up of Lorre's extra-filmic persona. Unlike the public image that came to define Lorre, Cairo is characterized as a professional thief rather than someone who has an uncontrollable psychological compulsion to kill. Unlike Sam Spade (Humphrey Bogart), he does not adhere to a closely held system of belief or morals: in his pursuit of financial gain he will attach himself to whoever appears most likely to succeed. Therefore, he cannot be trusted to be loyal to one particular party.

The association between Lorre and this type of character proved invaluable during the war years at Warner Bros., where professional ambiguities and mercenary tendencies could easily transform into political ambiguities and add layers to a story (as could an indistinguishable nationality). Lorre's commodity value was perceived almost exclusively in relation to this type of character rather than one which conformed to the boundaries of his extra-filmic persona, as shown by the repeated use of Lorre to play a professionally or politically 'unknowable' character in wartime narratives such as *All Through the Night* (1941), *Background to Danger* (1943), *Passage to Marseille* (1944) and *The Conspirators* (1944).

Whilst it is true that Lorre's extra-filmic persona is associated with untrustworthy characteristics, these are usually closely related to ideas of 'horror' iconography, psychotic compulsion and supernatural danger. It is also significant to note that the ambiguity of Lorre's screen roles was a plot function that usually had a positive outcome. Although always under suspicion, it was a rare occurrence for Lorre's characters to turn traitorous for profit or double-cross the protagonist. Within the narrative of a film, Lorre is almost wholly used as a diversionary tactic to distract the audience, rather than being the actual threat. Again, this use of Lorre in his supporting roles can also be attributed to his appearance as Cairo. Cairo's function within the film is primarily as a diversion: firstly, to delay Gutman's entrance, and secondly, to help distract from the actual focus of the story: Spade and Brigid's narrative.

Somewhat surprising, given the importance of the role in relation to Lorre's Hollywood career, one element of Lorre's extra-filmic persona is noticeably absent in the character of Joel Cairo: Cairo is not a killer. As with notions of sexuality, this is again a typical trait of Lorre's on-screen appearances. Despite the apparent link between the actor and his murderous persona in the films he made at the height of his fame between 1934 and 1950, his characters actually kill in only half of them. Furthermore, when his characters do kill, in twelve films the murders can be explained as having a professional or political cause, compared to the three films (*Mad Love*, *Stranger on the Third Floor* and *The Beast with Five Fingers*) in which they are unquestionably psychotically motivated.

Whilst he does not actually kill, Cairo does at least threaten to do so, and it is this position of the rationally motivated mercenary killer with which he is most closely aligned. He repeatedly threatens harm to those who stand in the way of his financial goal, including Spade. Despite the evidence present in the script, Cairo's threats and his willingness to brandish a gun, it remains questionable as to whether he is the professional thug he professes to be. The extent to which the audience believes his bravado comes down to how Lorre's performance as Cairo asks to be read. His performative choices do much to undermine the status of the character as outlined by the script at a superficial level.

This approach is not unique to Lorre. Deceptive dialogue and characterization revealed through performance rather than words are main tropes of *The Maltese Falcon*, a film in which almost all characters say one thing but mean another. As such, a questioning of the legitimacy of Cairo's threats is encouraged, but this is equally applicable to the other characters. What is a particular feature of Cairo – as performed by Lorre – is the degree to which the character is reinvented as the film progresses, merely as a comic foil to the unfolding events.

Much of Lorre's characterization is concerned with representing Cairo's homosexuality – a necessary inclusion because it forms a vital part of his storyline – explicitly enough for his relationship with the other characters to make sense, but implicitly enough to pass by the regulations stipulated by the Production Code, which forbade the depiction of obviously homosexual characters on-screen. The imposition of the censor led to the popularization of certain performative conventions and strategies which coded otherwise taboo characters as 'sissies' by their effeminate appearance or demeanour, including a fussy preoccupation with their costume, verbose dialogue, use of innuendo by themselves and others, and a tendency towards emotion rather than restraint. These characters could signal homosexuality subtextually, but were superficially presented as asexual, fey and frivolous contrasts to the conventional masculinity of the leading man, and examples of these performances were found across a range of genres – from light musicals or comedies (such as Edward Everett Horton and Eric Blore) to melodramatic thrillers (Clifton Webb) (Russo 1987: 30–34).

However, despite the implicit and therefore sanitized coding, performances of possibly homosexual characters continued to be monitored by Hollywood's censors. During the production of *The Maltese Falcon* there was a brief dialogue between the studio and Joseph Breen, as head of the Production Code Administration, over the representation of Cairo and the performance of Lorre. In a memo, Breen commented that the film 'couldn't characterise Cairo as a pansy as indicated by lavender perfume and a high pitched voice' (*The Maltese Falcon* Production File, 1941). Despite this statement, both the perfume (gardenia, not lavender) and Lorre's higher, softer intonation remained in the released film, possibly because the performance also readily conformed to the established 'sissy' conventions, rather than explicitly connoting homosexuality. The introduction of Cairo through an overblown musical flourish and his scented business card, and the misplaced concern he has for his bloodied clothing after being beaten up by Spade are played for comic effect and rely upon the heritage of 'sissified' representations, although they also contain subtextual signifiers of homosexuality. The lack of further comment by the Production Code Administration suggests that the finished performance was seen to be 'harmless' enough to warrant a PCA Seal of Approval. Much of the more explicit aspects of Cairo's homosexual behaviour – as written in the original novel – had already been omitted from Huston's adaptation before filming, such as Cairo's interaction (and growing infatuation) with Wilmer (Elisha Cook Jr). However, key moments remained within Lorre's performance which renders Cairo's sexuality visible. Even within Cairo's introduction, there is the opportunity for Lorre to develop his performance as a sexual and potentially threatening character in subtler ways than would seem to be suggested by the limits of the 'sissified' coding.

Despite his verbal threat to shoot Spade, the threat of Cairo is purely sexual as opposed to violent. Spade's disarming of Cairo can be seen as indicative of the detective's need to 'achieve dominance over almost everyone he comes in contact with' (Maxwell 1989: 256), but Lorre's performance of Cairo adds a further layer to the characterization of Spade. Lorre employs a tactic based around the social consequences of Cairo's sexuality. Cairo's first attempt at interacting with Spade is to flirt with him; Spade recognizes this as a 'threat' and brutally dismisses Cairo.

To convey this relationship, Lorre affects a coy and over-polite demeanour; he smiles continually when first speaking which emphasizes his white sparkling teeth which are mirrored by the lighting set-up that provides a sparkling gleam in his dark eyes. He also constantly plays with Cairo's elaborately phallic cane as he speaks and as he concludes his pleasantries he brings the cane up to his mouth. No mention of this prop is made in Huston's shooting script for the film, so it is possible that this prop was introduced during rehearsals by the performers. At this moment the camera moves from framing Cairo's face in isolated close-up to behind him, revealing his pose and Spade's impassive reaction to this flirtatious approach.

Furthermore, the catalyst for Spade's violence is when, during his frisking of the detective, Cairo's hand reaches for Spade's backside – again, the shooting script only calls for Cairo to reach for Spade's chest. At this physical contact, Spade turns swiftly and grabs the offending hand and knocks Cairo out. In line with Cairo's general function as a diversion, Spade easily defeats the 'danger' posed by Cairo, and subsequently he is not regarded as any real threat throughout the remainder of the film.

Instead Cairo develops into a more comic figure in his later scenes. Whilst elements of this characterization have their roots in representations of 'sissified' gay characters, much of Lorre's performance characterizes Cairo in isolation from these conventions. It should also be noted that *The Maltese Falcon* is not a film that relies upon these stereotypes in general, since it contains three homosexual characters (Cairo, Gutman and Wilmer) who share few characteristics based upon their sexuality. Lorre characterizes Cairo through a considered application of a deliberate verbal and physical performance strategy. This strategy firstly defines Cairo according to a sense of superficial seriousness and pomposity, but as the film progresses, seeks to break down the façade of the character as he becomes more entrenched in his pursuit of the Falcon, and the hysterical and excitable nature of Cairo's personality is revealed.

From a physical perspective, Lorre's portrayal of Cairo is a very carefully controlled performance. In some respects, it seems almost minimalist and overly restrictive as Lorre elects to use only sudden light movements for Cairo. These work both in isolation to the character – conveying certain aspects of his personality – but also in conjunction with the other performances of ensemble cast to demonstrate the inherently collaborative process of screen performance. The coherence and focus found within the ensemble's performances may have been significantly aided and enabled by Huston's insistence upon lengthy rehearsal sessions and a sequential filming schedule. Lorre's edgy physicality contrasts with the deliberately casual physicality used by Bogart's Spade and the immovable girth of Sydney Greenstreet's Gutman. These movements are employed at carefully chosen moments and in doing so they reveal the underlying fragility and panicked emotions of an outwardly calm figure. For instance, whilst the group waits through the night for the Falcon to be delivered, Cairo appears the most readily relaxed, lying apparently asleep with his legs hanging over the arm of his chair. And yet when the doorbell rings to announce the arrival of the package, Cairo leaps up and is standing taut and alert before anyone else has moved.

Lorre's physical presence is never oppressive, but it is most pronounced in this final sequence where Cairo has few lines but needs to present himself as an important element of the group. This is partly achieved by

Figure 4.1a Lorre as Joel Cairo in *The Maltese Falcon* (1941).

Figure 4.1b Cairo and Sam Spade (Bogart) in *The Maltese Falcon.*

Figure 4.1c Lorre centrally framed in *The Maltese Falcon.*

Figure 4.1d Lorre centrally framed in *The Maltese Falcon.*

framing, which places Cairo/Lorre in the centre of many of the group shots and keeps his face in focus during the sequence despite his background position. It is also partly due to Lorre's deliberate choice of gesture that draws attention to his wordless presence, ranging from a raised eyebrow or a cheeky grin, to the slow draw on a cigarette or reaching over to console Wilmer. Every particular movement that is captured in focus allows Cairo (and therefore Lorre) to appear part of the action when, in reality, he is quite inconsequential. Although Lorre restricts himself physically, he allows himself more freedom with Cairo's dialogue, and much of his construction of character is conveyed through Lorre's verbal performance. *The Maltese Falcon* is a self-consciously wordy film that places great emphasis on connecting storytelling and narrative strategies with power and dominance. In keeping with this, much of the 'action' occurs through the dialogue and repartee that the characters share, mainly through their dealings with Spade, who thrives on this kind of quick-witted interaction.

Just as he gives a stylized physical performance, Lorre also gives a stylized vocal performance. In the same way that aspects of Lorre's physical acting served to draw attention to the formal status of the actor within the frame, his verbal tactic is also used in a self-reflexive manner, because of the way it is used to highlight the process of constructing a character on-screen. Cairo's incoherencies and contradictions are revealed in the different ways Lorre chooses to speak at certain moments. Notable moments include the calculating display of a childlike lack of power (which seems authentically pathetic) when Cairo softly pleads, 'Oh, may I please have my gun back now', only to use the gun against Spade once he returns it; and the outraged serpentine hiss of 'This is the second time you have laid hands upon me!', to which Spade retorts 'When you're slapped, you'll take it and like it', revealing Cairo's lack of control within their relationship.

Lorre uses a slightly different accent to his own when speaking as Cairo which emphasizes the explicitly performative nature of the characterization (as does the curled hairstyle worn by Lorre, who is otherwise associated with a straight, slicked-back hairstyle). Additionally, his rhythmic intonation harks back to the type of performance style used in films like *Nancy Steele is Missing*, which highlighted the split between actor and character. In *The Maltese Falcon*, Lorre's speech emphasizes both the pleasure of the actor (in performing structurally complex lines) and the artifice of the character (through the non-naturalistic tone of Cairo's words themselves). By considering the following extract of an exchange between Cairo and Spade, one can see that the variations that Lorre makes in speed, volume and cadence efficiently demonstrate to the audience the falsity of Cairo's cultured persona: 'Shake out? Not one thing. I adhered to the course you indicated earlier in your rooms, but I certainly wish you would have invented a more reasonable story. I felt distinctly *like an idiot* repeating it.'

The italicized words (my emphasis) have been altered from those in the shooting script: 'I felt distinctly ridiculous repeating it.' This change serves a specific purpose because it, and through the way Lorre speaks the words, breaks the speech into two distinct halves. In the filmed version, Lorre shows Cairo struggling to make his way through the elongated and over-elaborate sounds of the first sentence, but then the actor quickly spits the sharp pithy sounds of the second sentence in order to reveal his character's bitterness, humiliation and easy tendency towards hysterical outbursts. This effect would not have occurred if the word had remained the equally elaborate 'ridiculous' instead of the sharper 'idiot'. Just as in his earlier supporting roles, examples such as this foreground the mechanics of a carefully managed performance as a moment of spectacle to be enjoyed by an audience in the way that it draws attention to itself as well as motivating character development.

From this and other moments, one can observe – as Stephen Karnot did in 1949 as part of a document produced for Warner Bros. entitled 'Character Analysis of Sam Spade' – that an intrinsic part of Lorre's characterization of Cairo (and one absent from the character in the original novel and earlier film versions) was a 'tendency towards hysteria [which] in the climax, bursts forth in full voice' (Karnot 1949: 60). The actor's vocalizations, particularly the explosive potential of his dialogue, became a key feature of Lorre's later performances. Throughout *The Maltese Falcon* the *mise-en-scène* encourages the viewer to prioritize Lorre's precise vocal delivery over his physical or gestural performance, as often he turns away from the camera, obscuring his face and relying solely on his voice. This strategy is a necessary tool developed to deal with Lorre's repositioning as a supporting actor, as there are times when he must turn from the camera towards the star. Within *The Maltese Falcon*, the majority of these examples occur during Cairo/Lorre's interactions with Spade/Bogart. Lorre utilizes this lack of visual attention and develops an appropriate mode of performance which does not require detailed photography of his face but prefers to develop characterization through speech patterns.

The particular method of vocalization that Lorre develops in *The Maltese Falcon* became an intrinsic part of his extra-filmic persona – hence the number of radio appearances made by the actor and the popularity of his voice with impressionists. It was certainly identified as having a specific filmic value by the producers and filmmakers at Warner Bros., as can be seen by the number of Lorre's appearances in studio productions which prioritized his voice in some way. In a significant number of the films made between 1941 and 1946, Lorre is given a short speech that effectively halts the narrative flow in order to present an aural interlude centred around the spectacle of the performer. This production strategy can be linked to Danae Clark's analysis of the way in which Hollywood producers attempted to construct actors as commodified and fetishized objects to be consumed in a system of exchange (Clark 1995). Whereas the 'object status' of an actor's commodification is often described in terms of a specific persona or a visually fetishized moment of representation (such as a 'star entrance'), the films that Lorre made at Warner Bros. demonstrate that his object status was partly constructed through aural representations.

This explicit association between 'spectacle' and 'voice' begins with Cairo's final hysterical outburst in *The Maltese Falcon*, where he calls Gutman (amongst other things) a 'fat bloated idiot'. The digressive nature of Lorre's scenes is explicitly identified in *Passage to Marseille* (1944). Here, he is literally figured as a diversion – his character Marius's first words are the elegantly phrased, 'As a pleasant diversion, may I introduce myself?', before recounting his own story. The other films are more implicit, but are 'spectacular' nonetheless. In *Casablanca*, Ugarte's two scenes are little more than an opportunity for Lorre to perform a career-defining speech and a typically emotional outburst in the face of death. In *Background to Danger*, Lorre's character repeatedly demands 'I want some vodka!' for no reason other than to hear Lorre shout it. And in *Hotel Berlin* (1945), amongst the myriad of characters and interweaving stories, Lorre performs two contrasting speeches – one filled with pessimism and the final one a message of hope. Even in the films in which he is undeniably underused, Lorre tended to deliver at least one 'star turn' in the form of a speech. Here an endlessly cyclic relationship can be observed: the supporting roles forced Lorre to rely upon his voice as an identifying tool, and subsequently the value of Lorre's vocal performance helped to shape the structure of his supporting appearances for Warner Bros.

That these moments have their genesis in *The Maltese Falcon* is emphasized most effectively through Lorre's wry speech from *Beat the Devil* (1953), a 'sequel' of sorts to the *Maltese Falcon* directed by John Huston and which re-teamed Lorre with Bogart. Despite being underused, Lorre is given one opportunity to take centre stage as he relays the following musings about time: 'Time, time, what is time? The Swiss manufacture it. The French hoard it. The Italians squander it. The Americans say it is money. Hindus say it does not exist. You know what I say? I say time is a crook.' Lorre's intonation and the two-part rhythm and pacing of this speech (soft sounds quickly juxtaposed with a sharper ending) are a virtual copy of the example of Cairo's lines discussed above. As a consequence, the prominence given to Lorre's vocal performance throughout this part of his career (and, as is the case with *Beat the Devil*, in moments which revisited this period), and the subsequent importance of the 'sound' of Peter Lorre in the extra-filmic discourses which constructed his persona, explicitly highlight that Lorre's own term of 'face-making' is a highly reductive and inaccurate description of both the on- and off-screen practices associated with Lorre's screen performance technique.

A detailed study of Lorre's performance as Joel Cairo enables a sense of coherence to be found in a text that bridges two apparently distinct periods of Lorre's career. Lorre's performance style continued to be constructed around his status as supporting actor, but also developed into a self-reflexive strategy that worked towards an articulation of his own labour position, and as an aid to characterization. This contrasts with his earlier self-reflexive supporting performances which sought only to demonstrate his professional status as an actor. The collaborative nature of such performances is also crucial, as they had to relate to and fit with those of other screen actors – both the more important 'star' (and leading) performance, and also within the wider ensemble cast.

Peter Lorre: The Émigré Actor in Wartime Hollywood: 1941–1946

As argued previously, readings of Lorre's career which prioritize the status of Lorre as an émigré actor tend to rely upon simplistic analyses of the work he undertook at Warner Bros. In particular, Lorre's roles for the studio did not always rely upon his inherent position as part of an émigré community – a group which has been described as having to overplay their differences in order to achieve acceptance within Hollywood and American society. Rather, they tended to accommodate him as an individual personality and 'star' figure.

Unlike the other Hollywood studios, Warner Bros. had developed a specifically anti-Nazi agenda throughout the late 1930s and early 1940s. The studio produced anti-Nazi films either through explicitly polemic narratives such as *Confessions of a Nazi Spy* (1939) or through interventionist allegories like *Sergeant York* (1941). Other studios were more reticent to take this stand whilst the United States remained officially neutral and whilst the studios themselves had considerable interest in European markets (and, it was argued at the time, for fear of adversely affecting the treatment of Jews in central Europe if the predominantly Jewish-run industry encouraged anti-Nazi opinion) (Birdwell 1999). The industry-wide policy changed after the attack on Pearl Harbour in December 1941 and the official entry of the United States into the war. Both Warner Bros. and the other studios quickly mobilized production of more explicitly anti-Nazi and anti-Japanese films. Towards the end of 1941 and for the next five years, Hollywood worked closely with the government's Office of War Information (OWI) and was mobilized to aid with the war effort.

One of the biggest impacts that this decision had was on the way in which the labour force of émigré actors was used within Hollywood production practices. The number of Europeans arriving in Hollywood had been steadily increasing since Hitler's rise to power in Germany in the early 1930s, as Jewish or left-wing directors, writers, actors and other industry personnel left their homelands. The scale of European migration remained somewhat hidden during the 1930s, but became much more visible during the 1940s – partly due to the increasing numbers, but also due to an increased on-screen representation. From 1941 onwards, Hollywood films readily depicted the war in Europe or used European settings as an evocative but implicit reminder of events occurring on the other side of the Atlantic. One of the most cost-effective ways of creating a sense of 'authenticity' around this Hollywood representation of Europe was to employ on-screen large numbers of accented émigré performers from the ready-made labour force that was settling in southern California.

In terms of labour practices, the war had a positive effect for the non-American actor within the industry. Not only did it provide increased job opportunities as 'foreign' roles became more prolific, but it was also seen as a period which expanded the types of role available to these actors. Ruth Vasey (1997) explores the rise of abstracted 'foreign' stereotypes in Hollywood films during the 1930s as 'a deliberate packaging of saleable elements' that sought to repress specific ethnic and national identities in favour of an amorphous category of non-American 'others', which would provide inoffensive characterizations that could be distributed amongst specific international markets without censorship and complaint. Following the trade crises in the late 1930s, whereby Germany and Italy restricted the distribution of American films, American producers were more inclined to produce nationally specific characters as parallels could be drawn between Hollywood's films and wider European national contexts.[5]

Thomas Doherty (1993: 50) suggests that the war provided an impetus to eradicate the representation of 'foreigners' as simply comedic or villainous characters:

> For the duration of the war, at least, foreigners were no longer funny folk with ridiculous accents and incongruous customs. The stock ethnic lowlifes and sinister foreign villains who had always freely stumbled and slithered across the screen were suddenly receiving blanket disapproval. Stereotypical or negative portrayals that might give offence to overseas allies, potential allies, or the anti-Axis underground hit the cutting room floor.

This use appeared to conform closely to the guidelines set out by the OWI, which encouraged a movement beyond the stereotyped view of the enemy, as the OWI believed this narrow representation would have a dangerous effect on American perceptions of the German and Japanese people in general (Koppes and Black 1997).

However, this is not to say that stereotypes were completely removed from Hollywood films during these years, as the OWI's guidelines were not rigorously enforced by studios that were unenthusiastic about such 'outside' interference. In particular, the enduring stereotype of the cold-hearted and sadistically brutal 'Nazi' was created during these years, having been remodelled from the earlier Hollywood incarnation of the 'Hun' that had been employed during the First World War (as was the image of the buck-toothed 'Jap' soldier). Despite early protests about the destructive image of the 'Hun' during the First World War, and the concerns of the OWI about harmful representations of the enemy during the Second World War, this image of the German enemy prevailed.

These observations are significant in relation to Lorre's career at this time because his off-screen circumstances (an Austrian/Hungarian actor who had come to Hollywood from Berlin) would seem to suggest that he possessed an obvious commodity value to employers as a 'foreign' or even 'Germanic' performer, and that this generic identity would be specifically emphasized within the roles the studio assigned to Lorre. However, looking in detail at the variety of screen work Lorre undertook during these war years shows how difficult it is accurately to define Lorre 'merely' as a supporting actor who specialized in 'foreigners'.

David Thomson (2005: 34) characterizes Lorre's Hollywood career in terms of having a 'vaguely useful foreignness' that was utilized most effectively during the Second World War. This description of Lorre as 'vaguely foreign' is accurate when one considers the nationalities of his characters in his Warner Bros. films: Spanish or Italian in *Casablanca*, Spanish in *Confidential Agent*, Russian in *Background to Danger*, French in *Passage to Marseille*, German in *Hotel Berlin* and *All Through the Night*, and in *The Conspirators* it is never made clear from where his character originates. In all, Lorre's accent is interchangeable and allows him to occupy a flexible position as a performer who is able to convey these different nationalities with relative ease. Furthermore, the indistinctness of his accent encourages an important element of characterization as it suggests that the individuals may be untrustworthy or unknowable because their identities are not wholly defined.

This employment strategy of an interchangeable nationality was not one that was unique to Lorre, nor was it restricted to supporting actors, as European stars such as Paul Henried and Charles Boyer often played roles that were neither Austrian nor French in origin. However, whilst the nationally specific star personae of actors such as Boyer compensated for this disparity between image and role, the same could not be said of Lorre, whose extra-filmic image conveyed a similarly generic 'foreignness' or positioning as an 'outsider' as his roles appeared to (Phillips 2002b). Lorre's own indistinct European nationality was problematic in terms of constructing a nationally specific and coherent 'public' persona, but it seemed to be considerably more valuable in terms of the actor's screen employment, as its vagueness was beneficial for a wide range of casting opportunities.

This indistinct quality also meant that Lorre himself, unlike many other émigré actors – even those with similarly 'vague' on-screen qualities – was not often cast as a Nazi, or even as a stock German character, during the war years. That this was relatively unusual, even given his non-German heritage, can be seen by comparing Lorre's work with other German-speaking actors during the same era, and can possibly be linked to his higher standing both within the industry and within the common American consciousness. Joseph Garncarz (2006: 108) writes that the rise in anti-Nazi films was a big break for exiled film personnel, as supporting and leading roles that could easily accommodate them grew significantly. Actors in exile only occasionally played refugees and resistance fighters on-screen, as more often than not they had to play stereotypical Nazis.

Lorre played a variety of roles during the Second World War, but in only three films was he explicitly cast as a German: *All Through the Night* (1942), *The Cross of Lorraine* (1943) and *Hotel Berlin* (1945). In his consideration of Lorre's career, Gerd Gemünden (2003: 89) implies that Lorre's apparent Germanic association restricted his roles by emphasizing that there was only one film in which he played a German who was not a Nazi (*Hotel Berlin*). Whilst this correctly identifies the ambiguous position that Lorre holds within the film, it overstates the appearance as a 'departure' for the actor, as it mirrors many of Lorre's equally ambiguous, but non-Germanic, Warner Bros. roles of the period.

In the large ensemble cast of *Hotel Berlin*, Lorre plays the relatively minor role of Koenig, an occupant of the eponymous hotel. The role was initially meant to be larger but was substantially edited in post-production, resulting in a somewhat unbalanced characterization. (One of Lorre's most sympathetic roles in *The Constant Nymph* was also subjected to similarly drastic editing after filming.) Koenig is a doctor who has worked for the Nazis at Dachau, but who also has associations with resistance forces. When the story begins he has been offered an escape package to South America by the Nazis with the proviso that he remains loyal to their cause. However, his spirit has been broken by bearing witness to the Nazis' concentration camps, and he prefers to hide in self-pitying drunken squalor where he has relinquished all hope of the possibility of Germany's rebirth, believing that, 'there are not ten good Germans left ... We shall be wiped off the face of the earth. Serves us right, absolutely right.' His final act in the last months of the war is one of redemption as he is moved to sobriety by the actions of the other inhabitants of the hotel: he takes charge of one arm of the resistance movement and ends the film with a rousing speech of hope for the future.

Lorre's portrayals of Nazi characters were minor and infrequent: he only played two in a career which spanned screen, stage and radio over thirty years: Pepi, a fifth columnist working on a plan to attack New York, in *All Through the Night*, and Sergeant Berger, a prison camp official, in *The Cross of Lorraine*. The brevity of his engagement with these types of roles demonstrates that Lorre was not defined in Hollywood as 'German' or 'Germanic'. Whereas one might assume that Lorre – with his psychotically murderous persona – carved a notable career playing a particular representation of America's enemy, or even, as film historians Robert and Carol Reimer (1992: 18) believe, that his persona helped to create Hollywood's representation of the 'Nazi', looking at his roles it becomes clear that there is little evidence to support either assumption.

Lorre's performances in *All Through the Night* and *The Cross of Lorraine* suggest a specific reason for his lack of sustained employment as a Hollywood Nazi. In both films, it is most apparent that, whether purposefully or not, Lorre makes a very unconvincing Nazi. In purely physical terms, Lorre's height and plainly non-Aryan features make him a nonstereotypical and unlikely Nazi. However, inappropriate physicality or Jewish identity rarely prevented actors in Hollywood from being employed as Nazis (Garncarz 2006). What set Lorre apart even more was the demonstrative and juxtapositional performance style developed by the actor between 1937 and 1941 which aimed to create a sense of distance between character and actor. This style was noticeably out of step with the prevailing Hollywood image of the fanatically devoted Nazi figure.

All Through the Night was made and released immediately prior to the attack on Pearl Harbour, and only conveys an implicit political message, preferring to emphasize its more entertaining qualities. The film's underlying seriousness is complemented by an irreverent tone, as it depicts the farcical attempts of a group of racketeers to prevent an attack on New York by fifth columnists. Within this setting, Lorre's performance as Pepi is equally irreverent, once again mixing lightness and darkness, and was described by *Variety* as 'a savage reptilian characterisation' (2 December 1941) and by the *New York Herald-Tribune* as 'the best screen acting [Lorre] has turned in for a long time' (24 January 1942). Pepi moves between being presented as an actual threat (carrying out torture and murder), an allegorical threat (Humphrey Bogart's character, 'Gloves' Donahue, repeatedly refuses to see how 'that little squirt' could be a danger; an attitude shared by isolationists in relation to Germany), and virtually no threat at all – and it is in these moments that Lorre demonstrates the ridiculousness of his employment as a Nazi.

The film pairs Pepi with his commander, Ebbing (Conrad Veidt). Ebbing is the stereotypical Nazi figure, and throughout the film his over-zealous fanaticism grates with Pepi's growing cynicism. This relationship culminates in Pepi's death as Ebbing shoots him for refusing to complete the bombing mission. What Ebbing sees as a glorious moment for the Reich, Pepi can only see as a 'silly act of suicide' that cannot be worth the consequences. Pepi is thus another of Lorre's 'mercenary' figures with an ability to shift loyalties if events turn too dangerous. This frivolous representation of the fifth column threat was more appropriate to domestic audiences prior to Pearl Harbour, but the representation of Axis forces changed somewhat on the United States' entry into the war.

The Cross of Lorraine depicts the internment of French soldiers in a prisoner-of-war camp and their treatment at the hands of their brutal captors. Made in 1943, at a time when the eventual outcome of the war was unclear, the story opted for a much more serious approach. Its depiction of the actions of the French resistance in the face of adversity fitted with the industry-wide policy of bringing to the American public the horrors faced by their European allies. This realistic agenda and aesthetic may partly explain why Lorre's performance is one of his flattest and most conventional, although *Variety* did describe his casting in more positive terms, saying he 'makes a most despicable German sergeant' (19 November 1943). Lorre conforms to the stereotypical image of the brutal and sadistic Nazi.

The decision to cast Lorre in *The Cross of Lorraine* was directly informed by the associations between the actor and his extra-filmic persona. MGM attempted to draw a parallel between the identity which promoted Lorre as murderous, horrific and abnormal, and the on-screen role of a sadistic Nazi. Lorre's character, Sergeant Berger, is presented as a monster that derives pleasure from the pain and torment of his French charges. He toys with the prisoners' lives: forces them to fight each other for food for his apparent amusement, shoots a priest for performing a religious ceremony, and takes great pleasure in breaking the body and spirit of one prisoner, La Biche (Gene Kelly).

According to his biographer, Lorre was hand-picked for the role by the director, Tay Garnett, because of the actor's apparent ability to deliver 'extra menace' (Youngkin 2005: 210). And yet, an analysis of Lorre's performance illustrates that Garnett's perceptions appear to come from a simplistic desire to appropriate vague elements of his persona rather than from an understanding of his attributes as a screen performer. This results in an incompatibility between Lorre's acting and the part he is playing. Despite his apparent value as a Nazi, his presence is virtually obscured within the film as Garnett downplays Lorre's identifying features: his appearance and his voice. Whereas Lorre's Warner Bros. films emphasized his vocal talents, in *The Cross of Lorraine* he has only isolated and relatively inconsequential lines dotted throughout the film. Additionally, Lorre's costuming effectively serves to disguise the actor, as he is forced to wear his cap and keep his uniform tightly buttoned-up throughout the story. He is also given a very limited number of close-ups, which means that his presence is easily missed by the viewer. All these restrictions make it difficult to recognize Lorre on-screen.

On the other hand, Lorre's casting undermines Berger's status as a loyal Nazi guard, especially when he is photographed in proximity to the other actors. Conversations with other German guards make Lorre's non-German status too explicit. His increasingly Americanized Austrian accent sounds softer and noticeably different to the harshly barked orders or quietly stern commands of those around him. In physical terms, Lorre's small stature is only emphasized in comparison with the overweight grotesque German officers and the tall, well-built French prisoners, and as such he is never truly intimidating – despite his characterization. Warner Bros. were more careful about revealing the physical limitations of their actors, including Lorre, and he tended to be paired with equally short leading men such as Bogart and George Raft unless his small physicality was used to highlight a particular contrast, such as in his 'partnership' with Sydney Greenstreet.

Berger's one extended scene further complicates his representation as a sadistic Nazi tyrant. As Berger is being driven towards the French border by the prisoner/interpreter Dupré (Jean-Pierre Aumont) – who has an escape plan involving himself and La Biche in operation – Lorre's performance momentarily humanizes Berger. He uses a very casual and relaxed tone, particularly when he comments on the arrogance of the SS who guard the border. This scene is immediately juxtaposed with the brutality of the prisoners when Dupré graphically stabs Berger in the neck and throws him out of the car. It is unclear whether this sequence is included as a means of illustrating the inconsistent behaviour of the general Nazi character or the way that the camp has dehumanized the French men. Either way, Lorre's performance serves to unbalance the 'reality' of the film and reveals his inherent unsuitability to play the Hollywood Nazi.

Lorre's remaining 'war' films were *Casablanca* (1942), *Background to Danger* (1943), *Passage to Marseille* (1944), *The Conspirators* (1944) and *Confidential Agent* (1945).[6] In each film, Lorre's characters serve a particular function rather than being fully sketched individuals. They either set the plot in motion (as in *Casablanca*), help to guide the protagonist in one direction (*Background to Danger*), or they are a diversionary tactic (*The Conspirators*). Within this limited scope of character function, Lorre's presence remains an significant element, and despite his reduced screen time and lack of narrative importance, his characters often stand out from many of the other second-level roles that are played by more minor actors.

This is demonstrated most clearly in *Passage to Marseille* in which Lorre has fourth billing, below Humphrey Bogart, Michèle Morgan and Sydney Greenstreet, but above Claude Rains. Lorre's character, Marius, is part of a group of French prisoners, led by Matrac (Bogart), who have escaped from Devil's Island in order to join the French Army. They are rescued by a boat and taken back to France. The focus of the narrative is on Matrac's spiritual redemption: as a political prisoner whose faith in France was broken during incarceration, he is only pretending to be patriotic so that he can escape and return to his wife (Morgan). His beliefs are changed by the challenges the men face as they journey towards the war zone, and the film ends with his death in combat: the ultimate patriotic act.

Initially Marius appears to serve very little purpose in the film apart from introducing Matrac to the group. Even when he dies whilst trying to attack a German plane with the boat's machine-gun – an action which could be interpreted as a valiant death which aids Matrac's final decision to fight for France – the film downplays this potentially heroic moment by keeping his death off-screen and quickly moving on to another set piece. The cinematic convention of an emotional final speech from a dying character is given to the more minor character of the cabin boy, who touches Matrac with his words of hope and patriotism.

In terms of plot and character, Lorre's is arguably a wasted presence in this film, despite his apparent value as a performer with the ability to portray 'foreign' characters. And yet, as an actor, Lorre is given a form of preferential treatment which serves to highlight his value to the film as a whole. This is demonstrated in the way the character is introduced through verbal and visual techniques. As already outlined, Marius is given a typically 'Lorre-esque' speech for his opening words – a move which draws attention to the actor rather than to the character. This verbal prioritizing of Lorre mirrors the visual mode used to literally introduce the actor into the film, as Lorre is photographed in a way which separates him from the other 'vaguely foreign' supporting actors. Instead he is linked to a treatment more commonly associated with leading actors.

As the men are pulled on board the boat and given some water, both Bogart (as the star) and Lorre are isolated from the rest of the men in two separate shots. Lorre also uses a more physical performance than the other supporting actors as he gulps and gasps and grabs the cup of liquid offered to Marius. Lorre occupies a space above the minor actors whose rescue is depicted only through the use of a wide shot which frames all the men. On the other hand, Lorre does not occupy the same level of importance as Bogart (as a conventional star). In Bogart's first medium close-up he is given lines of dialogue, whereas Lorre has to wait until the next sequence for his chance to speak. Lorre's value to Warner Bros. in the 1940s was linked to the understanding by his employers of the complex position he occupied as a highly recognizable and individual supporting actor. Not only was this acknowledged, but in these types of sequences there was also the subsequent provision of a forum in which Lorre was able to perform in virtual isolation from other supporting actors, many of whom were cast

Figure 4.2 *Passage to Marseille* (1944). Photo: Warner Bros./Photofest.

primarily because of their émigré status which worked to add a sense of authenticity to the wartime setting. Therefore, Lorre's value as a screen performer was not necessarily solely determined by his generic position as a 'foreign' or 'émigré' actor.

Using *Passage to Marseille* as an example allows for a distinction to be made, once again, between Lorre's cinematic labour and his extra-filmic persona. Archival material reveals that the emphasis on Lorre's individual (and unusual) star status was a deliberately acknowledged and considered – if not consistently recorded – feature of his years at Warner Bros. In preparing *Background to Danger* for production, a memo from Jack Warner to the advertising and publicity department requested that Lorre be promoted from fourth to second billing, stating that 'I feel Lorre in a chase film like this has a lot of value' (24 May 1943). Warner's words convey the perception that Lorre's commercial potential lay not in his position as a stock supporting actor, but in his power as a recognizable (and marketable) individual. This can also be seen in the different contracts that the actor held whilst at the studio. During the late 1930s and throughout the 1940s, it was relatively common for German-speaking actors to be offered picture-by-picture contracts rather than the more expensive one-year contracts (Garncarz 2006: 110). Whilst the first two years that Lorre spent at Warner Bros. conform to this pattern, the remaining years in which he held an extensive five-year contract suggest that the studio came to perceive him in different economic and cultural terms to other émigré supporting screen performers.

The Warner Bros. films illustrate the difficulty in characterizing Lorre's screen work from 1941 onwards as reliant upon his status as a 'foreigner'. In reality there was a much more complex negotiation within his employment at the studio. Lorre's commodity value was connected more to his individual identity as a recognizable and popular screen actor than to any particular cultural connotations. This can be discerned through every stage of a film's existence: at a textual level in *Passage to Marseille*, from casting and contract decisions in general and pre-release discourse surrounding *Background to Danger*, and in the reception of his work within the public sphere whereby contemporary reviews throughout the 1940s continued to single out Lorre out for praise, describing his brief performances in terms of the individual actor's skill rather than as stock characterizations.

Furthermore, a number of Warner Bros. films from this period made no overt reference to the war itself, or to Lorre's (or his character's) nationality as being a signifier of 'difference': for example, *The Constant Nymph* (1943), *The Mask of Dimitrios* (1944) (both produced by Henry Blanke), *Three Strangers* (1946) or *The Verdict* (1946). In addition to this – as is examined in Chapter 6 – Lorre's work within the horror genre during the 1940s actively questioned his position as an 'outsider', even going as far as to cast him as an American. A further change within Lorre's career was that in the Warner Bros.' wartime films – for the first time – Lorre's co-stars were predominantly other European actors. Prior to this, he had tended to be cast alongside American actors. Consequently, during this period Lorre no longer sounded as distinctly 'European' as he had done in the 1930s. Lorre's voice began to change dramatically, becoming more Americanized. The result of this was that by the end of the decade Lorre's voice was a mixture of the actor's own unusual vocal tones coupled with his curious appropriation of both European and American accents, and American slang.

Peter Lorre and Sydney Greenstreet: 'The Masters of Menace': 1941–1946

Lorre and Greenstreet's partnership was successful enough to still be considered today as one of the major defining features of Lorre's Hollywood career, and there is rarely a basic description of Lorre that does not mention his engaging on-screen relationship with 'the fat man'. The two are also described in terms that connect the actors to an image of 'evil' or 'menace': from the recycled sound-bites which construct them as 'the Laurel and Hardy of Crime' or 'Masters of Menace', to more thorough observations of their screen image, including Aljean Harmetz's (1993: 154) description: '[Greenstreet and Lorre] are complements of evil, yin and yang – the huge man, monstrously fat and monstrously corrupt, rolling into a scene like some landlocked ship, and, at his side, the dainty little man, whose evil was not of will, but of madness.'

The image associated with two actors was very popular and enduring, and their place within American popular culture can be illustrated by the darkly comic version of their partnership in the 1944 film, *Hollywood Canteen* (in which the actors themselves spoofed their own 'evil' screen image). This film was made only three years after they first appeared together in *The Maltese Falcon* and demonstrates the swiftness with which their partnership was constructed and consolidated. It is also an image that endured after their deaths, being particularly prevalent during the 1970s at the height of the cult appreciation of Humphrey Bogart.

The phrase 'the Laurel and Hardy of crime', which is so often used to characterize their partnership, came from a description of the relationship between the characters in *The Maltese Falcon*, Gutman and Cairo, written by Allen Eyles (1964: 50). This description is accurate in its consideration of the actors' contrasting physicality, but not in its exploration of their characters' relationship, as Cairo and Gutman only share a few words on-screen – both interact more with Spade. Possibly this summation has then been misquoted and misappropriated over time to come to define the actors, Greenstreet and Lorre, rather than the characters, Gutman and Cairo. This approach, which blurs the distinction between character and actor, is indicative of how perceptions concerning the duo have evolved, and how a convenient marketing image has come to supersede considerations of the screen work undertaken by both men. It can be argued that 'The Masters of Menace' partnership was constructed away from the cinema screen for a specific economic purpose, and that the majority of their on-screen appearances together do not conform to the remit of this popular image.

Of course, this mirrors the disparity that surrounds Lorre's position as an individual actor whose screen labour was connected to the development of his extra-filmic persona only by the most tenuous definitions. Indeed, much of the resonance of Greenstreet and Lorre as masters of menace and the macabre comes directly from the particular associations of Lorre's individual publically received extra-filmic identity. This means that the partnership is subject to the same kinds of misreadings that Lorre's own career was subjected to regarding the mismatch between role and image, as evidenced by the above quotation by Harmetz. Her evocative words seek to pique the reader's interest and they are successful in constructing an image of the two performers away from their brief appearances in *Casablanca* – but on closer inspection, the description is a wholly inaccurate picture of what the two men achieved on-screen.

The apparent partnership of 'Greenstreet and Lorre' enabled the easy marketing by the studio of two actors who were problematic to publicize as individual leading performers. This industrial strategy has then been repeated by critics and journalists as an accurate description of the Hollywood careers of both actors. It is especially useful regarding Lorre as it provides an easily defined image that sits conveniently in an otherwise heterogenic, incoherent and (apparently) 'tragic' career. It momentarily reduces the problematic nature of Lorre by defining his Hollywood years in terms of a popular partnership that existed between two recognizable character actors. However, this has led to an overemphasis of the importance of this 'duo'.

Lorre and Greenstreet appeared 'together' in nine films between 1941 and 1946: *The Maltese Falcon, Casablanca, Background to Danger, Passage to Marseille, The Mask of Dimitrios, The Conspirators, Hollywood Canteen, Three Strangers* and *The Verdict*.[7] Whilst this constitutes a solid body of work for the five years, it hardly amounts to an immortal cinematic partnership: a problem encountered by Ted Sennett (1979), whose book on the two actors struggles to reinforce this image.[8] In the nine films, the two actors only shared screen time in six of them (their characters do not meet in *Casablanca, Background to Danger* or *The Conspirators*); and the relationship between their characters only constitutes a 'partnership' in two of the films: *The Mask of Dimitrios* and *The Verdict*. The two barely speak to each other in *The Maltese Falcon*, their characters have opposing loyalties in *Passage to Marseille*, in the revue film *Hollywood Canteen* they play 'themselves' only for one short sequence, and in *Three Strangers* they only share two sequences with each other.

Despite the disparate nature of their screen work, Lorre and Greenstreet were promoted as an inseparable screen duo by the advertising and promotional department at Warner Bros., especially after 1944. Despite their lack of screen time together and little sense of 'terror' within the film itself, the trailer for *Three Strangers* inaccurately characterizes the film as 'another triumph of terror by the Masters of Mystery!'. It goes on to emphasize their contrasting physicality as a signifier of their apparent partnership – screen titles literally define Greenstreet as 'the Fat Man' and Lorre as 'the Little Man'. That this was a specific means of marketing these two particular actors (rather than the possibility that the association was created in the minds of an audience independent from studio management) can be seen in the absence of other partnership discourses surrounding Lorre. Looking at his screen career one can determine that Lorre had a far more engaging screen partnership in the scenes he played with Humphrey Bogart in the five films they made together, or with Vincent Price in the four films and one television programme that they subsequently collaborated on. Whilst an audience may have enjoyed these alternative pairings, there was no financial gain for their employers to encourage this perception. Both Bogart and Price were valuable to Warner Bros. and AIP as individual stand-alone stars.

Neither Lorre nor Greenstreet maintained this level of star power during the 1940s, although they had both proved themselves as more popular and valuable than conventional supporting actors. This status, coupled with their physical appearance, made them difficult actors for the studio to cast in appropriate leading roles. The solution was to use their contrasting physicality as a saleable quality and to 'reinvent' them as an eminently marketable double act. They achieved a new level of celebrity and popularity (which far exceeded that of other supporting actors such as Steven Geray or Victor Francen – both of whom 'supported' the duo in *The Mask of Dimitrios*), but only as a result of their appearances as a double act.

Central to the emergent image of Lorre and Greenstreet as an on-screen duo was their appearance in *Hollywood Canteen*. This 1944 patriotic flag-waver revolves around a naive GI, Slim (Robert Hutton), who visits the 'real' Hollywood Canteen and gets caught up in a love story with Joan Leslie. Within this framework, there are many cameos and interludes from the major stars of the period playing slightly fictionalized versions of their Hollywood personae. One of these cameos is a short sequence with Lorre and Greenstreet (demonstrating the level of their popularity in the mid-1940s) in which they scare Slim with the underlying threatening tone of their otherwise innocuous conversation. According to Lorre's biographer, both actors played an instrumental role in scripting their appearance, designed to showcase the two as gruesome 'masters of menace'. Youngkin (2005: 221–22) describes the scene as 'lampooning their familiar images as screen menaces. Lorre meekly whines, always the menacing milksop. Greenstreet is imperious but gracious, brimming over with malevolent affability.'

To describe this scene as a 'lampoon' is somewhat problematic: whilst it is clearly linked to promoting the image of the two as 'masters of menace', it is inaccurate to see it as a moment which spoofs their on-screen work together. It was filmed in 1944 at a time when their partnership consisted only of *The Mask of Dimitrios* – a film which does not conform to this image. It could be argued that the scene is linked to *The Maltese Falcon*, but the underlying psychotic nature of the sketch seems far removed from Gutman's and (especially) Cairo's professional mercenary position. Therefore, it can be argued that instead of lampooning their screen image, *Hollywood Canteen* depicts the moment that the image of the 'masters of menace' is created, partly by Lorre and Greenstreet, and partly with the aid of the writers, and wholly with the approval of studio management. The 'masters of menace' did not exist before they were specifically concocted for a sketch in a film, which, through its continual references to the extra-textual star images of certain performers in an on-screen format, constitutes in part an advert for Warner Bros. itself. The self-advertising nature of Warner Bros.' *Hollywood Canteen* explicitly highlights the connection between the 'masters of menace' partnership and the role of studio-managed promotion and advertising.

That this highly promotable image of the two actors drew heavily upon Lorre's already established extra-filmic persona is perhaps unsurprising, as by 1944 Lorre's persona had proved to be an economically sound marketing practice. Warner Bros. was able to profit from Lorre's murderous and menacing persona, without necessarily compromising how he was employed in other films for the studio. Lorre was not cast in these types of roles whilst he remained at Warner Bros., with the exception of Lorre's final film for the studio, *The Beast with Five Fingers*. Therefore, Lorre's extra-filmic persona had an impact on the conditions of his employment at the studio, even if it did not relate directly to the screen work undertaken by the actor. The persona continued to be utilized in order to lend a sense of unity to Lorre's otherwise disparate cinematic career.

Despite Lorre's extra-filmic persona, his films with Greenstreet tend to mirror his other screen roles of the time, and his characters rarely exhibited psychotic behaviour in their films together. The films in which the two played the leading roles (*The Mask of Dimitrios*, *Three Strangers* and *The Verdict*) always reveal Greenstreet's character to be the more unhinged and murderous member of the 'partnership'. Lorre's characters are always shown to be eccentric, but ultimately 'good'. These roles did not have such a dramatic effect on Greenstreet's individual persona and he cultivated a more jovial image both on- and off-screen.

This mismatch between the different types of characters played by the two actors and the unity of the overall image of the partnership is mirrored by the perception of the partnership as being an equal one. Although their employment in *The Mask of Dimitrios* and *Three Strangers* enabled Greenstreet and Lorre to share the status of lead actor, this equality was not reflected in the on-screen performances that both men gave in these films.[9] *The Mask of Dimitrios* and *Three Strangers* are unconventional because the films support two male leads who command approximately the same amount of narrative importance, screen time and levels of audience engagement. Despite this, neither film is wholly successful in its attempts to construct the two actors as a screen double act. Both contradict the assumption that both actors had 'the surest screen chemistry' (Thomson 2005: 34) with each other, further reinforcing the notion that their partnership was a deliberate studio strategy rather than an a posteriori construct of an appreciative cult audience. Whereas Lorre interacted with Humphrey Bogart with consummate ease in the scenes they shared, the interplay between Greenstreet and Lorre is far more laboured and served to unbalance their shared screen time, as one actor tended to shine at the expense of the other. In *The Mask of Dimitrios*, Sydney Greenstreet dominates the screen, whereas in *Three Strangers*, Lorre is more prominent.

The Mask of Dimitrios is a labyrinthine tale adapted from an Eric Ambler novel (*A Coffin for Dimitrios*) in which Lorre's character, Leyden, becomes obsessed with the puzzling life of Dimitrios (Zachary Scott), a notorious criminal and murderer, whose body has been found in mysterious circumstances in Istanbul. Joining him as he searches across Europe for the truth about Dimitrios is the equally mysterious Mr Peters/Mr Peterson (Greenstreet). As Leyden uncovers the history of the title character, it is revealed that Peters is a former acquaintance of Dimitrios who was betrayed by the criminal mastermind, and that Dimitrios is still alive and hiding in Paris. The story concludes with Peters murdering Dimitrios as an uncontrollable desire for vengeance consumes him.

As evidenced by this brief synopsis, although a main role, Lorre's character Leyden is not the focus of the film. He is characterized as a shy economics professor who writes detective stories, and whose desire to experience the kinds of worlds that he writes about leads him into the dangerous world of Dimitrios. Leyden quickly comes to conclude that, although he is fascinated by Dimitrios, he occupies a place that Leyden does not fit into or understand. Leyden is constructed as a character with no hidden motivations or secrets; a quality that again makes it clear he does not belong in the underworld environment of Dimitrios. This is in direct contrast to Peters, who forms a 'friendship' with Leyden only because he believes Leyden can tell him something about Dimitrios's death. It is also characteristic of the relationship formed between Leyden and the characters who retell Dimitrios's history to him. These characters constantly question Leyden because they cannot believe he is not motivated by either financial or emotional reasons for revenge. Throughout, Leyden is represented as a 'knowable' character; neither narrative nor *mise-en-scène* encourages the viewer to question his actions in the same way the other characters do. The story aligns the audience with Leyden, as they learn about Dimitrios and his fellow criminals only as he learns about them. Therefore, he occupies a position of respect and trust within the film.

It is accurate to suggest that there are few connections between Leyden and characteristics associated with Lorre's own persona or the image of the two actors as 'masters of menace'. Despite being a useful opportunity to encourage this distance between his work and the various ways that he was perceived and publicized within the industry, *The Mask of Dimitrios* is not one of Lorre's more interesting films. It is useful to cite a statement made by David Shipman (1972: 336), nominally about Lorre's portrayal of Mr Moto but perhaps more applicable to his performance as Leyden than to the 'oriental' detective: that 'Lorre did not know how to make "good" interesting'. With regards to Leyden, this comment has an element of accuracy to it. Part of this is undoubtedly due to the passive nature of the character himself: his function is to prompt the many flashbacks within the film – which contain most of the action – through his own questions. In keeping with this, Leyden is presented as an ordinary or invisible observer of life. This characteristic is further reflected by Lorre's physical representation of Leyden which uses glasses, greying hair and dark clothing to demonstrate the character's 'invisibility'. Somewhat paradoxically, this careful use of prop and costume acts to enhance Lorre's own presence as an actor within the film. Although Leyden is 'invisible', the performance remains 'visible' through these means which draw attention to his construction of the character. However, Lorre's foregrounding of his own performance is not as pronounced as in other films such as the Mr Moto series or *The Maltese Falcon*.

As illustrated by his performance in *The Maltese Falcon*, it was not especially hindering to Lorre for his characters to be on the periphery of the main action as he often utilized verbal and non-verbal techniques in order to focus an audience's attention on to him. However, whilst he uses some similar flourishes in *The Mask of Dimitrios* (such as his playful interplay with some kittens, and his equally playful benign delivery of the following exchange with Greenstreet's Peters: 'I can only conclude that you are a thief or a drunk. Are you drunk sir?'), there is no attempt to form these individual moments into a coherent leading performance. They remain isolated examples of disjointed 'scene-stealing', and for the most part, he is overwhelmed by the presence of Greenstreet who gives a bombastic and ambiguous performance as Peters.

The opposite is true of *Three Strangers*, where Lorre gives a much more cohesive performance and is a more dominant presence than Greenstreet – although this is perhaps because they only share a few scenes together. The narrative is made up from three separate stories concerning the three main characters; Johnny West (Lorre), Jerome K. Arbutny (Greenstreet) and Crystal Shackleford (Geraldine Fitzgerald), who become intertwined when, on Chinese New Year, Crystal invites the 'strangers' to enter into a pact with her to wish upon the statue of a Chinese goddess, Kwan-Yin, in the belief that this will mean they will hold a winning sweepstake ticket. Crystal's own story concerns her attempts to win back her estranged husband by increasingly desperate and misguided measures. Arbutny's story charts his descent into extreme panic after he loses a client's funds after misusing them to invest badly in some South African stocks. Their narratives converge again when Arbutny demands the sweepstake ticket from Crystal in order to raise the missing money. She refuses, and Arbutny kills her in a blind rage. Convinced he is going mad, he gives himself up to the police.

Lorre's Johnny is the only character who escapes unharmed from the pact, although this is not an obvious conclusion given his own story. He is an alcoholic who, in his drunken state, was involved in a disastrous robbery attempt. His accomplice killed a policeman and was arrested, but is later freed after betraying his fellow thieves. Framed by the real killer, Johnny is apprehended and sentenced to death. At the last minute, a second accomplice murders the killer and sacrifices his own freedom so that Johnny can go free. Johnny is released just in time to hear that the sweepstake ticket has won, only to then witness Crystal's murder at the hands of Arbutny. Since all three names were signed upon the ticket, he is unable to cash in his winnings, but he remains optimistic with life nonetheless.

Lorre's character is again a very passive one: he spends most of the time in a drunken stupor, incapable of much action. He is also seen as a 'good' character that 'bad' things happen to, a definition that can also be applied to Leyden in *The Mask of Dimitrios*. The difference is that in *Three Strangers* Lorre works very hard to make 'good' interesting. Ostensibly, Lorre plays Johnny as a charmingly pathetic drunk who is humorous, cultured, gentle and benevolent, despite his obvious addiction. However, he counters the superficiality of this representation of a souse with a heart of gold through specific techniques which attempt to reveal the underlying troubles implied by the character's addiction, despite this level of characterization being unnecessary to the development of the plot. He combines Johnny's more engaging qualities with a very casual and off-hand distracted manner in certain scenes in order to show the character's self-awareness of (and refusal to directly confront) his perilous situation. For example, he is able to recognize that the demands made on them by his suspicious and greedy landlady place her in danger from his more violent accomplice, so he quickly and calmly pays her off, which gives them both time to flee. In this film, Lorre employs a subtle duality (rather than a purposefully jarring juxtapositional style) within his acting to illustrate both the affability of Johnny-the-drunk and the cynical sober failure that hides behind the bottle. In doing so, he adds a further layer to an already ambiguous and fatalistic anti-hero operating within a noir-infused narrative framed around themes of determinism and existentialism.

Many of the instances in which Johnny reveals his more vulnerable characteristics occur in his scenes with Icey (Joan Lorring), the girlfriend of the 'real' killer, who is helping him hide from the police. His physical performance demonstrates the feelings he has towards her, but this is hidden by his cool and jocular verbal relationship with her. When she presses him further about his feelings, he casually replies that he is fearful of hurting her, and his distracted tone means that she refuses to accept this, believing it to be bravado. However, the continuities present throughout Lorre's subtly layered performance imply that there is an underlying truth to the superficiality of his words. As the film progresses, and as she comes to know him as a sober and sensitive man, Icey falls in love with Johnny and resolves to protect him from both the police and her boyfriend.

This touching relationship and its apparent success shows the degree to which Lorre's casting was capable of contrasting with the image associated with his extra-filmic persona. John Huston, who wrote *Three Strangers*, originally envisioned Humphrey Bogart in the role of Johnny, which explains the romantic narrative (Youngkin 2005: 227). The fact that it remained when Lorre was attached to the project is more surprising, given his relative lack of conventional romantic roles in his screen career, and the prominent place that the notion of sexual perversity played within his extra-filmic persona. Indeed this major discrepancy between his persona and his sensitive portrayal may explain why he has been considered by some to be miscast in this role (Sennett 1979: 100).

Three Strangers illustrates that Lorre was very effective at playing the romanticized existential lead and that Johnny, the philosophical fatalist, is one of his most fully realized characters. Extra-textual knowledge of his persona aids the character's story rather than hindering it. If a more conventional star, such as Bogart, had played Johnny, the outcome of the storyline would have been relatively predictable. Instead, Johnny's salvation and redemption (partly from the love of a 'good' woman and partly through his own journey) is more difficult to predict, precisely because he is played by Lorre; it is not unusual for his characters to die or to be abandoned by the conclusion of a film, rather than to be involved with a happy(ish) ending where they achieve romantic fulfilment. It also allows Lorre to occupy this leading status in virtual isolation from other male leads. Although he was only given this opportunity because of the perceived commodity value of his double act with Greenstreet, the two actors operate almost wholly independently of each other within the film, which enables Lorre to concentrate on his own performance rather than being overshadowed by his partner.

Notes

1. Lorre signed six single-picture contracts between 19 June 1941 and 1 October 1942 (*The Maltese Falcon, All Through the Night, Arsenic and Old Lace, The Constant Nymph, Casablanca* and *Background to Danger*). On 2 June 1943 he signed a multiple-picture contract, which was amended in November to stipulate the following conditions: Lorre was contracted to make three films per year at Warner Bros.; limited to appearing in two 'outside' films per year; and given the option to direct one film per year. Although reviewed and revised each year, the terms of this contract continued until 13 May 1946 when Lorre was released from it, 'by mutual agreement'. Warner Bros. Archive, University of Southern California, Los Angeles, USA.
2. The second film made under this contract was the hastily constructed horror-spoof, *You'll Find Out*, which will be discussed in Chapter 6.

3. This moment of having a character describe Lorre's physical appearance but being unable to recognize him, even when Lorre's character stands in front of him or her (unlike the viewer who has a privileged position and can easily recognize Lorre), is further developed to greater comic effect in *Arsenic and Old Lace* (Frank Capra, Warner Bros. 1944).

4. In both *The Chase* (1946) and *Double Confession* (1950) there is the potential to read the relationship between Lorre's characters, Gino and Paynter, and their respective bosses as having homosexual elements, but any suggestion is made far more implicitly than the relative explicitness of Cairo's homosexuality.

5. Although Vasey makes the point about changes in representation occurring within Hollywood as early as 1939, it should be noted that the specific examples cited by her on these pages are all Warner Bros. productions.

6. Lorre also made *Invisible Agent*, in which he played a Japanese Axis agent, for Universal in 1942, but I will not discuss it here because I have already explored Lorre's employment as an 'oriental' figure in Chapter 3. Out of the films listed here, the first three were produced by either Wallis and/or Wald, and the latter two produced by Jack Chertok and Robert Buckner, respectively.

7. Apart from the presence of Lorre and Greenstreet, there is little continuity within cast or production crew over the course of the nine films, even in terms of executive producers.

8. *Masters of Menace: Greenstreet and Lorre* is unable to maintain the overall focus of its title as Sennett's work is structured around chapters detailing their work pre-1941, *The Maltese Falcon*, their films together and their films apart. In all, 132 pages describe their careers as separate performers, but only 56 pages are devoted to their time together.

9. This shared status was further compromised by the other film in which they were paired on-screen, *The Verdict*, but since this uses Lorre in a more conventional supporting role, which employs his 'sinister' identity as a diversionary tactic (much like *The Maltese Falcon*), there is little to be gained from discussing it here.

Chapter 5

DER VERLORENE (THE LOST ONE) (1951)

Between 1946 and 1950, in the final months of Lorre's contract with Warner Bros., and in his tentative return to freelance acting, a lack of artistic direction in the way Lorre was employed and also within the detail of his performances can be observed. By 1946, it also became clear that Warner Bros. were unlikely to deliver on a clause in Lorre's contract that he had himself insisted upon: the option to direct one film per year.[1] In films such as *The Chase* (1946), *My Favorite Brunette* (1947) and *Double Confession* (1950), a tendency towards self-parody became more prominent which has often (erroneously) been seen to characterize much of Lorre's career. In terms of characterization, Lorre's roles more readily conformed to the prescribed extra-filmic persona of the actor and were written as little more than sadistic thugs who were eager (if not necessarily compelled) to kill. Lorre's individual performances also seemed to conform to his stereotypical extra-filmic image, whereby no further complexity was added to the films through a considered deployment of acting styles or techniques. Lorre played these thuggish roles with little imaginative flair and incorporated none of the pluralistic or reflexive qualities that were in evidence in much of his previous work. It is in these instances that the actor's description of acting – as merely 'face-making' – becomes a more accurate summation of his screen work.

This period of cinematic stagnation was partly due to a downturn in his financial fortunes, which became especially pronounced following the termination of his regular employment with Warner Bros. and his decision to set up his own production company, Lorre Inc. Throughout the late 1940s, Lorre had little artistic freedom regarding the work offered to him or how to play these roles. Many such roles were reliant upon the marketability of Lorre's extra-filmic persona and his own celebrity, and as such, they deviated little from that stereotypical association.[2] In addition to Lorre's screen work, this was a period in which the actor was appearing regularly on American radio in roles which also subscribed closely to his particular extra-filmic image of menace and horror.

By 1949, Lorre was forced to declare himself bankrupt (Youngkin 2005: 308–10). In June of that year, he left the United States for the UK (where he made *Double Confession*), and by October 1950 he had returned to Germany for the first time since 1934. Between late 1950 and mid-1951, Lorre directed *Der Verlorene* (1951). The film was commercially unsuccessful, having only a limited European release (although it was submitted for the Venice Biennale in 1951). It ran for only ten days in Germany, and this lack of attention from the German public has been suggested as reflecting the more general widespread distaste for crime and horror films that were deemed inappropriate during the aftermath of the war (Bergfelder 2007a: 149). Additionally, the German press had been following the production of the film intensely, as Lorre's return to the country was a high-profile event. Throughout filming, newspapers published rumours about the controversial nature of the film, and on its release it garnered mixed reviews from critics (Youngkin 2005: 344–55).

The historical circumstances that surrounded Lorre's return to Germany in 1950 have resulted in the short period during which he filmed and released *Der Verlorene* (translated as either 'The Lost One' or 'The Lost Man') being awarded a great deal of significance within the actor's career and life. One of the staunchest detractors of Lorre's Hollywood career, Bertolt Brecht, had asked the actor to rejoin him in Germany in 1948, the year the playwright returned to Berlin.[3] Brecht perceived that Hollywood had corrupted the 'artistry' of the actor, and in turn, believed that a return to the Berlin stage where Lorre had first tasted fame would encourage him to recapture the glories of his youth. Given the way his career was progressing towards the late 1940s, it is very likely that Lorre shared Brecht's viewpoint, at least regarding his immediate prospects and artistic value within Hollywood during this period, and also concerning the chance to explore once more the different working practices of the Berlin stage.[4] This perception of the desire of a figure in exile to escape the commercialism of the Hollywood machine through a return to the European setting of past artistic achievements has certainly influenced how critical discussions pertaining to *Der Verlorene* have been shaped.

However, it should also be noted that when Lorre returned to mainland Europe, he did not return to Berlin to seek out Brecht. Instead, he settled in areas of West Germany that he had not previously worked in, first briefly in Munich and then in Hamburg, and the close relationship he had forged with the playwright in both Berlin and Hollywood soon dissolved. Whilst Brecht's swift return to Berlin signalled an artistic agenda influenced by political circumstances and his exilic status as an 'outsider' in America, Lorre's own motivations for returning to Germany are much less distinct and difficult to define simply along these lines.

Lorre's directorial debut, *Der Verlorene*, can certainly be read as a statement about the emblematic post-war figure of the returning exile. Within this mode of discourse surrounding the film, the central figure of Peter Lorre occupies a particular role: the tragic figure of the 'lost' man who is constructed as one (like many others) who is unable to find his place within post-war Europe. In addition to acknowledging this dominant discourse which markedly contributes to an overall understanding of the film, I will consider a secondary interpretation which takes a more individualistic approach to Lorre's work. Rather than solely defining Lorre as a refugee figure conflicted by his European identity and his American career at this specific moment in 1950–51, it is also possible to place *Der Verlorene* within the wider realm of Lorre's successful transnational career. In doing this, it becomes a complex and highly self-reflexive text in which references to Lorre's public image and the entirety of his career (making no particular cultural distinction between Hollywood and Europe) are employed by the director/actor as a filmmaking tool which allows for an examination of political and social contexts and the creation of a highly pluralistic, multi-faceted text. Both approaches define Lorre's *Der Verlorene* as a specifically autobiographical film at a textual level. This personal self-reflexive relationship between film and filmmaker is, of course, emphasized by the off-screen roles attributed to Lorre: not only did he direct *Der Verlorene*, but he also co-produced it (with Arnold Pressburger) and developed the original story (co-writing the screenplay with Axel Eggebrecht and Benno Vigny). Due to his extensive involvement throughout the whole production process, and because of the nature of the themes examined within the narrative, Lorre's film can be characterized as an allegorical text in which – from the outset and the very title – the actor's own central and complex cultural and industrial position is explicitly foregrounded.

Not all critical interpretations of this film define it in solely autobiographical terms. It can be situated within other critical discourses which downplay the presence of Lorre in favour of other aesthetic contexts.[5] Whilst readings of the film which are not Lorre-centric are available, emphasis on the central presence of the actor and the particular way that he, as a returning exile, chose to represent post-war Germany has been the conventional point of scholarly engagement with *Der Verlorene*. As such, existing critical assessments of the actor have tended to colour interpretations of the film, hence the reading of it according to discourses of exile and typecasting, and the reconstruction of it as a narrative which relates to Lorre's own seemingly 'tragic' life as an 'outsider' working in Hollywood.

Defining *Der Verlorene* as an 'Accented Film': Lorre's Exilic Status

Discourses concerning national identities and post-war German cinema are central to an understanding of *Der Verlorene*. It is a film that explicitly references the Second World War in the context of the effect the Nazi regime had upon apolitical German citizens, and the subsequent complicity of those citizens in allowing the horrors of the war to develop, through its careful deployment of a story which foregrounds the figure of the serial killer. Furthermore, it was one of the first German films to be made after the war that presented these dark motifs of collective guilt and a damaged national psychology. The film's commercial failure in Germany is often attributed to a combination of the story itself, the pessimism of the underlying message, and that it was offered by a man who was easily defined as an 'outsider'; whose experiences of the war were shaped, at the expense of his Mitteleuropean identity, by Hollywood narratives and the comfortable lifestyle of an Americanized celebrity.

The film itself is ostensibly set in the bleak post-war environment of a refugee camp, but is mainly told through a series of flashbacks to the bombed-out streets of Hamburg during the war. The main character, Dr Rothe (Lorre), is routinely working at the camp until the arrival of a man from his past, Hösch (Karl John), forces him to confront actions and emotions that he has long since managed to repress. The two men spend the night drinking in the camp canteen, during which Rothe retells his story to his increasingly drunken and boorish companion. Rothe describes his former life as a research scientist, and how his lab was infiltrated by a Gestapo agent (Hösch) and his superior officer, Winkler (Helmut Rudolph), who suspected Rothe's fiancé, Inge (Renate Mannhardt), of selling the doctor's research to the Allies. Initially ambivalent about this betrayal, Rothe murders Inge upon the revelation that this information had been learnt during the course of Inge's affair with Hösch.

Realizing the importance of Rothe's work to the regime, Hösch and Winkler conspire to cover up the murder. However, Rothe's existence becomes characterized by both his guilt over this 'state-sanctioned' crime and the hitherto hidden impulse that compels him to seek out female victims so that he may kill again. Tormented by his insatiable desires, Rothe resolves to kill Hösch and then himself, but he becomes entangled (along with Hösch and Winkler) in an assassination conspiracy and fails to carry out his revenge. He lives out the war wandering aimlessly; becoming the eponymous 'lost man', until the encounter with Hösch at the camp (and the beginning of the film). Once Rothe has revisited and confronted his existence, which defines him as a sexually motivated killer, he is able to shoot Hösch and throw himself under a train. He acknowledges his own murderous identity and, through its destruction, is finally able to find peace.

Readings of *Der Verlorene* which favour a semi-autobiographical approach highlight Lorre's own exilic status in order to reveal a meta-text that, to some degree, mirrors the plot of the film, but is ultimately more concerned with identifying the idea of emigration (as opposed to the act of murder) as the point at which everything that was once familiar is made strange and unknowable, even the sense of one's own identity and place within modern urban society. In these readings there is the desire to read the title, *Der Verlorene*, as a reflection of Lorre's own position. (The most notable example is the use of the phrase in the title of Stephen D. Youngkin's biography which explicitly defines Lorre as a 'lost man'.) The exiled actor takes on the emblematic role of the 'lost man', and the film itself becomes a more general treatise on what it means to be an émigré who returns 'home' in order to find and confront his own identity and place within post-war German society, rather than a straightforward thriller constructed around the presence of a serial killer.

Drawing on Hamid Naficy's concept, Jennifer M. Kapczynski (2003) describes *Der Verlorene* as an 'accented film' which 'stages the complex negotiations between the filmmaker's interconnected but divergent lives in exile'. Autobiographical readings suggest that the film is constructed around the central extra-textual identity of Peter Lorre, whose personal dilemmas and complex identity take precedence over those of Rothe. This distinct strategy which aims to create a self-reflexive separation between the roles of 'character' and 'actor' within a specific text can be found throughout Lorre's career – from the Berlin stage, through his years at Warner Bros., and even through to his last films with AIP. Interpretations of *Der Verlorene* which view it primarily as an 'accented' text, read Lorre's position as an 'actor' only through a categorization of him as an 'actor-in-exile'. This émigré position becomes Lorre's defining characteristic as a performer, and this feature is displayed most transparently within *Der Verlorene*.

For Kapczynski, even the most basic formal components of the film are influenced by Lorre's position as a returning exile. As an example, she cites the structure of the text, which moves effortlessly between past and present with minimal visual disruption or unnecessary set-up through the use of flashbacks. The movement is conveyed through a variety of techniques: from the visual example of Rothe lighting a cigarette in his Hamburg apartment only to extinguish his match underfoot in the camp canteen as he continues his story; to the aural continuity of Rothe's voiceover, which continues his narration even when his witness, Hösch, is shown at times to be either sleeping or listening to the doctor. The flashbacks and fractured narratives of Rothe and Hösch are thus seen to reflect a desire to set up a dialogue between Lorre (the émigré) and the former countrymen that he sought to engage with about Germany's immediate past and its present. Kapczynski writes that these techniques demonstrate that, 'through the film's complex and fragmented narrative structure, Lorre repeatedly represents the nation's present and past as closely intertwined'.

This interpretation relies upon first using Lorre's emblematic position as an émigré in order to construct him as an 'outsider' within post-war Germany. Not only does he occupy a dislocated position, but his experiences in exile in the United States further complicate his own Mitteleuropean identity by giving him a privileged and objective viewpoint, from which he could survey post-war German society. Defining Lorre as an 'outsider' within German society is also relatively easy given the imprecise nature of his own identity, which is why I use the term 'Mitteleuropean': he was born in Hungary (in a town which is now part of

Slovakia), grew up in Romania and Austria, and spent only five years working in Germany before he became an exile in France and the UK, before settling for sixteen years in the USA. From this perspective of an 'outsider', Lorre presented a film which explicitly confronted the continuities between history and the present; an attitude explored because, as Tony Williams (2007) suggests, Lorre felt the new German society risked ignoring or forgetting the immediate past in their anxiousness to distance themselves from the Nazi era.

However, readings of this film (and of Lorre's career) which prioritize his status as an émigré do not just define Lorre as an 'outsider': they define him as 'insider as outsider', both in the United States and in Germany (Youngkin 2005; Gemünden 2003; Kapczynski 2003; and McCullough 2004). In doing so, Lorre is assigned a symbolic status where he is constructed as a figure that is able to represent the tragic and impossible position of the émigré: like many exiles, Lorre is simultaneously someone who 'belongs' and yet 'does not belong'. Furthermore, *Der Verlorene* can be seen as an attempt to reconcile these two opposing positions. One way in which this position of 'insider as outsider' is confronted by the film is through the way in which the theme of 'guilt' is referenced both as a motif within the text and also contextually through the figure of Lorre. It has been argued by Kapczynski and Ulrike Ottinger (2000) that the source of the underlying sense of guilt which pervades Rothe's actions throughout the film can be identified as the guilt felt by Lorre himself as a European who remained absent and isolated from the conflict in Europe, and also from Germany's crimes and eventual defeat by the Allies. Lorre's perception of his own 'Germanic' identity (although as stated before, this is a problematic definition) led him to create the narrative of *Der Verlorene* and also to cast himself as the sociopathic murderer Dr Rothe, who seeks justice through his own destruction; a decision which led to Lorre appearing to incriminate himself within his polemical indictment of German society.

I have already discussed the limitations of the definition of Lorre as 'insider as outsider' with regards to his employment within Hollywood; whereby defining Lorre's position within Hollywood as an 'insider', who was forced to play the 'outsider' in order to be accepted, requires a somewhat limited understanding of the conditions of Lorre's Hollywood employment and the nature of his screen roles. By highlighting the problematic nature of this phrase regarding the majority of Lorre's career and his status as an 'other' within American society, it also becomes a term which needs further exploration in relation to *Der Verlorene*.

This argument which highlights the somewhat ambiguous nature of Lorre's 'foreign' or 'othered' status has a particular impact upon readings of *Der Verlorene* in two ways. Firstly, it reveals that approaching Lorre solely as an émigré figure relies upon a simplistic interpretation of his film career. Secondly, it also shows that analyses based around Lorre's specific definition as 'insider as outsider' are structured along binary divisions which are unhelpful to a consideration of the actor's complex history and performative methods: Europe/the United States; and European 'Art' Cinema/Commercial Hollywood Cinema. Rather than being an almost unique and lucid self-reflexive statement within Lorre's career, that his émigré position 'allowed' him to make, *Der Verlorene* can be seen as being wholly consistent with strategies used throughout Lorre's work (for different effect) in both Europe and Hollywood. Therefore, the references made to Lorre's supposed cinematic and cultural heritage may not necessarily be solely tied up around subjective and personal ideas of guilt or belonging felt within this specific moment.

Readings which fasten upon Lorre's émigré status attempt to define the actor as an emblematic symbol who can be used to represent the experiences of the 'émigré', ignoring the complex position that Lorre occupied within Hollywood: an actor who was continually shifting status between leading and supporting actor; a performer who developed a public 'extra-filmic' persona in virtual isolation from his actual screen roles; an actor who was increasingly visible within American popular culture and his own assimilation of American styles and mannerisms; and the precise (and often self-reflexive) performative techniques used by Lorre throughout these years. These complex issues around the notion of identity and modes of representation make it increasingly difficult for Lorre to serve as a standardized representative for any type of émigré actor.

The purpose of transforming Lorre into an emblem of the émigré is similar to the way that the figure of Bertolt Brecht is also invoked in relation to the actor. In both cases (which are obviously both linked to the idea of exile), there is a need to 'explain' Lorre using established subjects or discourses in order to legitimize studies of the actor. However, an implicit element of these arguments is the underlying notion that Lorre's European status and the work he undertook in Europe is of a higher critical value than his position and employment within Hollywood. Highlighting Lorre's émigré identity and his roles in pre-war and post-war German cinema suggests that his emigration somehow destroyed the creative potential of the actor, because the most 'significant' films that he made appear to be *M* and *Der Verlorene*. Therefore, to some degree, every other film becomes incidental in comparison to the artistry of these two German films. Within this context, *Der Verlorene* is read, firstly as a commentary on *M* itself, but secondly as a commentary on an actor whose life appeared to be defined and trapped by an image that had its genesis in *M*.

Across interpretations which favour an implicit or explicit opposition between the artistic opportunities of European cinema and the crass commercialism of Hollywood cinema, Lorre is reinvented as a tragic figure whose life can be characterized by the unfulfilled opportunities which resulted from the enforced emigration from Europe to the corrupting forces of the Hollywood film industry. Lorre's dual moments of 'exile' and 'return' become the defining events of his life, where everything in between can be linked to those moments in order to make his American work meaningful: for instance, that his Hollywood career can be seen as little more than Lorre trying (and perhaps failing) to recapture the artistry of his European performances; or that in certain films Lorre was referencing and coming to terms with his émigré status through performances that were 'enactments of displacement'.

Furthermore, the apparent 'tragic' nature of Lorre's life is further emphasized by the actor's level of celebrity within Hollywood. His popularity within the United States overshadowed his position as a meaningful artist, as his Hollywood success was seen to have negative connotations; such as his passive acceptance of 'typecasting' in certain roles, the erosion of his position as a 'star' performer, the limiting nature of his persona and his disillusionment with this situation – often conveyed through apathetic or parodic performances. Therefore, his greatest artistic achievements (his performance in *M* and his directorial effort, *Der Verlorene*), were never as popular as the 'Peter Lorre' that was seen to be created by Hollywood. However, these assumptions about Lorre's Hollywood career can all be challenged through evidence which determines that there is a distinct separation between Lorre's screen work and the various transmedial methods that were used to manage the actor's extra-filmic persona.

Separating 'Image', 'Labour' and 'Reality': Objectivity within *Der Verlorene*

Considering *Der Verlorene* in relation to the management of Lorre's on-screen and off-screen career, by both himself and those around him, it is possible to read the film beyond its status as an 'accented film': as more than one isolated moment of self-reflection that was only enabled through Lorre's exilic position and his return to Germany. It is illustrative of a consistent strategy that Lorre utilized throughout his working life that can be categorized as 'self-reflexive' in reference to a variety of different techniques and modes of reference. Generally, this strategy was concerned with the way in which performances are constructed, especially in the creation of a distinction separation between the 'actor', and the 'character', in addition to an articulation of the relationship between an actor's labour and the development of his marketable image or extra-filmic persona.

Within *Der Verlorene*, these distinctions are repeated, enabling a reading of the film in which the dialogue presented is not just between Lorre's American and European sensibilities, but also between the placement of practices and images found throughout his career within an overtly political context. It is as much one man's attempt to explore a political and social context through an objective acknowledgement of his cinematic past and the nature of his own prescribed persona, as it is a subjective document of the emotional experience of the exile who returns 'home'. This is achieved in part because of the different labour space occupied by Lorre in *Der Verlorene*. Here he plays the leading protagonist who appears in the majority of the scenes, rather than limited to brief character roles. Additionally, his central creative position off the screen, particularly in his role as director, is hugely important in shaping the representations and juxtapositions offered within the film because this also allows them to extend beyond the performative frame. This new level of creative control and his extended screen time enables Lorre to develop a discourse that utilizes his own life as a means of exploring post-war Germany.

That Lorre's only attempt at directing adheres so closely to his established extra-filmic persona, in its return to the subject of the serial killer, and its extended references to elements of his screen work, has been seen as an extraordinary move. This is partly because of Nazi propaganda which had co-opted the image of Lorre in *M*, and through its usage – most notably in *Der ewige Jude* (The Eternal Jew) in 1940 – aimed to blur the boundaries between character (the mentally ill serial killer), performance (Lorre's acting in the trial sequence) and reality (Lorre's Jewish identity) in order to depict Jewish figures as subversive, deviant and morally suspect (Bergfelder 2007a: 150). Away from the resonance that Lorre had as serial killer within the recent past of the Nazi regime, his revisiting of this character-type was also perceived as a moment of tragic irony that, when given the freedom to undertake a personal and artistic project, Lorre appeared to fall back on the safety net of *M* and his public image rather than try to develop an alternative representation (Kapszynski 2003: 155).

However, Lorre was more than aware that the continuities with his past could serve a specific function in order to situate and explore the political discourse within the film. The close parallels between Lorre's persona and the character of Rothe was commented on by the actor in an interview conducted soon after the film's completion. In it, Lorre rather objectively suggests that his public image is a framework through which to construct the film text as much as it is about personally inflected reflections upon cultural belonging or national identity:

> It was just common sense to take the line I have become known for in the United States … As you can see, 'The Lost One' is a man who glides into murder. But I certainly did not want to repeat myself. So we set the story of my psychopathic hero against the background of Hitler Germany. (Quoted in Manfred George, 23 September 1951: 113)

That this bid for artistic freedom does not deviate from Lorre's prescribed image is not so much 'poignant' or 'tragic', as demonstrative of the way that certain representations of an individual actor can be used as a filmmaking tool in order to support the narrative or to emphasize meanings which are also implicitly conveyed via other formal techniques such as dialogue, staging or plot. The film visually depicts the destructive and corrupting effects the Nazi regime had upon German society through an interplay between the figures of Lorre and Rothe. As the director and developer, Lorre put his persona and screen history to work in order to serve political ends. The references made by the film to Peter Lorre can be defined as the repetition of specific moments from his life, but these examples also present a homogenized representation of Lorre's career and image, that make no obvious distinction between the 'Hollywood' and 'European' elements of his career, preferring to investigate it from a holistic, rather than national, perspective. However, in doing so and within the characterization of Rothe, it makes distinctions between Lorre's off-screen reality, his performative labour and his public image.

Through the self-reflexive aesthetics (within Lorre's own performance, the overall visual style, and the narrative structure) *Der Verlorene* becomes a film with a highly pluralistic outlook. As it shifts between a variety of

Figure 5.1 Lorre as Dr Rothe, *Der Verlorene*, 1951, Arnold Pressburger Prods.

tones and techniques, image and filmic references, it offers itself as a political parable, aiming to create a sense of objective distance between the diegesis and the viewer. The pluralistic tactics that Lorre had become skilled at, in both his Hollywood and his earlier European work, are put into practice in a context beyond an articulation of screen labour.

The proliferation of self-reflexive references within *Der Verlorene* have led to it being described as a reprise of *M* (1931), whereby the significance of Lorre's film is contained within how he develops certain similarities or contrasting juxtapositions with Lang's earlier film. Foregrounding this association suggests that Lorre was primarily concerned with making most explicit the link between Dr Rothe and his character from *M*, Hans Beckert. Lorre's film repeats specific motifs from *M* when representing the murderous capabilities of its central protagonist. In both films, Lorre's characters are marked as murderers through a study of their reflected images. On learning of Inge's betrayal, Rothe attempts to gather his thoughts alone in his laboratory. He wanders over to a mirror and rubs his hands over his face. In doing so, he transfers the blood of a rabbit (from his experiments) from his hand to his cheek. He quickly reacts with fear and shame at the bloody mark on his face, which serves as a visual representation of his subconscious desires. In keeping with the way Lang chose to represent Becket in *M*, Lorre – in his roles as both actor and director – also uses the reflected image to 'unmask' Rothe as a 'monster'.

In addition to the repetition of certain scenes and motifs, *Der Verlorene* also takes from *M* its overall narrative theme of the serial killer. In particular, it uses Lang's film and the reactions of the diegetic world to the killer's crimes as a counterpoint, to highlight the inherent changes that occurred within German society between the 1930s and the 1950s as a consequence of the Nazi regime. Lorre contrasts the concern of the urban society with catching the killer whose crimes have brought the city to a virtual standstill through paranoia and fear, as depicted in *M*, with the indifferent postwar urban society found in *Der Verlorene* which barely registers the crimes committed by a compulsive killer.

Many of the references made to Lorre's other Hollywood films within *Der Verlorene* are often explained by their apparent close relationship with *M* and the notion that Lorre was typecast in Hollywood through his appearance as Beckert. This is especially true of *Mad Love* (1935), *Stranger on the Third Floor* (1940), and *The Beast with Five Fingers* (1946) – the three films with narratives closest to both *M* and *Der Verlorene*. These three films, in which the central role of the 'deranged killer' is played by Lorre, are taken as evidence that Lorre could not escape the influence of *M*, despite these being the only three Hollywood roles where he played a deranged killer (Kapczynski 2003: 163). However, the references made to these films within *Der Verlorene* can be seen as reflections in their own right, away from readings which attempt to establish a direct linear relationship between *M*, the Hollywood 'psycho-killer' roles, his public image, and Lorre's own film.

At its most simplistic level, this relationship between Lorre's history and Rothe's world can be seen by the way that continuities between the two are highlighted through the manner that motifs from Lorre's earlier films, or those that are generally associated with the actor, are repeated here in order to represent Rothe. These brief references take the form of gestures, lines of dialogue (and the performance of these lines), use of props, and framing compositions, which are all highly suggestive of familiar moments from Lorre's past. In some sequences, particular prominence is given to Rothe's hands, which are shown to wander over every available surface almost as if they have a mind of their own: not only is this gesture found in many of Lorre's performances, but it also recalls the actor's roles in both *Mad Love* and *The Beast with Five Fingers* – films that create horror from the idea of murderous hands that act independently from their 'owners'. In all three films, Lorre's characters kill (or attempt to kill) another character by strangulation.

Whilst references to Lorre's earlier films appear to be used only in passing, such as the prominence given to his hands, some play a more important role and are employed to add layers of meaning to the characterization of Rothe, in a similar way to the references made to *M*. One such example is the direct allusion to *Stranger on the Third Floor* within Lorre's film. In trying to deal with his murderous desire, Rothe approaches a prostitute and they return to her apartment. Before entering, she identifies him as a *Totmacher* (death maker) and runs from her door, screaming for help. As she does this, Rothe hides in the shadowy stairwell, with only his brightly lit, white hand on display. This corresponds to a sequence from *Stranger on the Third Floor* when Lorre's character, The Stranger, has just committed murder and is also attempting to escape from an apartment building by running down the main staircase.

The most prominent difference between the two films is that in the earlier film through visual, aural and narrative cues, 'The Stranger' is easily identified as a 'horrific', 'insane' or 'other-worldly' figure, especially in the way he does not speak within the sequence and almost magically manages to evade capture. In *Der Verlorene*, whilst the narrative context and the expressionistic set design are virtually the same, the characterization is markedly different. As the prostitute wakes up the apartment block, Rothe is forced to defend himself against her accusations. Whereas The Stranger was silent, panicked and abnormal, Rothe is lucid, calm and normal: he easily interacts with the residents and charms his way out of the situation by explaining that the woman is drunk. Furthermore, The Stranger's crimes are not contextualized by the urban or historical environment in which he operates. Unlike The Stranger – but much like Hans Beckert – Rothe can hide his 'monstrous' nature behind a façade of petit bourgeois normality. However, as Tim Bergfelder (2007a: 152) observes, despite this momentary similarity between Beckert and Rothe, elsewhere they remain markedly antithetical characters: Beckert – the social symptom is manic, hysterical, unreflective and childish, whilst Rothe – the existential avenger is passive, melancholy, and painfully aware of his actions, environment and age. Therefore, the differences between these three ostensibly similar serial killers (The Stranger, Beckert and Rothe) suggest a difficulty in charting each one as a mere echo of the previous incarnation.

Whilst *Der Verlorene*'s narrative clearly draws upon *M* through its anchoring of social critique through the figure of the serial killer, the overall narrative structure and tone of *Der Verlorene* is quite different. *M* moves from objective police procedural to a subjective and emotionally charged close-up of the killer in order to complicate conventional thinking around crime, justice and social structures. The tonal shifts and organization of narrative events in Lorre's film are similarly used to demonstrate the ambiguity inherent within apparently absolutist political, social and ethical positions, but the constant changes of direction and motivation that follow Rothe make it difficult to see the film as engaging in a moral debate that might enable forward momentum and social action. Instead, it seems to suggest the impossibility of such a discourse in the immediate post-war environment, preferring to emphasize the sense of hopelessness through the blurring between timeframes and individual and political crimes. However, this position of irreconcilability and collective guilt is also undercut by allusions to Lorre that foreground the artifice of the text, and problematize the notion that Rothe 'stands' for Lorre, through the distinct differences between Rothe and earlier screen incarnations of Lorre. The use of Lorre's screen history separates this character from the actor's own identity, and their positioning as 'quotations' suggests a technique more akin to a distancing effect rather than the construction of Rothe as the embodiment of Lorre's public image.

Der Verlorene's plot is dependent upon coincidence and contrivance, as events beyond Rothe's control unfold around him causing distinct shifts within the tone of the film. Towards the end, Rothe's desire for revenge against Hösch is temporarily distracted by his involvement in an assassination plot that pits Hösch against Winkler. This dramatic change in narrative direction is jarring and has been criticized as absurd (Reimer and Reimer 1992: 21 and Gow 1973: 70). That Lorre is being purposefully absurdist can also be suggested, as this ties in neatly with the overall existentialist framework around the character and the ambiguous moral and political outlook throughout the whole film. This is further reinforced by Rothe's description of the conspiracy in general, which explicitly draws attention to the ridiculousness of the situation: 'It was like a detective story. I had to laugh. I laughed myself into a strange world.'

The intertextual references made to Lorre's career within this sequence work to support it as an absurdist diversion. One implicitly reflexive example from this sequence involves the easy disarmament of Rothe by a dismissive Winkler, a moment which jars with the previous determination of the doctor to carry out his murderous revenge. The insouciant tone of the scene – affected through Lorre's deliberately disinterested performance –

is in keeping with Rothe's fatalism, but it, along with the composition of the shot which emphasizes Lorre's short stature in the face of his adversary, is highly reminiscent of the sequence in *The Maltese Falcon* (1941) where Sam Spade is confronted by an armed Joel Cairo but easily divests him of the gun, and their subsequent cautiously casual interaction with each other. As such, the tension of the sequence in *Der Verlorene* is wholly dissipated because of the reference made to the comic absurdity of Huston's film, and to Lorre's own screen history as a somewhat harmless and pathetic figure within the detective film.

Whereas the example cited above references the comic tone of an earlier film in order to undermine the contrived gravity of the political narrative of the final third of Lorre's film, other comic references are invoked for a very different effect. Hösch's questioning description of Rothe as they drink together in the bar, which asks 'You're either insane doctor, or drunk!', not only summarizes characteristics of both Lorre's persona ('insane') and his screen work ('drunk'), but also replays a line that Lorre speaks to Sydney Greenstreet in *The Mask of Dimitrios* (1944). However, it crucially removes the humour of that previous exchange in which Lorre enquires of Greenstreet, 'I can only conclude that you are a thief or a drunk. Are you drunk sir?'. In *The Mask of Dimitrios*, the playful delivery of this line is used by Lorre as a mode of engagement with his perceived audience. In *Der Verlorene*, these references create an objective distance between the character (and the diegetic world within the film) and the audience, because they make reference to Lorre's status as an actor with a cinematic past. Lorre uses his own presence to draw attention to the artifice of the film – where a moment from *The Maltese Falcon* interrupts the tension between Rothe and Winkler; and an abridged quotation from *The Mask of Dimitrios* foregrounds the purposeful objectivity of Lorre's film.

Other self-reflexive elements performed by Lorre, and emphasized by his directorial choices and visual framing, become increasingly complex in the way that they encourage an awareness of both performative labour and the relationship between 'character', 'actor' and 'image' in order to create the political underpinnings around the film. This draws on the strategy frequently used by Lorre in his Hollywood performances, expanding it into a more coherent tool of representation as a result of his position as director. One motif that is continually employed throughout *Der Verlorene* is the use of cigarettes as a prop. The nature of these references is more abstract than the repetition of one specific sequence because the association between Lorre and this particular prop was constructed by much of his on-screen work, and also formed an intrinsic visual aspect of his extra-filmic persona. Indeed, the position that the cigarette occupies for Lorre's career articulates the dichotomy between Lorre's labour and his image, and in part, this is how the prop is used within the film. Cigarettes and the process of smoking constitute one of the more iconic constituent elements of the actor's public image. Whilst the continual presence of this prop throughout Lorre's career and throughout the various transmedial representations of the actor could be seen merely as a signifier of the image of 'Peter Lorre', cigarettes play a much more important role than just that of a visual cue or shorthand for the actor. Instead they become a signifier of filmmaking labour; and this complex relationship between image and labour is articulated within *Der Verlorene*.

Lorre smokes in virtually every film he made, and even admitted that by the end of his career he felt unable to perform without the 'security' of a cigarette in his hands (Youngkin 2005: 339). Even in *M*, where he does not light up on-screen, the fact that Beckert smokes the brand Ariston is a major clue to his identity. Smoking is conspicuous by its absence in *The Face Behind the Mask* (1941), as Janos's (Lorre) admission that he does not smoke firstly sets up a humorous exchange concerning his excitement at arriving in the United States, and secondly adds a layer of irony to the knowledge that his life will be virtually destroyed through fire. Lorre uses cigarettes to aid characterization in many of his brief sequences as a supporting actor; such as in *Casablanca* (1942) where the attempted bravado of his character, Ugarte, is undermined by his nervous habit of continuously lighting new cigarettes from old butts.

Conversely, there are examples of Lorre using cigarettes in a more playful manner in order to draw attention to himself (as a performer) within the cinematic frame. This tendency is confirmed by an anecdote from the set of *Background to Danger* (1943) where Lorre explicitly informed the star, George Raft, that he was waving a cigarette around in order to 'steal the scene' from Raft, saying, 'They're [the audience] like you, they'll all watch me'. Raft is reported to have responded by punching Lorre (Youngkin 2005: 208). Whatever the motivation behind Lorre's use of the cigarette, it is an obvious performative device that either develops the character or makes explicit the position of the actor, rather than merely being a prop that reinforces a particular marketable image.

In *Der Verlorene*, the complex way that Lorre introduces cigarettes takes on a more ritualistic function which foregrounds their position as both a filmmaking tool and mode of visual performance. At the level of characterization and performance, cigarettes signify the internal processes of Rothe's mind that Lorre's performance otherwise obscures. Rothe describes them as a 'life force', and the act of smoking defines his sense of choice and intent within the film. This is most apparent in the sequences where he acts upon the compulsion to kill. Minutes before Rothe strangles Inge, he pointedly refuses to take a light from her, and as he reaches for her neck, he violently stubs out his own cigarette. These gestures depict his decision-making process, whereas Lorre's other performative choices mean that Rothe's face remains blank and unreadable.

Cigarettes are also used to signify the continuities between Rothe's past crimes and compulsions and his new anonymous life in the refugee camp. As already mentioned, one transition between past and present is illustrated by Rothe lighting a cigarette in the past only to extinguish the match in the present. Whilst this sequence has been observed only in terms of Lorre, as a first-time director, taking 'a cineaste's pleasure in toying with the medium' (Gow 1973: 69), it serves a more coherent function than mere flamboyance as it acts as a visual aid which cues the audience towards a particular perception; that Rothe (now called Neumeister) is unable to maintain a clean break from the former murderous identity that he describes in the flashbacks. This moment is indicative of the agenda with which Lorre employs his most visually effective prop. The continual references to smoking may appear merely to suggest continuities of the image associated with the actor, but it is much more accurate to read these moments as more pointed filmmaking practices and performative techniques regularly used by the screen actor, and given extended prominence in order to reveal the wider implications about continuities between the actions of the past and the behaviour of the present.

The visual aesthetics of the film also become an increasingly complex network of references and juxtapositions that make key separations between different elements and representations within the film. At times, the visual style clearly refers back to Lorre's own films, particularly in the expressionistic mirroring of *Stranger on the Third Floor* or *M*, but it can also be seen to reference cinematic aesthetics away from Lorre's specific history. Use of expressionistic motifs run throughout *Der Verlorene* linking it to film noir (beyond Lorre's few appearances within genre) and to the earlier German expressionist period which had influenced Hollywood noir. The opening sequence set around the refugee camp has been described as recalling both *Das Kabinett des Doktor Caligari* (The Cabinet of Doctor Caligari) and *Nosferatu*, as – in silhouette – Rothe moves through a bleak and abstracted landscape dotted with black telegraph poles and a low white sky (Bergfelder 2007a: 153; and Keser 2007).

This same sequence also uses conventions of naturalism influenced by Italian post-war neo-realism as the inhabitants of the camp are presented to Rothe for vaccination using flat, naturalistic light and realistic setting, costume and make-up. The momentary interplay between naturalism (not a style Lorre was hitherto associated with) and abstract expressionism bookends the film, returning as Rothe makes his way through the desolate landscape down to the train tracks. Elsewhere, the juxtaposition is between the noir-infused flashbacks to the war, the urban setting of Hamburg and Rothe's crimes – which dominate the film – and the scenes between Rothe and Hösch in the bar. The increasingly drunken interaction between these two is photographed using techniques associated with standard classical realism. Much like their narrative function, the visual style of the bar scenes positions them as 'bridges' between different extremes of social situation and political ambiguity: the post-war hardship of the internment camp, and the strange unfathomable nightmare of the war itself. The constant shifting between aesthetic styles draws attention to the artifice of narrative and its allegorical intent, also aiming towards a disorientating and disrupting effect on the viewer.

Like Hollywood film noir, the expressionism at the centre of scenes in Hamburg functions as representations of psychological anxiety. It is also within these sequences that the self-reflexive references to Lorre dominate. Defining *Der Verlorene* as an 'accented film', these references conflate Lorre's own psychological guilt with that of Rothe's; however, away from this subjective definition, Lorre's use of them (in conjunction with other formal techniques) also works more objectively, to actively reduce psychological or empathetic engagement with Rothe. Although through his admission of guilt and his eventual role as an 'avenger', Rothe (and his individual crimes) occupies a moral superiority over the military figures (and state-sanctioned crimes) in the film, ambiguity and pessimism remain around the protagonist, not least in the overt suggestion that Rothe's psychotic impulses continue to exist under the surface and after the war (Bergfelder 2007a: 152).

Whereas films such as *M* or *Stranger on the Third Floor* rely upon a narrative trajectory that aims to develop the humanity of their killers through the depiction of their suffering before 'punishing' them (and, in the case of *M*, encourages the audience to rethink their attitudes) *Der Verlorene* offers deliberately few opportunities to similarly engage with Rothe in this way, or through Lorre's performance, in spite of the character's self-awareness. Its narrative progression hints that Rothe is beyond salvation, just as the cigarette motif depicts that he still harbours the same murderous desires but has learnt to temporarily repress them. The use of coincidental event to shape the plot positions Rothe as passive, ironic observer, and the meandering plotlines convey a lack of purpose and underlying existential outlook. But the constant allusions to Lorre's Hollywood films suggest that even these quasi-philosophical positions are not stable throughout the film. Through his voiceover, Rothe may present himself as the bemused commentator – caught up with, but coolly distanced from, the machinations of the war – but he remains an active agent in both time periods, determining the course of his own actions, killing Inge, the woman on the train and Hösch. Unlike Lorre's other role as passive observer, Leyden in *The Mask of Dimitrios*, Rothe is unreliable and unknowable, continually denying information to the viewer about his personal actions.

Rothe faces an inescapable destiny that has been argued to reflect Lorre's position as an émigré – the impossibility of returning 'home'. The existentialist tone and construction of Rothe as a fatalistic anti-hero also mirrors Lorre's engaging performance as Johnny in *Three Strangers*, but the differences between his performances are highly revealing. Lorre seamlessly conveys Johnny's duality (his drunken bravado and underlying sorrow), but the shifts within Rothe remain jarring, episodic and inscrutable. During decisive sequences, Rothe is often filmed from behind; in doing so, Lorre obscures his face and prevents the viewer from a close reading of the character's emotional state. This is most apparent in the scene where Rothe entertains his new young female lodger, Ursula (Eva Ingeborg Scholz) in his room. Rothe has already strangled his fiancée, so his murderous intentions towards women have already been established. And yet, because the camera is positioned to obscure Rothe's face – especially during moments when Inge's death is mentioned – his motivations towards Ursula in this scene remain unknown. Even in the shots which show his face, Lorre utilizes a particularly blank or mask-like expression throughout, along with deliberately slowed-down, almost robotic movements, to create a purposefully ambiguous and (implicit in Lorre's filming of him) potentially deceptive figure. Despite the shared fatalism of Johnny in *Three Strangers* and Rothe in *Der Verlorene*, there are marked differences. Johnny occupies an acknowledged space of powerlessness, is presented with a playful energy, and finds redemption. By contrast, Rothe – despite his resigned attitude – remains in an active position of power (he acts and this has consequences), is presented with a lumbering somnambulism, and is complicit in the crimes he avenges. This is no longer a complicity between Lorre and Rothe in terms of their collective 'guilt', but a positioning of Rothe (separate from the actor) that links his individual crimes to the collective crimes committed during the Nazi regime.

Der Verlorene actively underplays the possibility of emotional connection between 'audience' and 'character' via performance and *mise-en-scène*, but there are a number of shots within the film which remain problematic. Rothe's face is mainly obscured during sequences which prioritize the development of the story, such as scenes which rely upon the tension created as Rothe interacts with a potential victim. In contrast to this, there are shots which depict Rothe in deep contemplation and actively isolate him within the frame in a series of medium close-ups, usually accompanied by his voiceover which continues over the image. Rather than promoting a moment of engagement with Rothe, the focus of these shots is 'Peter Lorre' himself. Lorre's slow and heavy movements afford the actor a sense of stillness within the frame, often freezing his image on-screen for a number of seconds, forcing the viewer to gaze directly at Lorre. These moments become a series of 'star shots' which arrest the narrative, and offer Lorre as a visual spectacle. In doing so, the shots emphasize the role of contemplative viewing as a mode of representation which prioritizes the position of the actor, Peter Lorre, over the character, Rothe.

In terms of conventional star discourse, these moments might appear to encourage identification or empathy because of the familiarity of a star's image. However, Lorre's deployment of his star status challenges this in two ways. Firstly, there are the obvious visual differences between Lorre in *Der Verlorene* and in the cinematic and photographic images from his heyday of the 1930s and 1940s. This frozen visual presence of the now seemingly frail actor offers this further mode of self-reflexive representation, as Lorre's position as a man with a cinematic past is implicitly highlighted via the contrast between his body in 1951 and the younger, more energetic film star that was captured on-screen during the previous two decades. 'Peter Lorre' here is rendered strange and unfamiliar through his obviously aging body and expression of permanent exhaustion. Secondly, these shots tend to occur at the most unsettling moments (as Rothe kills, or when he is contemplating the existence of his impulses). The sharp continuity between the leading character and the 'horrific' extra-filmic image of Lorre is unsettling because of the potency of that image, and its relative infrequency in close-up on the screen.

It should be noted that these types of shots become less prevalent as the film progresses (only returning in the final moments of the film). The visual treatment of Lorre in the assassination-plot sequences becomes more 'inclusive', mirroring the supporting function of Rothe (and Lorre) in these scenes. Lorre is photographed using a style that is more in keeping with how supporting actors were traditionally shot: he is placed on the edge of brightly lit group compositions which do not impede the narrative progression, rather than being framed alone in the shadows. With the inclusion of these two contrasting methods of framing, Lorre effectively summarizes on-screen within *Der Verlorene* the two positions held by the actor during his career: the leading actor and the supporting actor.

The presence of Lorre's 'autobiography' within *Der Verlorene* is consistently split into different elements: references to his screen labour, his performative styles, his public image, and the underlying reality of the actor – as a figure whose return to Germany allowed him to bear witness to the changes that the country had undergone since the early 1930s. As such, Lorre does not occupy an objective position in relation to what he presents on-screen – it remains a highly personal undertaking, leading to readings which define both Lorre and Rothe as 'lost ones' who conduct a dialogue between Hollywood, Europe and the émigré figure. However, the aesthetics and modes of representation used by Lorre – particularly the references to his own history – turn 'autobiography' into a more objective filmmaking tool, whereby political allegory is created via a series of dislocations, juxtapositions and quotations that aim to disrupt and disorientate the viewer, rather than drawing them into the serial killer narrative, in order to examine the complexities of recent German history.

Lorre's disruptive self-reflexive strategies are consistent with many of his Hollywood performances that distinguish between image, performative labour and the actor's own 'reality', but here extend them across the entire film text, rather than containing them within brief supporting sequences. Lorre's appropriation of his own visual and cinematic history as a discursive framework runs counter to how Nazi propaganda used the actor and sought to present him to the German public. In 1940, the placement of footage from *M* in *Der ewige Jude* blurred the boundaries between the different facets of Lorre's life in order to create political and social discourse; here Lorre keeps these facets decidedly separate, and develops the frame of reference beyond Germany's cinematic past by including earlier work from Hollywood cinema in order to document post-war attitudes and positions in the aftermath of the Nazi regime.

Notes

1. Peter Lorre's Warner Bros.' multiple-picture contract 1943–46; Warner Bros. Archive, USC, Los Angeles, USA.
2. There were some exceptions, such as his performance as the sympathetic investigating officer, Slimane, in *Casbah* (John Berry, Universal, 1948). This film was the second remake of *Pépé Le Moko* (Julien Duvivier, Paris Film, 1937, France), following *Algiers* (John Cromwell, United Artists, 1938, USA).
3. In addition to Brecht's critique of Lorre's time in Hollywood in the poem, 'Der Sumpf' (The Swamp), (discussed in Chapter 1), and the invitations sent by the playwright to Lorre about joining the newly formed Berlin Ensemble, Brecht also wrote an emotive poem to Lorre on his return to Berlin (circa 1948), entitled 'To the actor, P.L, in exile':

   Listen, we are calling you back. Driven out
   You must now return. The country
   Out of which you were driven flowed once
   With milk and honey. You are being called back
   To a country which has been destroyed.
   And we have nothing more
   To offer you than the fact that you are needed.
   Poor or rich
   Sick or healthy
   Forget everything
   And come.
   (John Willet and Ralph Manheim, 1979a: 418)
4. The differences between Hollywood and Germany, as experienced by an actor, can be perceived in comments made by Lorre during an interview in 1951 with the *New York Times* after *Der Verlorene* had been completed. The following quotation explicitly outlines the more favourable working practices experienced by Lorre, but also implicitly constructs the theatrical world of Brecht's Berlin as a more artistic and fulfilling environment in which to work:

   I am trying to realize an old dream. I have always wanted to achieve real teamwork in the movies – team, *équipe*, *Mannshaft* – you know. Only if you have a team, can you realize your plans and achieve that harmonious cooperation which has a creative counterpart in the 'ensemble' of the European Theatre. I want to dream – dream of ideas and their realization, but as long as one has to work on a career, one cannot dream. (Manfred George, 23 September 1951: 113)
5. See for example, Tim Bergfelder 2007a; Gordon Gow 1973: 70; Robert Keser 2007.

Chapter 6

THE FINAL SCREEN ROLES (1954–1964)

In traditional overviews of Peter Lorre's career, the years between 1954 and 1964 (the year of Lorre's death) are viewed with a certain sense of embarrassment. It is felt that the once great star of German cinema or the famous supporting actor of Hollywood's Golden Age suffered a slow drift into the lowest levels of Hollywood mediocrity. This downward trajectory has been seen as the result of two events. The first was Lorre's permanent return to Hollywood from Germany following *Der Verlorene*, a move which implied that his career as a legitimate 'artist' stalled, as it had appeared to do in the 1930s: he did not take up the invitation from Bertolt Brecht (who returned to Germany in 1948) to join the playwright's theatre ensemble in Berlin, and Lorre's status as a potential director was ignored by Hollywood on his return in 1952.

Secondly, Lorre made a series of disastrous business decisions after he left Warner Bros. which severely compromised the course of his career post-1946. After his contract ended, he had been approached by the entrepreneur Sam Stiefel who suggested that Lorre embrace his new-found freelance status and set up his own production company, Lorre Inc., in order to maintain careful control over the terms of his own employment and his image. (Stiefel had brokered a similar deal with Mickey Rooney, and his involvement with both actors led to the production of *Quicksand* in 1949.) However, the formation of Lorre Inc. provided neither new opportunities nor financial security for the actor. Stiefel was put in charge of running the business, but continually mismanaged the company's funds. By 1949, Lorre was forced to declare bankruptcy and his financial situation never fully recovered from this precarious position (Youngkin 2005). He remained a freelance actor who was dependent on individual pay cheques for most of the following two decades, making it virtually impossible to make any long-term career plans and severely reducing the amount of control he had over the projects he worked upon.

Many of the screen roles played by Lorre during his last years are defined as lazy parodies of his own persona (rather than fully developed characters in their own right), seemingly in line with Lorre's own apparent admission that by this stage in his career he considered himself an actor who merely 'made faces' rather than one whose performances were executed with much forethought. This increased use of parody is seen to demonstrate the failure of Hollywood to consider Lorre as a valuable creative artist – preferring the cheaper investment of recycling an already established marketable identity and performative style. In many retrospectives of Lorre's career it is common to describe his later roles as especially negative engagements that were 'largely given over to self parody' (Dyer 1964: 125) in which he 'played his own caricature' (Kapczynski 2003: 170), or that he was used as 'a gimmick in rotten pictures' (Thomson 2005: 35). Repeatedly insisted upon is the definite association between Lorre's extra-filmic persona and the types of roles he was playing during this decade.

Throughout his Hollywood career, Lorre was continually positioned within critical analyses of his work as 'outsider', or as a signifier of 'otherness'. This position is claimed to be at its height during the 1950s and 1960s, as critics have sought to align the apparent 'otherness' of his roles with the seemingly helpless position that the financially stricken actor now held within the industry, and the emotionally charged phrase, 'insider as outsider', is taken to describe accurately Lorre's later career. Whereas in other periods there is evidence that Lorre was able to subtly undermine the 'outsider' position, the dominant perception remains that, during the 1950s and 1960s, the tragedy of Lorre's life was that he no longer seemed willing to fight against the Hollywood system which appeared to have imposed massive limitations upon him.

Thirdly, there is the association of Lorre with 'horror'. Whilst Lorre had a prevalent (if ambiguous) association with horror throughout his career, it was during these later years that analyses of Lorre make explicit his identification with the horror genre. This is partly due to the increased 'outsider'/'other' status that he increasingly appeared to maintain, and partly through the importance of horror to Lorre's by now firmly established extra-filmic persona.

Changes to how Hollywood operated, and the effects this had upon performative decisions in general, meant that Lorre's screen life developed in two different ways during the final ten years of his career. The first was that Lorre was reinvented as a 'family' entertainer in 'blockbuster' films, usually within the action/adventure genre. The second was that Lorre became associated with a new form of independently produced horror film in which he used a self-reflexive performance style for an increasingly comic effect. Linked to his screen appearances of the 1950s and 1960s is a largely ignored aspect of Lorre's life which needs further exploration: the 'Americanization' of Peter Lorre. These films and genres offer an alternative screen representation of Peter Lorre that was constructed around his status as an 'insider' (rather than an 'outsider') through a position which aligns the actor with the newly dominant youth consumer cultures who became the target audiences for these films.

'Family-friendly Lorre': Action/Adventure Films for a 'Universal' Audience

From 1954 onwards, Lorre's screen roles and mode of acting altered dramatically away from the template that had been developed during his tenure at Warner Bros. As before, Lorre played a range of character types throughout these years, but his performance style was no longer in line with the mannered and consistent performative techniques at Warner Bros. Lorre's shift in acting style was due in great part to the changing filmmaking environment of the 1950s, as the industry began to move away from the stability of the studio system and to operate less as a production line – a move which had a profound effect on the on- and off-screen position of actors within the industry (including both leading and supporting actors).

Between 1954 and 1964, Peter Lorre made eighteen films; a small number compared with the twenty-eight films he made between 1940 and 1946. The majority of these later films were orientated towards special effects or lavish spectacle, including *20,000 Leagues under the Sea* (1954), *Congo Crossing* (1956), *Around the World in 80 Days* (1956), *Silk Stockings* (1957), *The Story of Mankind* (1957), *The Sad Sack* (1957), *The Big Circus* (1959), *Scent of Mystery* (1960), *Voyage to the Bottom of the Sea* (1961) and *Five Weeks in a Balloon* (1962).[1]

Whilst some of these 'action' films used Lorre in a way that parodied his extra-filmic persona in order to generate screen menace (such as *The Sad Sack*), this type of employment of the actor was rare. In fact, many of Lorre's roles after 1954 are remarkably similar in tone to his first major studio role of the decade, Disney's *20,000 Leagues under the Sea*. Here, Lorre played Conseil, the bumbling, good-natured (if a little irascible) sidekick to Ned Land (Kirk Douglas). The template quickly came to characterize Lorre's roles of the 1950s and early 1960s, and signified a major change in how Lorre was perceived by the industry itself and presented to audiences. Instead of being consigned to the status of an exotic or mysterious menace, he was continually employed as a harmless character that was often the source of a film's comedy. Thus Lorre's roles of the 1950s and 1960s can be seen to actively continue the distance created between the work of the actor and his extra-filmic persona, rather than to directly parody that image through various repeated on-screen representations of Lorre.

Recognizing the significance of Lorre's employment in the action/adventure genre also reveals that Lorre did not necessarily occupy an isolated position as an actor. Instead of being interpreted as one unlucky individual's decline, the way that these films use Lorre (and the way that Lorre performs within them) can also be seen as illustrative of an industry undergoing considerable structural change at many levels.

As has been extensively examined by film historians, the 1950s was a time of immense change within Hollywood. The American film industry had entered a period of conservatism and uncertainty as a result of exter-

nal factors, primarily as a result of the 1948 Paramount Decree which sep-
arated the studios from their means of exhibition. This had a significant
impact on how the studios produced films, as the production line process
of the 1930s and 1940s was no longer financially appropriate and was replaced by a 'picture-by-picture' scheme. Fewer films were being made; they
were individually financed with considerably larger budgets than before,
and because of this, they had to recoup their costs on an individual basis.
The dominant genres also changed to those best suited to big budgets and
lavish treatment such as epics and musicals, and 'B' movie production was
also phased out as cinemas concentrated on the major releases. Hollywood
increasingly favoured the 'pre-sold' film which had a ready-made audience and guaranteed box office returns and profits. The industry also invested in new technology as a means of product differentiation. In order to
compete with new media such as television, cinema emphasized its size,
scale and innovation as a public space attraction by introducing widescreen
technologies, and increasing the use of colour and various other techniques
which became increasingly reliant on 'gimmicks' such as 3-D (or the more
extreme 'Smell-O-Vision' used in the 1960 film *Scent of Mystery* which also
featured Peter Lorre).

In the early part of the decade, the industry also continued to see its audience in terms of a homogenized mass that required 'universal' pictures
suitable for all ages. Audiences were beginning to splinter into certain de-
mographic groups (such as teenagers), and whilst wider filmmaking trends
towards the end of the decade would eventually recognize this, throughout the 1950s the whole family remained a primary target audience (Caspar
2007: 83–89). In addition to the late-1950s fragmentation of the market, the
increasing challenges to censorship made by certain films, particularly
social dramas that contained more outwardly controversial themes, meant
that a two-tier system slowly began to arise in Hollywood which categorized films as either having some 'adult' content, or being safer and family-
oriented. Although an important part of 1950s Hollywood production, the
more mature 'adult' films tended to be in the minority, and so the
family/universal category of filmmaking dominated the industry and the
box office. Therefore, many of the action/adventure films that Lorre was
cast in were major releases, and instead of existing on the sidelines as he
had done during the late 1930s and late 1940s, Lorre continued to work
very much in the mainstream and enjoyed the popularity associated with
mainstream success, as he had done during the war years. This genre's reliance on the new large-scale technologies and increased use of colour
meant that the post-war years were a boom-time for the adventure film
and it entered its 'third flourish' (ibid.: 161).

In general, Hollywood was slow to realize that their audience had been
in the process of changing dramatically since the end of the Second World
War. As the 1950s progressed, it was recognized that 'families' were no
longer the main consumers at the cinema. Suburbanization of American

cities resulted in the trend of falling cinema audiences as income was spent on other leisure activities in different locations, such as the rise of television sets in the home. As a result of the migration from the inner cities and the 1948 Paramount Decree, which forced the major studios to divest themselves of the theatre chains that they owned, many of the small neighbourhood theatres closed (later to be replaced by the 'Drive-In' on the outskirts of built-up areas). The remaining cinema audience was also becoming younger as the teenage group began to dominate the consumption of American popular culture. These later developments of the Drive-In and the teenage audience were important with regards to Lorre's work for the independent production company AIP, as will be seen later in the chapter.

The changing industry also had an important impact on the way that actors were used; both in a film itself and in terms of the conditions of their employment. The most significant development was the increasing 'freelance' status of performers who were no longer contracted to a specific studio (either through the choice of the actor or of the studio). The operating system of having a ready-made pool of stars and supporting players who were contracted to a studio, which in turn closely controlled actors' careers via the allocation of roles and the careful management of publicity (which characterized Lorre's own employment during the 1930s and 1940s), was beginning to break down. There was a growth in small independently run and actor-owned production companies set up to organize a performer's individual career. Because of the revenue needed to start such a company, this solution was mainly adopted by actors who were already established and who had achieved a certain level of success. Despite this, many companies – such as Lorre Inc. – failed to prove themselves as adequate business solutions. In addition to being a personal catastrophe, Lorre's financial position can also be seen as typical of the industry as a whole. Actors became more independent from studio control, but also occupied a precarious position, as the 'incorporated actor ... was forced to make day-to-day decisions for immediate profit' and tended to 'accept roles which [gave] him immediate big opportunities rather than solid development' (Dyer MacCann 1962: 57).

For a few actors, the structural shifts in Hollywood meant freedom and control, but for the majority it meant being cut loose from a paternalistic system and left to fend for themselves. It would be simple to suggest that the group who flourished were stars and the group who floundered were supporting actors. This split can certainly be demonstrated at a textual level whereby the two types of performers were given very different filmic treatment – as I will explore in relation to Lorre.

Barry King (1986) argues that the production of public personae and star images became increasingly complicated during the period after 1948 and Divorcement due to the difference in filmmaking practice. Because films were now being made on an individual basis, the risk of failure was greater and was more costly to all involved, including stars. Therefore to produce a distance between the star image and the character portrayed on-screen became necessary, in order to 'protect' the star: in effect, the star image was no longer primarily produced by the on-screen 'product' (character). This process was also linked to the lessening of studio control over an actor and his/her image. This new era of stardom saw stars become 'proprietors of their own image' rather than being subservient to the image that the studios wanted to promote. The one unified image of a particular star was reshaped to take on a more reflexive nature, with performers able to comment on their own image through their own work or through other media (such as television and the press) which further distanced them from the 'old' studio system of control.

This new, more complex public persona could be applied in at least two different ways, both of which sought to create distance between the star image and the character.[2] Firstly, it was used to challenge an actor's star status when a performer was seen to effectively relinquish their stardom in order to 'submerge' themselves in character. Secondly, this distance sought to maintain a unity between the actor and the star image, at the expense of the character, in order to enhance the impact of their image, regardless of what was being portrayed on-screen.

The former category appears to be the more positive one, as is evidenced by the reputation of those stars who followed the practice of containing 'character acting' within a 'star performance' (King uses Burt Lancaster as an example; another obvious case study would be James Stewart). Significantly, the same terminology could be utilized to describe a number of Lorre's leading roles of the 1930s and 1940s. However, the different timescales are an important factor: Lorre's character performances belonged to an era which privileged conventional star performances over the character-actor-as-star. It should also be noted that critical reputation might also be linked to issues of genre: Lancaster and Stewart were associated with the new mature-themed and often independently produced social dramas and thrillers, whereas Lorre was associated with 'frothy' family entertainment.

Despite the apparent freedom of freelance status, the further Lorre moved away from studio control, the more clearly defined his particular 'star image' seemed to be; hence the repeated analysis of his work during this period as representations which fed the perceived image of 'Peter Lorre' through parody. Maintaining the star image/extra-filmic persona of Peter Lorre was a means of ensuring that the actor maintained his economic value within the media industries, and, as King argues, an actor's persona need not necessarily be sustained through screen labour or screen product: it could be completely extra-filmic. In terms of maintaining his profitability as a performer, Lorre had a responsibility to sustain his extra-filmic persona, even at the expense of his screen labour: if his roles did not match this persona, the association would have to be maintained elsewhere – through alternative transmedial representations and by the actor's own analyses of his career.

The ease with which Lorre readily conformed to his persona (albeit, for the most part, away from the cinema screen) during these years – when contrasted with the alternative and more challenging use of star personae by other actors in the 1950s, Lorre's own earlier self-reflexive performances and his complex position within the industry hierarchy of actors, as well as the relative value of the types of films that were being produced ('adult' versus 'family') – reveals why this period is so often characterized as a moment of failure and resignation on the part of Lorre. It is perhaps no coincidence that Lorre's only roles which were widely praised by critics during these years were the Poe adaptations directed by Roger Corman for AIP. This is perhaps because in his AIP films, Lorre returned to a partly self-reflexive mode of performance: a method he had used elsewhere throughout his career, but had abandoned to some degree during the 1950s. However, only considering Lorre's roles of the 1950s and 1960s to be evidence of the failure of an individual performer to capitalize on early success is a problematic stance to perpetuate, as it ignores the wider industrial positions of actors in the 1950s, the types of characters that Lorre was playing during this period, how he chose to play them, and the relationship that these roles had towards his extra-filmic persona.

In reality, Lorre's position within the industry of the 1950s and early 1960s can be seen in many ways as almost identical to the position he occupied during the years of the Second World War. The roles offered to him tended to be first support to the lead performer (usually a sidekick of some description), and the films often used his character as a plot function that aided or temporarily impeded the main narrative. The most significant difference between the films of the 1940s and the films of the 1950s and early 1960s was the formal screen treatment afforded to Lorre, in line with his status as a supporting actor. In order to illustrate the nature of Lorre's appearances in these action/adventure films, I want to consider two Irwin Allen productions in further detail: *The Big Circus* (1959) and *Voyage to the Bottom of the Sea* (1960). Both films are spectacular adventures whose narratives are constructed around set pieces, stunts and special effects. The first is a lavish drama set inside a travelling 'big top' circus as it attempts to outdo the competition by staging increasingly dangerous stunts (amid fears of sabotage), where Lorre plays Skeeter, an amiable old clown prone to bouts of drinking. The second is a science-fiction film about a scientific genius's attempts to save the world from climatic disaster using his futuristic atomic submarine (again, amid fears of sabotage), where Lorre plays the second-in-command, Commodore Emery, a mathematically gifted seaman.

The most obvious difference between these 'action' films and Lorre's Warner Bros. films is the absence of sequences where Lorre's performance is foregrounded as a spectacle, included for the benefit of the audience. There are virtually no stand-alone scenes of Lorre spouting quotable dialogue or acting in a manner that draws attention to his position as an actor who is performing for an audience. Compared to his appearances in *The*

Maltese Falcon (1941) or *Passage to Marseille* (1944), Lorre is a peripheral supporting presence in *The Big Circus* and in *Voyage to the Bottom of the Sea*. When there are moments that do foreground the actor, these scenes occur early on and fail to be fully integrated into the characterization: for example, the forced eccentricity of Lorre's bizarre first appearance as Commodore Emery which depicts him 'walking a shark' in a tank inside the submarine. In the action/adventure films of the 1950s and early 1960s, the presence of the character (Skeeter or Emery) is more important than the presence of the actor (Peter Lorre), and there is the absence of a purposefully self-reflexive relationship between the two elements of character and performer. This is in direct opposition to many of Lorre's earlier supporting roles, where Lorre's performance of characters like Joel Cairo or Marius were as much a comment upon the actor's own identity and status as they were an exercise in characterization in their own right.

This formal treatment of Lorre – which served to make him an 'invisible' supporting presence – was not limited to him alone. Unlike his Warner Bros. films, which tended to place Lorre in an isolated position between the lead actor and the supporting cast (as in *Passage to Marseille*), the position held by Lorre in Allen's action/adventure films mirrored the treatment of the supporting cast as a whole. Generally speaking, because of the spectacular nature of these films, supporting actors (and even some lead performers) were given very limited opportunities on-screen other than to react to the unfolding dramatic events. The narratives of *The Big Circus* and *Voyage to the Bottom of the Sea* are fast-paced and action-packed, containing many characters, complicated plots, and isolated moments of spectacle which temporarily suspend the forward momentum of the narrative. Therefore, the screen time and cinematic space left for actors to perform in is severely reduced, and much of the characterization of the supporting roles can only occur through the necessary exposition of the story. For example, in *The Big Circus*, the set piece of an acrobat walking across Niagara Falls and a stunt on a trapeze involving a criminally insane aerialist and the young female love interest are both vital to the overall narrative. They take precedence over any scenes involving Skeeter, because his actions have little effect on the overall plot; he is relegated to the sidelines even during the scenes of the clowns' circus act.[3]

In addition to spectacular moments in these action/adventure films, they also had substantially larger casts. As outlined by Thomas Doherty (2002: 177), films of the late 1950s and early 1960s utilized large casts as a means of maintaining their 'universal' audiences, whilst trying to include the somewhat separate teenage audience that the industry had finally begun to recognize. The strategy of 'casting to everyone's taste' gave films a so-called 'youth insurance' which reflected the changing audience tastes, but severely reduced the on-screen time available for the cast. In *The Big Circus* this can be seen by the inclusion of four leading roles which are split into one 'older' romantic couple (Victor Mature and Rhonda Fleming) and one 'younger' romantic couple (Red Buttons and Kathryn Grant); whilst in *Voyage*, this strategy translates into significant narratives constructed around the older authorities (Walter Pidgeon and Joan Fontaine), the intermediate couple (Barbara Eden and Robert Sterling) and the young men of the crew (Frankie Avalon and Mark Slade). Acting opportunities were thus limited (especially since the stars were prioritized over the supporting cast) and the performances were wholly subordinate to the visual spectacles on display.

With specific regard to Lorre, screen time was so limited, given that he was not perceived by the filmmakers as being instrumental to the 'youth' audience, that there was no room for him to utilize the condensed performative style that he had first developed as a supporting actor in the late 1930s. In *The Big Circus* and *Voyage*, Lorre shifts away from using the performative mannerisms, vocal techniques and placement or prop decisions that had informed many of his earlier supporting roles. He does not enunciate clearly, he rarely moves about within the shot (and is often seated), and he rarely uses props as a means of making his presence more felt. They do not appear to be multi-layered character presentations, they have no self-reflexive qualities, and they do not offer themselves up as spectacular or contemplative moments which emphasize the actor himself.

However, this critical dismissal ignores certain acting choices that were made by Lorre and the filmmakers he worked with. In many ways, just as Lorre's performance as Joel Cairo was a reflection of his supporting status as a screen actor, his performances in these films serve a similar, though much less explicit, function which suggests an awareness of Lorre's position as an actor/worker in a changing industrial context. They reflect an adaptability of performance style and demonstrate that both the actor and the filmmakers who employed him were willing to move beyond the established public image of Lorre.

In the brief sequences in *The Big Circus* and *Voyage* which prioritize Lorre, the actor plays a certain type of character which, rather than parodying Lorre's extra-filmic persona, is more accurately defined as working against that image. Firstly, at a basic level of characterization, Lorre's roles are avuncular characters that are genuine in their affections, unthreatening, playful and friendly. This is not necessarily an accidental representation or one merely dictated by the script, as revealed in a comment by scriptwriter Charles Bennett (1978: 335) about Lorre's performance in Allen's *Five Weeks in a Balloon* (which Bennett had written), where the actor appeared to turn the unsavoury role of a slave trader into a much more benign sidekick: 'From an actor's viewpoint, the dealer wasn't exactly an endearing character. Yet in spite of his viciousness, Peter immediately established himself as " Mr Adorable" and remained so until the movie's fade-out. Looking back, I'm not sure that the screenplay intended it that way.'

There was a definite attempt by Lorre to incorporate a more broadly comedic and approachable element in his screen performances. In these films, Lorre's comedic acting is very much distanced from notions of horror or menace, whereas that ironic juxtaposition was an intrinsic part of his earlier supporting roles. This change in style is linked to the perceived audiences for these films – although nominally described as 'universal', this more specifically meant that they were designed to appeal to children. Therefore a more straightforward application of comedy or characterization was more appropriate than the shifting duality of many of Lorre's previous performances. Through these 'family' films, Lorre was virtually reinvented as a performer who had the potential to appeal directly to younger audiences.

In addition to the different way Lorre performed on-screen, his formal cinematic treatment by the filmmakers he worked with mirrored this less ambiguous approach. In both *The Big Circus* and *Voyage*, there is never any question, in the script or in the *mise-en-scène*, that Lorre's characters have any involvement in the sabotage plots that create much of the tension within the narrative. Neither Skeeter nor Emery are used as diversionary tactics to misdirect the audience until the 'real' saboteur can be revealed. Indeed, the *mise-en-scène* of *The Big Circus* is organized to first implicate the ringmaster (Vincent Price) through formal techniques such as close-ups which linger upon Price during discussions about the saboteur's actions. In this film, Price occupies the position of the necessary plot 'distraction' – a cinematic technique that had so often characterized Lorre's 1940s wartime roles – as it is finally revealed in the final reel that the ringmaster is innocent and the aerialist is guilty. Not to suggest that Peter Lorre's characters were a possible threat would have been unthinkable in many of his earlier roles, especially during his employment at Warner Bros. where (with the exception of *The Mask of Dimitrios*) his characters were – at least initially – constructed through their potential untrustworthiness. Instead, the loyalties of Skeeter and Commodore Emery are shown to be steadfast, even in spite of audiences' potential awareness of both Lorre's cinematic history and the behavioural elements which contribute to his extra-filmic persona.

Therefore, rather than being reliant upon parodying Lorre's performances or his public image, these action/adventure films show a very obvious willingness to operate outside the boundaries of both Lorre's infamous extra-filmic persona and the limits of his previous screen roles. The absence of the signifying conventions of a 'typical' Peter Lorre performance in these films cannot be seen merely as an example of lazy filmmaking. At the very least, this absence is indicative of the reduction of the screen significance of the supporting actor in general within the industry. In addition to this, it also demonstrates the continuing agency and flexibility of a performer such as Lorre by revealing the choices to use the constraints of genre, audience and new post-Divorcement filmmaking practices as a means of moving beyond the constraints of his former roles and his extra-filmic persona.

Horror, Comedy and the 'Americanization' of Peter Lorre

The second genre with which Lorre is associated during his later decades is the horror film. Between 1962 and 1964, Lorre appeared in three hugely successful horror films for the independent company American International Pictures (AIP): *Tales of Terror* (1962), *The Raven* (1963) and *The Comedy of Terrors* (1964). These iconic films ensured the actor would continue be associated with the genre for years to come. The first two were loosely based on works by Edgar Allan Poe and were produced and directed by Roger Corman as part of his 'Poe cycle' of films, whilst the third one was an original tale directed by Jacques Tourneur made to capitalize on the success of the earlier films. In these, Lorre co-starred once more with Vincent Price; and the use of Lorre, Price and other actors such as Boris Karloff and Basil Rathbone who were closely associated with the horror genre made a clear reference to the 'golden age' of classical horror within these films.

In their casting of Lorre, Corman and AIP were building the notorious association between the actor and 'horror' iconography. Given the central importance of 'horror' to Lorre's American career and to the formation of Lorre's extra-filmic persona, it is necessary to reflect upon his position within the cinematic genre and to discuss how the association impacted upon the manner in which public perceptions around the actor were encouraged. Horror films did not constitute a significant part of the actor's Hollywood screen work. Only eight of his films can accurately be described as belonging to the this genre: *Mad Love* (1935), *You'll Find Out* (1940), *Arsenic and Old Lace* (filmed 1941 but released 1944), *The Boogie Man Will Get You* (1942), *The Beast with Five Fingers* (1946), and the three AIP productions already listed. Indeed, despite their remit of covering horror film icons in their 'Midnight Marquee Actors Series', Gary J. and Susan Svehla (1999: 9) concede in the introduction that Lorre can only be seen as a 'quasi-horror man'.

Unlike *Mad Love* and *The Beast with Five Fingers*, the other six films can all be described as 'comic horror' films and, as such, seek to amuse the viewer as much as scare them. Despite this, Lorre was never defined as a 'comic' performer in the same way as he came to be defined as a 'horror' actor. Prior to his roles in the AIP 'gothic' films of the 1960s, Lorre's work within the genre can be categorized in three ways: the pseudo-Universal horror of MGM's *Mad Love* in 1935; the slapstick horror films of the 1940s: *You'll Find Out* (1940), *The Boogie Man Will Get You* (1942) and *Arsenic and Old Lace* (1944); and the 'straight' horror of *The Beast with Five Fingers* in 1946.

After *Mad Love*, which has been discussed previously, Lorre had a wide and varied career working for a number of different studios and did not appear in another horror film until *You'll Find Out* in 1940.[4] This vehicle for the popular radio personality/band leader, Kay Kyser, teamed Lorre with two legitimate horror stars, Boris Karloff and Bela Lugosi. The plot concerned a conspiracy between the characters played by Lorre, Karloff and

Lugosi to murder an heiress and steal her inheritance, which is foiled by the bumbling investigations of Kyser and his band. Despite Lorre's absence from the genre for five years and sixteen films, much of the promotional discourse connected with the film emphasized the actor's apparent position as an established horror icon. In particular, posters described the combination of Karloff, Lugosi and Lorre as 'those 3 bad-humour men' or 'the three horror men'.

Audiences were thus encouraged by the film's publicity to see Lorre's character (Prof. Karl Fenninger) as having affinities with both horror films in general and with previous roles played by Lorre. In retrospect, the role of Fenninger appears to conform to the extra-filmic persona of Peter Lorre (the charming but devious murderer operating within the confines of the horror genre); defining it as parodical is inaccurate because the character of Fenninger is not a direct reference to any previous role played by Lorre. The linkage made between him and the horror iconography suggested by Karloff and Lugosi – who both had a legitimate screen relationship to each other and to the horror genre, having starred in at least five horror films together (and many more as individual performers) – is inexplicable. Lorre did not possess the association with horror cinema that his co-stars had; in 1940 he was still most recognizable to cinema audiences as the 'oriental' detective, Mr Moto.

However, at a wider industrial level, the logic behind this strategy becomes much clearer. Stephen D. Youngkin (2005: 168–70, 179) notes that the director, David Butler, wanted to cast some 'notable heavies' alongside Kyser (as this was only his second film following *That's Right, You're Wrong* in 1939), as this casting strategy could potentially increase box-office returns. Executives at RKO, who had signed a two-picture deal with Lorre in order to make *Stranger on the Third Floor* (1940), saw this as the perfect opportunity to fulfil their side of the contract as quickly as possible, which was a necessity since the terms of the contract stated that Lorre was to be paid the substantial fee of US$3,500 per week.[5] As with *Stranger*, Lorre's screen time in the low-budget production of *You'll Find Out* was minimal and therefore cheap.[6] Additionally, in *You'll Find Out*, Lorre's representatives at the William Morris Agency negotiated that the actor had first feature billing. That this was agreed to by RKO, despite the presence of Karloff and Lugosi, implies that Lorre was perceived to hold greater box-office weight than the two horror stars, which is a possibility given that the turn of the decade saw the conventionally 'straight' horror film enter into a period of decline after the heyday of the early 1930s. However, Karloff and Lugosi had a much sharper screen image to exploit than Lorre did at this stage, especially since the Mr Moto association was of little relevance to this film. Therefore, the presence of the two horror icons shaped the narrative and determined the image of the film: Lorre was swept up within the genre associations, and his minor place within the history of screen horror reinvented and overemphasized.

You'll Find Out was also a horror film that attempted to confront the decline of the genre's popularity by prioritizing comedy over terror. Lorre continued this association with comic horrors in his next two appearances within the genre. *Arsenic and Old Lace* was a stage-to-screen adaptation of a hugely successful Broadway play of the early 1940s. The play had starred Boris Karloff in a highly self-referential role – as a character who 'looked like Boris Karloff'; a physicality which signified his 'evil' intent. The film version was directed by Frank Capra in 1941, soon after the play opened. However, due to contractual arrangements with the play's authors, the film could not be released until the play finished its run, which meant that it was not seen publicly until 1944. The producers blocked Karloff's appearance in the film version, fearing his absence onstage would affect receipts. The narrative chronicles the discovery by Mortimer Brewster (Cary Grant) that his long-lost brother, Jonathon (Raymond Massey in the Karloff role) – who returns to the family home with his sidekick, Dr Einstein (Lorre) – is a criminally insane murderer, on the same night that Mortimer's elderly aunts reveal that that they have secretly been poisoning lonely old men and burying them in the cellar for many years.

As a film, *Arsenic and Old Lace* is distanced somewhat from the horror genre for a number of reasons. Firstly, unlike many horror films of the 1940s, it was an 'A' picture that involved highly regarded personnel who were associated with major productions and comedy (Cary Grant, Frank Capra, and screenwriters Julius and Philip Epstein). It was also seen to be a relatively safe gamble, even considering the decline in popularity of horror films, because the success of the stage show meant that it was a 'known' commodity. As a studio, Warner Bros. had no long-standing associations with the horror genre, and the studio only released one conventional horror film during the 1940s: *The Beast with Five Fingers* in 1946 (which also starred Lorre). The release date of 1944 is also important in distancing audiences from the genre as a whole. The mid-1940s was a time where Lorre's screen identity had significantly altered as a consequence of the wartime roles he undertook at Warner Bros., and he – as the actor within the film most easily identifiable with horror – was even further removed from the idea of screen horror than he had been in 1941.

Indicative of the complex nature of the association between Lorre and horror is *The Boogie Man Will Get You*, a horror film which paired Lorre once more with Karloff, but which is not considered a canonical film in the careers of either two 'horror icons'. The film was produced by Columbia in 1942 and was made between Lorre's freelance employment on *Casablanca* and the signing of his permanent Warner Bros. contract in 1943. The pairing of Karloff and Lorre in an original narrative was seen as the best way for a competing studio to capitalize upon Warner Bros.' misfortune of owning an unreleasable film and an unusable star by releasing a cheap imitation of *Arsenic and Old Lace* which combined the horror iconography of the stage show and the (as yet unseen) film in the hiring of both Karloff and Lorre.

In the film, Karloff plays Professor Billings: a mad scientist – albeit an affable and patriotic one – who sells his house (but remains a tenant) so that he may raise the income to keep an 'experiment' running in the basement. The experiment is revealed to be the creation of a race of 'supermen' that Billings believes will help defeat the Axis forces and win the war for the Allies. Lorre plays Dr Lorencz (pronounced by all the film's characters as 'Lawrence'), nominally the town sheriff, who first investigates the experiment but who soon becomes convinced of the validity of Billings's plans.[7] As this summary suggests, the wartime context is very significant to the film, and the patriotic desire of Billings to help his country reveals his good motivations, and moves the film into the realm of comedy rather than outright horror.

On a textual level, both Einstein and Lorencz have more in common with Lorre's supporting roles of the late 1930s and 1940s than with the more generically horrific or murderous extra-filmic persona associated with the actor. In both films (and unlike Lorre's later supporting roles in the action/adventure genre), Lorre's contrived and self-reflexive performance style takes precedence over the actual characterizations. In a manner reminiscent of *Stranger on the Third Floor* (a film from the same period) the potential awareness that an audience would have concerning Lorre's extra-filmic persona and cinematic history is used as a means of engagement with the characters. The ways in which these moments of engagement are constructed vary between the *Arsenic and Old Lace* and *The Boogie Man Will Get You*, and also change from scene to scene during the course of each individual film. Sometimes they are used only for brief comic characterization; in other instances they operate on a more multileveled basis which incorporates a distancing technique on the part of Lorre that serves to remove both the character and the actor from conventional notions of horror, in particular, concerning the role of the 'other' or the 'outsider'.

In *Arsenic and Old Lace*, the 'uniqueness' of Lorre's physical features is played for laughs – just as it was used to create tension in *Stranger on the Third Floor*. A bumbling police officer fails to identify Dr Einstein as a wanted criminal, despite being given the following description over the telephone as the doctor stands before him: 'about 40, 5 foot 3, 140 pounds, pop eyes, talks with a German accent, poses as a doctor'. The comedy is heightened even more as Lorre carefully emphasizes each of the features as they are recounted, culminating in a string of Germanic 'obscenities' muttered under his breath. In the same film, the potentially negative characteristics of Einstein are turned around by Lorre so that the character is presented as sympathetic precisely as a result of his subservience, his drunkenness and his sneakiness. By the conclusion, the film – through formal and performative means – has encouraged the viewer to accept that it is the 'right' decision for Einstein to escape the police. The duality of Lorre's performance goes further than 'merely' humanizing a criminal (as it does in *M*): it effectively removes the threat and makes him an innocent party.

In *The Boogie Man Will Get You*, the performative techniques of Lorre build significantly upon the script to provide the character with depth and colour. Familiar horror tropes are present throughout the film, such as the dark basement setting and hidden passageways within the old house. The melodramatic and overwrought performances of the supporting cast also belong firmly to traditions of that genre. However, Karloff's and (especially) Lorre's energetic overplaying transcends this, and is more in keeping with a black comedy about the war effort rather than with generic horror cinema. Lorencz himself has an eccentric physical demeanour. He is dressed in a costume that combines the look of the 'Wild West' with that of a Mid-West preacher, comprising a wide-brimmed 'cowboy' hat, long dark frock-coat, ribbon neck-tie, sheriff's badge and six-shooter. He also carries a small kitten in his coat pocket and frequently holds exasperated and amusing conversations with the animal that are obviously off-the-cuff remarks by Lorre.

The most important scripted aspect of the film to note in further detail is the standing that Lorencz has within the small-town community. This is significant when one considers the wider industrial and political contexts in which the film was made. *The Boogie Man Will Get You* was conceived as a vehicle for Karloff and Lorre, to best harness the commodity value of their particular marketable identities. In spite of this, Lorencz is far-removed from the conventionally 'monstrous' extra-filmic persona of Lorre. The film becomes an even more unusual text to consider given the political context of the production, made, as it was, just after the USA's entry into the Second World War, since it makes no issue of Lorre's other assumed commodity value – his position as a foreign actor working in Hollywood.

Dr Lorencz is first introduced as the sheriff of Jenksville, a small American town. During the course of the story, he is revealed to hold all the major positions of local authority, including justice of the peace, general practitioner, coroner, realtor, notary and creditor. He is also depicted as American (one of the few that Lorre ever played). Not only does his accent, name and standing within the community pass without explanation, but the obvious Americana iconography of his cowboy-esque outfit is reflected in his whole environment – even down to the white picket fence which surrounds his home, and it is made explicit that his actions throughout the film are motivated by a mixture of patriotism and capitalist entrepreneurship. The conventional association of Lorre (either as an émigré actor or through his persona) with everything that is 'un-American' or 'abnormal' is reversed in this generic B-movie horror knock-off as Lorre (and Lorencz – the similarities between names may not be entirely coincidental) is presented as a legitimate and genuine representative of an American community. Within the confines of this minor horror film, Lorre is given the opportunity to occupy the space of the 'insider' at a time when the cultural identities of European actors were being employed for a very different effect within Hollywood filmmaking.

Figure 6.1 *The Boogie Man Will Get You* (1942). Photo: Columbia Pictures/Photofest.

Both the comic nature of Lorre's early-1940s films, and the complex reception surrounding his 'straight' horror films, emphasizes the disjunction between Lorre and the genre he was most associated with throughout his Hollywood career. In turn, this allows one to view Lorre's final few years working for AIP as more than an unavoidable descent into forms of parody constructed around a 'monstrous' or 'horrific' extra-filmic persona. Much of AIP's output (in particular, the films of Roger Corman) has come to be seen as a body of significant creative works, as analyses of horror cinema, cult films and independent filmmaking have increased. In part, this realization that cult AIP films, such as Corman's Poe cycle, have challenged horror conventions through their application of parodic and reflexive filmmaking techniques has legitimized further academic study of them. However, through this discussion of self-parody in relation to these films, there has been a continuation of the argument that Lorre's performances can also be defined as reliant upon parodical techniques. By analysing the history of the company in terms of its impact on Hollywood and its own marketing and employment strategies, and Lorre's performances in the films, I want to challenge this view and expand upon Youngkin's (2005: 408) nominal notion that Lorre's roles in Corman's Poe films should be interpreted as an opportunity which the actor grasped to 'stop being "Peter Lorre"'.

AIP (formerly American Releasing Corporation) had emerged as a successful independent producer during the 1950s, as a direct result of the changing industry as discussed at the beginning of this chapter. The abolition of 'B' Movie production, the closure of second-run theatres and the opening of Drive-In theatres left a gap in the market for cheaply made films. Furthermore, AIP explicitly targeted the teenage audience with its focus on 'exploitation' narratives such as juvenile delinquency, monster horror, and 'teenpics', at a time when this growing audience was ignored by the major studios. They developed a strategy called 'The Peter Pan Syndrome', whereby the company identified that they should target their films at nineteen-year-old males in order to generate the largest possible audience and most profitable returns (Shary 2005: 27). They also pioneered the release of complementary films as double features, in particular marketing them as 'Midnite Movies', which was another commercially successful strategy. In spite of their 'low' beginnings, AIP proved to be a hugely influential filmmaking force from the late 1950s through to the mid-1960s, as their production cycles and their understanding of the available audience helped to shape the output of the rest of the industry.

One of the main reasons AIP (unlike many other independent companies) did not fade away after its initial successes was that the company actively strove to expand upon its beginnings in 'exploitation' filmmaking. After the success of British-made Hammer films in the American market, such as *The Curse of Frankenstein* in 1957, AIP's owners, Samuel Z. Arkoff and James H. Nicholson, in conjunction with their leading producer/director, Roger Corman, recognized that the heyday of cheap black-and-white combination features was over by 1959 and implemented a series of bigger budget colour features with literary origins, made in 'Cinemascope', in order to maintain AIP's audience share and increase the respectability of the company. The first of these was *The Fall of the House of Usher* (1960), an adaptation of Edgar Allan Poe's story, written by Richard Matheson and starring Vincent Price. Its box office success led to the production of a new cycle of films based upon Poe stories which were lavish in style, increasingly tongue-in-cheek in tone, and employed major stars who were perceived to have established connections with the horror genre.

The use of recognizable stars had always been instrumental to AIP's plans for respectability, since the preference for former contract stars in leading roles (as opposed to amateurs who were cheap but performed badly) had helped establish the company in a competitive market (McGee 1984: 27). The cost of an established star performer was seen as worthwhile expenditure for a notoriously financially stringent company. Although Vincent Price became the 'face' of AIP, they had wanted to employ Lorre as far back as 1956. In a strategy reminiscent of Columbia's plans to use Lorre as a means of raising the cultural profile of the studio in the 1930s, Lorre was approached to make *The She-Creature* with Edward Arnold – his co-star from *Crime and Punishment* (1935). However, *The She-Creature* was no prestigious literary adaptation, and once Lorre read the script he refused the offer of employment and reportedly fired his agent, Sam Jaffe, to avoid fulfilling the commitment, even though 1956 was one of his poorest cinematic years (cameos in *Meet Me in Las Vegas* and *Around the World in Eighty Days*, and a minor role in *Congo Crossing*) (ibid.: 42). Therefore, Lorre's decision to work for AIP in 1962 can be seen as being connected more with AIP's rising reputation, rather than with his own downward fortune.

Lorre shared AIP's and Corman's view of Edgar Allan Poe as a potential source of legitimate cultural value. Corman saw Poe's value as a literary figure whose work could be appropriated without alienating the core teenage audience who were hungry for gore and schlock. During the 1940s, Lorre had already formed an association with the writer's work through stage performances based upon 'The Tell-Tale Heart' and through his appearances on American radio, including programmes which often retold Poe stories. Whilst these performances undoubtedly encouraged the perception of Lorre with 'horror', they also served to emphasize his talent as an actor and his continuing cultural aspirations. According to Youngkin (2005: 282), they also helped to create a link between Lorre and younger audiences, who made up a large part of the audience for Lorre's stage appearances. During one stage show matinee, Lorre's dark monologue quelled the riotous actions of a particularly rowdy group of youngsters, and his popularity ensured his continued employment, provoking the actor to comment, 'Those kids! For some extraordinary reasons they have started going for me.'

This level of interaction between Lorre and teenage audiences is vital to understanding what Lorre achieved on-screen for AIP, and to shift an analysis of his performances away from notions of 'parody'. The complementary relationship between tone, audience and performance is most fully realized in the second of Lorre's appearances in Corman's Poe cycle, *The Raven* (1963). *The Raven* is a very loose interpretation of Poe's poem of the same name. One evening, Dr Craven (Vincent Price), who is in mourning for his dead wife Lenore (Hazel Court), is visited by a raven. The raven reveals to Craven that he is a magician named Bedlo (Lorre) who has been turned into a bird by the evil magician, Scarabus (Boris Karloff). After Craven returns Bedlo to human form, Bedlo informs Craven that Lenore is not dead but is living in Scarabus's castle. Accompanied by their offspring, Estelle Craven (Olive Sturgess) and Rexford Bedlo (Jack Nicholson), the two magicians rush to the castle, only for Scarabus to reveal that the plan was to lure Craven to the castle and trap him (aided by Lenore and Bedlo). Craven, Estelle and Rexford are imprisoned but Bedlo, realizing the error of his ways, helps them to escape. The final act sees Craven and Scarabus face off in an effects-laden 'magicians' duel'.

Whilst I will predominantly draw upon examples from this film, it is important to note that significant continuities exist between Lorre's performance as Bedlo and his appearances in his other two AIP films, *Tales of Terror* and *The Comedy of Terrors*. However, there are differences between the films which somewhat dilute the overall effect of attempting to engage with the audience in a particular way. In the portmanteau film *Tales of*

Terror, Lorre appears in one 'tale' as a brutal antagonist (Montresor). Here he is constrained far more by tighter narrative function and only presents a sympathetic character in one sequence. As suggested by the title, the tone in *The Comedy of Terrors* is overarchingly farcical throughout, so Lorre is not the sole provider of the broadest comedic moments. Furthermore, during filming he was more restricted by ill health than he had been on previous sets and this had a serious impact on what he was physically able to achieve.

Mark Jancovich explains that *The Raven* was the most extreme version of Corman's reworking of Poe's American gothic style into an excessively sensationalist, humorous and vulgar appropriation of gothic horror conventions. In general, Corman's Poe films were over-the-top, with ludicrously portentous dialogue, wild use of colour and impressively lavish, but still obviously cheap sets. Jancovich argues that through the careful management of these excessive elements, the films appeared intentionally camp rather than merely inept. This strategy emphasized the position of the texts, in the minds of their intended audience of young men, as cult films based around ideas of pastiche or parody. Corman's use of generic conventions in this particular way meant that the success of these films required an audience who were able to recognize this playful application of conventions. As such, both the teenage or young adult audience and the cult filmmaker shared 'a common position of distance from, and involvement with, the material' (Jancovich 1996: 282–83).

One of the ways that *The Raven* created this simultaneous 'involvement with' and 'distancing from' was through the performances of its leading actors. Despite his status as a 'cult auteur', it is difficult to credit Corman alone with this strategy: there is much anecdotal evidence that suggests he preferred to concentrate on the formal aspects of filmmaking and allowed actors (especially the more experienced ones) to develop their own performances without too much guidance.[8] Therefore, a certain amount of creative agency may be due to the performers themselves for deciding how to achieve this duality on-screen. In particular, and because of his presence throughout the Poe cycle, there are a number of useful analyses of Vincent Price's 'excessive' acting style which explore the way in which his performances mirror Corman's own development of the formal style and tone of the films.

Vincent Price's carefully honed and knowingly melodramatic technique is on display in *The Raven*. However, also in evidence is a contrasting technique employed by Lorre which does not rely upon aspects of excess and parody. Despite the very obvious difference in style, Lorre's performance is just as coherent and has the same overall effect of engaging the viewer within the horror conventions, whilst also maintaining a sense of distance between the two. Price used an appropriately extravagant on-screen persona in these films, and Kevin Heffernan (2004: 106) describes his delivery in *The Pit and the Pendulum* (1961) as stylized and self-conscious, suggesting 'both nineteenth-century melodrama and popular notions of "high-brow" or "Shakespearean" stage performance'. This purposefully old-fashioned 'European gothic' style is repeated throughout *The Raven*, from Price's ponderous reading of Poe's 'The Raven' which opens the film, to the excessively polite and gentlemanly demeanour which characterizes Craven's behaviour in the face of extraordinary magical occurrences. It is a performance which attempts to engage the viewer through Price's total immersion in the gothic world, whilst it manages to create a distancing effect through the increasingly comical underplayed reactions of Craven to the unfolding chaos and danger. Through this juxtaposition, Craven is effectively presented as a character who recognizes he is trapped in the middle of a horror story and sets about making the best of it.

In contrast to Price, Lorre favoured a performance style which emphasized an 'anti-gothic' stance, and was very much reliant on conveying the contemporary 'American' modernism of both the character and the actor. As is typical of his supporting performances from the 1930s and 1940s, but unlike his performances in the action/adventure films of the 1950s and early 1960s, in *The Raven* the significance of Lorre's presence as a performer far outweighs the importance of the presence of Bedlo as a character. Whereas Price's performance as Craven does not challenge visual horror conventions or the generic dialogue, Lorre – through Bedlo – purposefully takes every opportunity to cut through the melodrama and the horror rhetoric as a means of drawing attention to the genre and to the artifice of the illusion of reality.

The most obvious examples of Bedlo's anti-gothicism come from lines improvised by Lorre which are excessively 'modern' in tone and vocabulary, and jar with the faux nineteenth-century language used elsewhere.[9] Bedlo's first lines (as a raven) are a suitably terse response to Craven's meandering rhetorical questions: 'How the hell should I know? What am I – a fortune teller?'; and when offered some milk, he replies, 'Urgh, how vomitable!'. As well as positioning himself as separate from the traditional performative horror conventions typified by Price's melodramatic playing, Lorre also mounts a challenge to the formal representations of horror cinema by virtually stepping outside of the story in order to explicitly draw attention to the artifice of the surroundings: Bedlo takes one look at the cobweb-covered crypt (nominally a place of tension and terror within horror films) and quips 'Hard place to keep clean, huh?'. Having grown accustomed to the use of improvisation in *The Raven*, Lorre continued the practice throughout *The Comedy of Terrors* with similar effect of 'modernizing' the tone, and ripping through stereotypically old-fashioned exchanges around romance and class relations. When the object of his character's (Felix Gillie) affection pleads with him to 'forbear', he responds with a frustrated, 'I don't know what that word means ...'; and having been harangued by his officious boss (Vincent Price again) once too often, Lorre/Felix turns and audibly calls him an 'Ungrateful employer'.

The use of improvisation in this way could have had an unsettling effect whereby Lorre/Bedlo/Felix would only momentarily upset the gothic nature of the film, before returning to its confines. However, certainly within *The Raven*, it can be seen as a coherent performance because the anti-gothic element is continued through Lorre's physical performance.[10] Despite his size, Lorre's physicality in *The Raven* is an example of carefully worked-out light physical comedy – very much removed from Lorre's own slowly menacing movements in a film like *Der Verlorene*, and also from the traditional use of an actor's body in horror films to suggest tension. From the relaxed facial and loose body movements that reveal Bedlo to be a souse incapable of controlling his tongue or his actions, to the playfully loose double act between himself and Jack Nicholson, Lorre is unconstrained by costume or convention. The combination of Lorre's verbal and physical performance suggests a figure rebelling against the genre conventions: an irreverently 'modern' man in an old-fashioned world.

The decision by Lorre to utilize this particular performance style clearly created a sense of distance between the viewer and the horror story unfolding on-screen. Whilst a performance like Price's seems to allow for a more successful engagement between the audience and the genre, a similar sense of engagement can also be discerned within Lorre's performance. Acknowledging this is partly down to recognizing the type of audience that the film would have been targeting: the American youth culture of young adults and teenagers. Lorre's exceptionally contemporary perform-

Figure 6.2 Lorre and Jack Nicholson in *The Raven* (1963). Photo: American International Pictures.

ance style uses elements that had clear associations with youth cultures of the 1950s and 1960s: American slang, sexual innuendo, rebellious and iconoclastic attitudes, and ambivalence towards authority. Furthermore, whilst positive representations of these forms of teenage culture had formed an important part of AIP's earlier filmmaking cycles (and had used young actors on-screen), the 'teenpics' of the early 1960s were concentrating on more conservative representations of 'good' teens (such as AIP's 'Beach Series'). Therefore, to some extent, the rebellious screen youth had briefly disappeared from the cinema.

What *The Raven* does, through the performance of Lorre, is subtly offer a viewpoint familiar to teen audiences within the confines of the more 'alien' literary and gothic aspects of the traditional horror film, and away from screen incarnations of 'the teenager'. Lorre/Bedlo is presented as the most likely figure of identification for the viewer – the nineteen-year-old male described in the 'Peter Pan Syndrome' – because of the ways in which his performance references recognizable American youth cultures and the 'low-brow'. Craven/Price may be engaging, but is too melodramatic and high-brow, and Jack Nicholson's Rexford (as the only young male character) is too ineffectual and appears too briefly to be considered an alternative. Significantly this identification is primarily created through Lorre's agency as a performer, not through Bedlo as a character – after all, Bedlo is a pathetic failed magician who bullies his son and forces Craven into a trap.

The representation of Lorre as an 'ordinary' figure who actively challenges high-brow snobbery is also evident in *Tales of Terror*. Here, the 'everyday' and 'anti-gothic' does not wholly characterize Lorre's appearance as these thematic concerns exist only in the isolated wine-tasting sequence between Fortunato (Price) and Montresor (Lorre). The remainder of Lorre's scenes rely on his more conventional narrative position as a violent antagonist. However, Lorre/Montresor momentarily engages with the viewer in a different way as he is pitted against Price/Fortunato, the 'civilized' wine expert. In doing so, Montresor is revealed to be both 'average' and 'heroic' as he is equally adept at identifying the expensive wines as Fortunato. As Montresor gulps down copious amounts of alcohol and drunkenly undermines Fortunato's 'proper' wine-tasting technique, Lorre (as he went on to develop more fully with Bedlo) refuses to perform in an appropriately 'old-fashioned' way, using modern, to-the-point vernacular, loose-limbed movements and giggling insouciance. In doing so, Montresor becomes highly engaging, especially as he finds something to praise in each glass, whereas Fortunato only criticizes the wine that is placed before him. Unlike *The Raven*, this exuberantly iconoclastic performance from Lorre is only temporary, as the narrative builds and the extraordinarily brutal aspects of Monstresor's personality soon return once he discovers Fortunato's affair with his wife.

Within the context of Lorre's career, the way that Lorre is subtly aligned with the perceived audience of *The Raven* (and at various moments within

Tales of Terror and *The Comedy of Terrors*), primarily through performative methods but additionally supported by formal filmmaking decisions, is of vital importance. Lorre does not exist as an 'outsider' or 'othered' figure (however 'bad' Bedlo's actions may be, or even when he does not possess human form having been turned into a bird) that stands as a contrast to the 'normality' of the viewer. Instead he occupies the same position as his apparent audience. It has to be noted that this is at a moment within the history of a cinematic genre where the audience is perceived to be a group at odds with conventional society in a much wider sense: the 'American Youth' of the 1950s and 1960s were perceived to be 'outsiders' in their own right. However, it does raise the issue that it is inaccurate to suggest that the cinematic representation of Peter Lorre always occupied the space of the 'outsider' in relation to his audience, and that this strategy of 'othering' was achieved through the use of Lorre in an increasingly parodic manner. By stepping away from notions of parody, many of Lorre's 'horror' roles, especially in the AIP horror films, can be seen as the filmic examples which most closely align Lorre with American society, as opposed to the genre which creates the greatest distance between the actor and his adopted home.

Rather than being seen as a period of decline and failure, Lorre's films of the 1950s and 1960s should be seen from both a textual and contextual basis as a vitally significant part of his career. In terms of their textual, or filmic, value, Lorre's appearances should be understood in two ways. In the first instance, they work in effect to 'Americanize' the actor, removing the 'vaguely foreign' and mysterious associations that helped to characterize the actor's extra-filmic image, and were present to a relative degree in a number of his screen roles in other genres or from earlier decades. Secondly, the nature of the roles themselves and the way that Lorre performed these characters contradicts the notion that his later screen work can be defined as reliant upon 'lazy parody' or even as the 'face-making' of a frustrated performer.

These years were an important period of Lorre's life, precisely due to the audience who were perceived to be consuming his films. The 1950s saw the rise of the 'cult film', the 'cult icon' and the 'cult audience', whereby marginalized audiences were seen to reject mainstream definitions of value and decide for themselves what was (and was not) important. Although this began with seemingly rebellious figures such as James Dean and Marlon Brando, by the 1960s and 1970s with the increasing importance of teen audiences, the parameters of 'cult fandom' had dramatically widened. Given the nature of Lorre's AIP films, he (and other actors closely associated with 'horror') became a focus for cult appreciation; added to this was his apparent affiliation with youth cultures (as demonstrated in *The Raven*), and then his early death in 1964 at the age of fifty-nine – all contributed to the formation of his cult profile.

Lorre's cinematic history played an important role in his final reinvention as a cult figure. Many of the significant early champions of cult and horror cinema in the 1960s grew up during the 1930s and 1940s, and already held Lorre in high regard. One such person was Forrest J. Ackerman, who published the magazine *Famous Monsters of Filmland* between 1958 and 1983 and was an instrumental force in maintaining the association between Lorre and 'horror' during these years due to the manner in which his publication discussed the actor.

In addition to this older generation of fans, Lorre was already familiar to the teenage viewers who watched the AIP films, since the young adults of the early 1960s had been the children who would have been a significant part of the target audience for Lorre's Disney and Irwin Allen action/adventure films during the 1950s. This age group was also discovering older Hollywood films (especially horror) through the syndication of classic films on television (Heffernan 2004: 154–79). Without this particular relationship of older and younger consumers that helped establish 'cult' fandom from the 1950s onwards, Lorre's image and fame as an actor would not have developed in the way that it did, despite his skills as an actor and the popularity of his screen identity. Although Lorre's extra-filmic persona did not accurately describe his film work at virtually any moment during his career, the combination of the publicity discourses, non-cinematic performances and transmedial references to Lorre which constructed the image of the actor as a 'film monster', together with an appreciation of the cinematic labour of Peter Lorre, are all central to the increasing cult recognition of the actor during the second half of the twentieth century.

Notes

1. Four of these films were directed or produced by Irwin Allen, who would go on to produce many of the disaster movie blockbusters of the 1970s such as *The Towering Inferno* (Irwin Allen and John Guillermin, Twentieth Century-Fox, 1974).
2. King also acknowledges that examples of this new 'complex' form of public persona did not mark a complete shift away from the more conventional star persona, which conformed to and maintained the star image via the on-screen product, as examples of this type of persona still existed during this period.
3. The most significant action that Skeeter is involved in is to force the interaction of Randy (Red Buttons) with the circus. However, this occurs through Skeeter's (and Lorre's) absence: the clown becomes so intoxicated that he cannot perform in his act and Randy is forced to take his place. (This narrative element may also be due to the severe ill-health of Lorre in the late 1950s which prevented him from doing anything too physically straining.)
4. However, Lorre continued to be publicized using terminology which encouraged an association between actor and 'horror' during this period.
5. For comparison: drawing on a similar Freelancer's contract, Lorre was only paid $2,000 per week to make *The Maltese Falcon*, and throughout his centrally contracted years at Warner Bros. his weekly salary varied between $1,750 and $2,500 per week, depending on which film he was working on. Source: Payroll folders (*Mask of Dimitrios*, *The Conspirators*, *Hollywood Canteen*, *Hotel Berlin*, *Three Strangers*, *Confidential Agent*, *The Verdict*, *The Beast with Five Fingers*), Warner Bros. Archive, USC, Los Angeles, USA.
6. According to a report from *Time Magazine*, 2 December 1940, the budget for *You'll Find Out* was 'a paltry $300,000'.

7. The name is spelled 'Lorencz' within the film, but 'Lorentz' in the published cast list.
8. For example, see Youngkin 2005: 408; McGee 1984: 119; di Franco 1979: 29; Corman (with Jerome) 1990: 85–86.
9. There is much anecdotal evidence which details Lorre's improvisations on *The Raven* and *The Comedy of Terrors*, including those taken directly from Roger Corman (Corman [with Jerome] 1990: 85); and interviews conducted by Youngkin with Vincent Price, Hazel Court and Richard Matheson (Youngkin 2005: 415–16).
10. Since Lorre was in such poor health during the filming of *The Comedy of Terrors* a body double was used in a number of scenes requiring excessive physical action.

Chapter 7

ALTERNATIVE 'HOLLYWOOD' MEDIA CONTEXTS

Between Europe and Hollywood, Peter Lorre maintained a varied and disparate film career from the 1930s to the 1960s. Specifically within the American studio system structure, he occupied different labour positions, conveyed a range of cultural connotations and played markedly contrasting characters on-screen. In order to compensate for this, 'Hollywood' worked to construct a coherent public persona around Peter Lorre, not through its cinematic representations of the actor, but through his employment in associated industries and through the marketing practices of the studios that he was contracted to, in order to maintain his commodity value. The dominant feature of this persona was a sense of the macabre and the horrific: defining Lorre as a 'one-man chamber of horrors'. Whilst it may have had roots in the German cinema of *M*, the primary factor in the creation of Lorre's extra-filmic persona was the Hollywood transmedial infrastructures of the classical era.

Through a figure such as Lorre, one can observe that the 'Hollywood' industry of this period was heterogeneous and based around symbiotic relationships with a number of different popular media forms and modes of representation, rather than homogeneous and based solely around the singular medium of film. An examination of Lorre's appearances in the different media contexts which helped consolidate Lorre's extra-filmic persona offers an alternative to the notion that Lorre was employed and defined by his Hollywood films as little more than a strange and macabre 'outsider'. This also challenges the implicit discourse that follows such a statement: firstly that his employers undervalued his talents as an individual screen actor, reducing the actor merely to a 'type' via their casting practices, and secondly, that these limitations can be taken as a reflection of the tragic personal experience of the émigré actor in Hollywood.

The media platforms discussed in this chapter – radio, television, and popular culture and caricature, and a further analysis of promotional and publicity material – provided the space for Lorre's persona to exist. Between the 1930s and the 1960s, these alternative arenas effectively operated in parallel to Lorre's cinematic career. Both publicity material and the caricatures began in the mid-1930s (1937 being a key year) and existed throughout Lorre's life – and even beyond it. These discourses are supplemented by Lorre's radio appearances which were predominantly concentrated in the 1940s and 1950s, and his television work during the 1950s and 1960s.

Publicity and Promotional Material

Throughout this book, I have drawn out elements of promotional discourse in relation to specific films, cycles or moments within Lorre's career, most prominently during the 1930s and the concept of typecasting. Here, I want to provide a more general overview of the promotional strategies that were in operation around Lorre, and how they deliberately worked to create and perpetuate his public image over the course of his whole Hollywood career. The horrific nature of Lorre's image was derived from a repeated emphasis on his apparent connection to horror filmmaking and horror iconography, but it can also be attributed to personal characteristics that were presented to the public, such as a tendency towards murderous psychopathology and monstrous abnormality, within promotional and journalistic material, including press releases, biographies, posters, reviews, interviews, career overviews and even obituaries, produced either independently from, or by, the studios that employed Lorre.

Certain perspectives, phrases or quotations which describe the actor's extra-filmic persona are repeatedly used, even in material produced by different Hollywood studios. As such, generic themes and threads that appeared to characterize Lorre's life can be identified. This rhetoric around Lorre should be viewed more as evidence of various press department's 'recycling' strategies in the promotion of established actors rather than as testament to any coherence within Lorre's cinematic employment. Lorre's publicity claimed that his screen work could be easily defined by its repetitive, and therefore homogeneous, elements. What this strategy effectively achieved was the reconstruction of Lorre's acting experiences into an abstracted version of the actor – which was then further distanced from the reality of Lorre's employment in the way that this abstracted image was continually repeated by different sources – in studio-produced publicity and in interviews that were published with the express aim of promoting and publicizing the star actor – throughout his career.

In 1937, the *Detroit Free Press* called him 'Europe's one-man chamber of horrors' (4 January 1937), a quote that was reworked into his 1940 Twentieth Century-Fox biography to re-emphasize Lorre's place within the cinematic medium, as 'the movies' one-man chamber of horrors' (Brand 1940). The same 1940 document quoted Lorre on his relation with *M* as 'that picture *M* has haunted me everywhere I've gone. I've been the sinister menace constantly'; and his 1954 Walt Disney biography stated that 'his first international success as the child-murderer in *M* has blinded producers to his possibilities other than murder and mayhem'. In a 1946 interview written to promote *My Favorite Brunette*, he recounts his experiences off-screen as 'Most of the neighborhood kids have seen me on the screen and think I'm the devil reincarnated. I've tried to be friendly with them but it's no-go – they think it's a trap' (Anonymous 'Peter Lorre interviewed by his stand in, Russel Coles' 1946).

Other promotional tactics emphasized the actor's position within horror iconography, not through an insistence that his screen roles could be defined according to a specific type or genre, but in an emphasis on the supposed 'authenticity' of the actor's extra-filmic persona. There are examples of articles and interviews which seek to create a sense of cohesion between Lorre's 'evil' public image and the 'reality' of the actor. This strategy, where promotional discourses are used as a means of authenticating an actor's prescribed image, is linked to wider concepts associated specifically with conventions of stardom whereby extra-textual discourses attempt to maintain continuity between a star's on-screen and off-screen life, through publicizing the star in terms which suggest they are the same sort of person that they tend to play on the cinema screen.

Although it remains problematic to define Lorre as a 'star' in a conventional sense (mainly due to his increasing employment in supporting or character roles), the implicit insistence within written discourses of the similarities between the 'real' Peter Lorre and his 'star' persona remains a key feature of Lorre's public image. This mode of advertising comes into existence around 1937, as prior to this, public perceptions regarding Lorre were constructed to emphasize the discontinuities between his roles and his 'reality'. From 1937 onwards, official biographies of Lorre published by his employers began to include a sentence which revealed that the actor was born in a remote Hungarian village at the foot of the Carpathian Mountains. This immediately created a link to classic horror iconography in the implicit association between Lorre and the definitive icon of modern gothic horror, 'Dracula'. Twentieth Century-Fox were the first studio to advertise Lorre using these terms in 1937, but other studios including Warner Bros. and Universal maintained the trend, and recycled the phrase throughout the actor's career. [1]

In addition to the wording of these biographies, the 'authentic' aura of menace and horror regarding Lorre was also reinforced through interviews conducted with, or quotations credited to, the actor. A key component of interviews conducted with Lorre is the repeated intimation of foreboding on the part of the interviewer, where the journalist conveys uneasiness about his/her meeting with Lorre because of the inherent 'abnormal' qualities associated with the actor's public persona. Surprisingly, a meeting with the 'real' Peter Lorre typically appears to confirm this image rather than dispelling it. In part, and especially in examples from the later years of his career, this is conveyed by Lorre himself, who proffers quotations which are in keeping with his image, but are often bizarrely inaccurate summations of his career, such as his quip in the 1954 Walt Disney Pictures biography that the giant squid from *20,000 Leagues under the Sea* was 'the part I usually play'. Even Lorre's term for acting – 'face-making' – alluded to the monstrous qualities associated with the actor in the implied grotesquery of the phrase. This deliberate form of self-representation can be explained by Barry King's (1985) notion of a 'professional persona', whereby an actor utilized aspects of his extra-textual/star persona during engagements within a public sphere in order to maintain a coherent – and therefore, marketable – public personality.

However, in part, this sense of horror is also created away from the behaviour of the actor himself, and is constructed by the way in which the written style and structural choices of the author insist upon fictionalizing an aura of murderous menace around Lorre. Significantly, this mode of representation existed long before Lorre's own published statements began to support his public image. Again, 1937 marks a turning point. For the majority of her article, Alice L. Tildersley's 1937 interview for *The Post*, is a conventionally sedate piece of writing, but she chooses to end it very abruptly with a quotation from Lorre in which he asks, 'Shall I scare you?' (*Post*, 25 April 1937). The positioning of this question effectively removes his words from their actual context (a discussion relating to performative practices) by offering it as characteristic behaviour of the actor himself.

Also from 1937, Gladys Hall's interview in *Screenland* outlines Lorre's thoughts on Freudian analysis and performance theory, but the decision to entitle it, 'Are You Insane?' belies the pseudo-intellectual tone of the piece by emphasizing the more 'abnormal' qualities associated with the actor (2 October 1937). This stance, which prioritized elements of Lorre's persona over the reality of the man and specifics of his screen roles, continued throughout the next several decades. In a later interview from 1953, which publicizes Lorre's role in *Beat the Devil* (1953), the comedic nature of Lorre's character is ignored, in favour of a pronounced focus on the subject of 'murder', not least in the decision to call the piece, 'Mr Murder' (Frishauer, 30 May 1953: 9). This is constructed by erroneous claims about Lorre's cinematic career – that he has already 'killed' co-star Humphrey Bogart on-screen seven times (in their films together, not once do the actions of Lorre's characters lead to Bogart's characters' death); and bizarrely mistaken beliefs about his European past – that the actor was a suspect in the 'Düsseldorf Vampire' murders that partly inspired *M*. The association between Lorre and murder is compounded by the final sentences of the interview in which the author makes the absurd confession that although he had 'befriended' Lorre, during the night '[he] had a most fearful dream. Even for a friend it seems impossible to keep Peter Lorre and murder apart.'

Despite the proliferation of instances within studio-produced or studio-influenced promotional material which sought to connect Lorre with concepts of horror, psychosis or murder, it remains difficult to prove conclusively that this was a deliberate and collaboratively strategized policy regarding the way that Lorre was perceived by the studios he worked for, even on the part of Twentieth Century-Fox, the studio that Lorre was under contract to in 1937. Lorre worked for many studios under varying conditions throughout his career (and was represented by a number of different agents), making it virtually impossible to understand how a long-term strategy for managing his career could have been coordinated.[2] This lack of coherence is further supported by the fact of Lorre's non-engagement within the screen horror genre – both in terms of the actual screen work he undertook, and the small number of horror films that he was optioned to appear in but which did not make it to production with him in the cast.[3] Instead, it is more accurate to argue that it was the wide variety of studio-produced and independent forms of advertising copy that created and contributed to the continued existence of Lorre's highly coherent and easily recognizable extra-filmic persona.

Radio Appearances

One persuasive explanation as to why the association between Lorre's career, his extra-filmic persona and the subject of 'horror' became so indelibly linked within American public consciousness may be found through a consideration of the actor's extensive work on American radio.[4] Between the mid-1930s and early 1960s, Lorre made 143 appearances on either American network radio, or the Armed Forces Radio Service (AFRS) which broadcast to serving forces stationed overseas (60 per cent of which occurred during the 1940s). In the same period, Lorre made sixty-eight feature films. A large number of the radio programmes which employed Lorre were closely associated with the horror genre, and the image of Lorre as a dark creature in possession of murderous, monstrous or psychotic characteristics, can be found more readily and concisely within Lorre's radio appearances than in any other form of media representation, particularly from the 1940s onwards. Lorre's radio roles can be generally categorized in three ways: his appearance as a 'guest star', his position as a 'host' who introduced different radio dramas each week, and his work as a 'lead performer' in a series of self-contained one-off dramas.

The radio work undertaken by actors hitherto associated with the cinema can be seen as instrumental in shaping public awareness of them as individual performers. By the end of the 1930s, more than 80 per cent of homes in the United States had access to at least one radio receiver, and ownership continued to rise during the following decade (Hilmes 1999). As Richard J. Hand (2006: 46) notes (in specific regard to dramatic radio programming, but nonetheless relevant to radio broadcasting as a whole), between the 1930s and 1950s, 'radio drama [served] to enhance or consolidate the careers of Hollywood stars, ensuring that they were household names through the instantaneousness of radio'. Therefore, potentially, many more Americans heard Peter Lorre star in radio broadcasts than paid to see the actor on the cinema screen. He was a frequent presence within radio programming during the height of the medium's popularity within American culture, and made repeated guest appearances on many of the most prominent radio shows that dominated the monthly ratings between 1937 and 1953. Given the prolonged and prominent position that Lorre occupied within the medium, radio representations of the actor can be seen to have had a direct impact on the popularity and notoriety of his extra-filmic persona.

From 1940 onwards, Lorre was a celebrity guest performer in sketches written for some of the most popular radio shows being broadcast within the United States and for American troops fighting overseas. In addition to appearing on leading radio shows, such as *Amos 'n' Andy*, or those hosted by Fred Allen, Jack Benny and Eddie Cantor, Lorre also guested on other notable variety and comedy shows including; *Kay Kyser's Kollege of Musical Knowledge* (1938–1949) in 1940, *The Abbott and Costello Show* (1940, 1942–1947, 1949) in 1943, *Duffy's Tavern* (1940–1951) in 1943, *The Frank Sinatra Show* (1944), *Arch Oboler's Plays* (Series Two)(1945), *Baby Snooks Show* (1944–1951) in 1945, and *The Martin and Lewis Show* (1949–1953) in 1949.

In these guest slots on established radio variety and comedy shows, Lorre appeared as 'himself', or more accurately, a highly fictionalized version of 'Peter Lorre', who was purported to be a genuine representation of the actor, but who acted exclusively within the remit of Lorre's extra-filmic persona and presented him as an iconic horror star. Despite the obviously fabricated nature of Lorre's personality in the guest slots, the comedy of the sketches in which he was involved was – for the most part – constructed from an insistence that Lorre was being presented 'as he really was'. For example, in response to a question posed by Dean Martin on *The Martin and Lewis Show* which makes reference to Lorre's sinister screen characters, Peter Lorre replies to Martin, 'What makes you think I'm acting?' (NBC, tx. 8 May 1949). On *The Abbott and Costello Show*, 'Peter Lorre' was reinvented as a 'mad doctor' figure living in 1940s California. Despite this contemporary placement, Lorre is also presented as a mysterious and mythic figure who knew Dracula (Lorre: 'I caught him stealing from my blood bank!') (NBC, tx. 11 February 1943). This type of characterization is repeated throughout virtually all of Lorre's guest appearances, and worked to make the connection between Lorre and traditional horror iconography far more explicit than even his studio biographies.

In addition to representing Lorre in a certain manner, these guest appearances also seek to reinforce the connection between Lorre, 'horror' and his cinematic roles. The radio scripts continually infer a connection between the repetitive nature of Lorre's screen work, the terrifying qualities of his characters, and the violent death of those who share the screen with him. On *Duffy's Tavern*, Lorre is introduced with the following sentence: 'Here he is, kids – Jack the Ripper' (NBC, tx. 19 October 1943). On *Texaco Star Theatre*, one cast member comments: 'In the pictures, Mr Lorre is always killing people – I'm scared!', and Fred Allen says to Lorre, 'You're supposed to be a brutal killer!' (CBS, tx. 4 June 1944). During *Spotlight Review* (1947–1949) in 1948, host, Spike Jones, whispers 'Everyone at Warner Bros. is scared of him!' (CBS, tx. 19 December 1948). On *The Martin and Lewis Show*, Jerry Lewis remembers, 'One time I took my girl to see Peter Lorre in a picture. He was so sinister and menacing, when I came out, I had the creeps!'

These statements are not accurate characterizations of the vast majority of Lorre's screen roles. However, the continual repetition through the popular and accessible medium of radio meant that these types of broadcasts effectively taught American audiences how to perceive Peter Lorre – in relative isolation from his film roles – through the way that the actor's guest appearances on the radio made constant reference to his 'monstrously murderous' persona.

Away from these comedy guest appearances, the association with horror and murder was also constructed through Lorre's employment as a host and as a leading performer in radio drama throughout the 1940s and 1950s. Many of the series that Lorre performed in were categorized as programmes which broadcast horror stories or mysteries, including *Inner Sanctum Mysteries* (1941–1952), *Suspense* (1942–1962), *Creeps by Night* (1944), *Mystery Playhouse* (1944–1945), *Mystery in the Air* (1947) and *Nightmare* (1953–1954).

Over the course of the series which employed Lorre as a host of dark tales of mystery and suspense, such as *Mystery Playhouse* (which broadcast old episodes of *Inner Sanctum Mysteries* and other programmes with new introductions by Lorre on the AFRS), the extra-filmic persona of Lorre was used as a cohesive tool which bound together a series of otherwise unrelated stories, whose sources ranged from adaptations of Robert Louis Stevenson and Edgar Allan Poe, to Nero Wolfe mysteries and original science-fiction-style stories. Lorre only appeared briefly at the beginning and end of each broadcast to perform a short monologue.[5] These monologues, which Lorre usually began with the greeting 'Good evening kreeps [sic], this is Peter Lorre', mirrored the basic way Lorre was presented in his guest appearances – as a source of psychotic mayhem and murder – as evidenced by his introduction to the episode 'Randall's Discovery': 'If you like mystery and suspense; if your tastes run to the macabre or the supernatural; if sweetness and light bores you – then my friends – you've come to the right place. I promise you, there is nothing sweet and very little light here' (AFRS, tx. 30 April 1944).

In a basic sense, and given the disparate nature of the stories themselves, Lorre's monologues, which closely adhered to the actor's extra-filmic persona, gave the series a cohesive identity of its own. Furthermore, the relationship between the stories and Lorre's public image was one of mutual reinforcement. The decision to employ Lorre as host encouraged the perception of the series in terms pertaining to 'horror' and 'mystery' because of the notoriety of his persona; but the reverse is equally suggestive, and as a result of performing in this type of broadcast Lorre came to be defined as an actor who commonly appeared in programmes about murder and mystery.

The vast majority of Lorre's leading performances within radio drama further confirmed this association. In these dramas, Lorre played (or at least appeared to play) the types of role that were central to the development of his public image: torturers, killers, lunatics, psychotics, dangerous criminals, and mysterious strangers. Furthermore, Lorre's characters in these dramatic broadcasts were written and performed expressly to scare the audience as opposed to amuse them. Sometimes the 'scare' was undercut by narrative twists or the reassuring voice of the host (sometimes Lorre himself), but in general terms, the objective was to create 'tension' rather than 'humour'.

Even in the moments when Lorre stepped 'outside' of the narrative itself and drew attention to his own position as a performer, as he did in an episode of *Mystery in the Air* based upon Guy De Maupassant's 'The Horla', the self-reflexive nature of the performance only added to (rather than offered relief from) the uncertain atmosphere created through Lorre's performance (NBC, tx. 21 August 1947). At the conclusion of his retelling of 'The Horla', Lorre moves from the fictional character he has been playing to portraying a version of 'himself' (similar to the role he occupied within his radio comedy appearances). At the end of the broadcast, Lorre's performance 'expands the horror beyond the narrative frame' (Hand 2006: 58–59) as the fictionalized 'Peter Lorre' also finds himself at risk from the destructive force contained within De Maupassant's story. Lorre concludes the show with the following outburst:

> There's one thing I can do, I … I can destroy myself … yes, yes, yes! I must destroy myself! Destroy! Yes! Let me go! Yes! I know I feel alright! Let me go! Yes I know I'm Peter Lorre, I know it's a story, I know it's by De Maupassant, I know it's Thursday and we are on the air, but it's the Horla! …
>
> Oh, I … I beg your pardon. I … I'm sorry I got so excited but I … I warned you at the beginning, it's a very uncomfortable story.

Lorre's final words may restore a sense of normality and balance to the listener through their wry black humour, but its intense tone does not aim to situate the horror story within a broadly comic setting in which an ironic performance encourages a distancing effect between the audience and the action. Instead, Lorre's acting foregrounds the more terrifying aspects of the narrative. Therefore, when those who somewhat mistakenly describe being scared witless by the 'screen exploits' of Peter Lorre, it may be possible that the 'frights' they are remembering came from the radio rather than the cinema (Hadley Garcia 1983).

Considering the way that the medium of radio tended to represent Peter Lorre, it is possible to suggest why there was perhaps such a virulent notion of the actor as a 'horror' star. Radio may not have initially created the extra-filmic persona of 'Peter Lorre', but the medium certainly perpetuated the image throughout the 1940s and 1950s (and to some degree, the 1960s, although Lorre only made five radio appearances between 1962 and 1963). Furthermore, the prominent place that the medium occupied within the forefront of American popular culture during these decades also suggests why the 'monstrous' or 'murderous' view of Lorre (as defined by his extra-filmic persona) remains dominant, and how Lorre's less horrific screen performances have been partly obscured by the image that was promoted through the more 'intimate' and 'immediate' domestic medium of radio. Examples of Lorre's performative labour were most accessible when they were in the form of his frequent radio appearances. The fact that the majority of his radio roles conformed (albeit in a variety of ways) to the public image of him as a psychotic murderer can be seen as a major factor in determining why the rest of his work, especially within the cinematic field, has so often been characterized in accordance with this extra-filmic persona.

Television Roles

Unlike Lorre's radio appearances, the actor's career on American television did not have the same significant impact upon public perceptions of him. Whilst this may be considered somewhat surprising given the equally domestic nature of the televisual mass medium, the majority of Lorre's television appearances occurred during the medium's more developmental phase of the early 1950s, and therefore did not reach the comparable 'mass' audience that radio had achieved in its heyday of the 1940s. Furthermore, Lorre's television career only began in the years after the actor had already achieved a considerable level of fame, both on the cinema screen, and on the radio.

Although it did not play as important a role in the shaping of Lorre's public image as radio or promotional materials, television certainly reinforced the dominant perceptions of the actor, heavily relying upon his prescribed image. Between 1949 and 1963, Lorre made eighty-two appearances on American television in a wide variety of programming: from variety hours *Celebrity Time* (1952) and *The All-Star Revue* (1953); game shows *What's My Line* (1950–1967) in 1952 and *I've Got a Secret* (1952–1967) in 1955; one-off dramas *Suspense* (1949–1952) in 1952 and *Producer's Showcase* (1954–1957) in 1955; repeated guest roles and cameos in *Climax!* (1954–1958) and *The Red Skelton Show* (1951–1971); and appearances on established drama serials such as *Rawhide* (1959–1966) in 1960 and *Route 66* (1960–1964) in 1962.

It should be noted that there are a number of examples of television shows which did not employ Lorre according to the limitations of his extra-filmic persona – a far greater number than the handful of radio broadcasts to do so. Television (at times) found a greater variety of uses for Lorre's talents, such as Lorre's role as an eccentric Mexican policeman in a farcical episode of *Alfred Hitchcock Presents* entitled 'The Diplomatic Corpse' (CBS, tx. 8 December 1957), or his role as the suicidal cameraman in *Playhouse 90's* adaptation of F. Scott Fitzgerald's *The Last Tycoon* (CBS, tx. 14 March 1957). As such, Lorre's television work can be seen to have elements in common with his film work as well as with his radio appearances, not least because of the similar performative methods used within film and television.

However, much more so than during his film career, Lorre was frequently employed on television according to the established remit of his persona. As with the other modes of representation discussed in this chapter, this was primarily achieved through an association with horror iconography. Many of Lorre's small screen cameos mirrored his radio guest slots in the way that they positioned the actor in line with established horror tropes. Some of the radio stars that had used Lorre's public image in this way had moved to television in the 1950s (after the decline of radio's popularity) and Lorre made similar appearances on Milton Berle's (NBC, tx. 24 December 1958) and Eddie Cantor's (synd. tx. 2 May 1955) television programmes, as he had done on their radio shows. In addition to this, throughout his eight appearances on *The Red Skelton Show* between 1954 and 1960, Lorre's persona was repeatedly used for comedic effect through his casting as a 'mad scientist', 'the phantom of the ballet', or his role in a 'haunted house sketch'. This association with horror continued through his roles in individual drama broadcasts, including 'The Tortured Hand' for the television version of the *Suspense* radio show (CBS, tx. 16 December 1952).

It was also on the television screen that Lorre's association with the genre was emphasized through casting decisions which combined the presence of Lorre with that of established screen horror personnel. This expanded the tendency within promotional material and radio to discuss Lorre in the same breath as Boris Karloff and Bela Lugosi. It also harked back to the two films Lorre had already made with Karloff (one of which was also with Lugosi), and, in turn, presaged the films of the early 1960s where Lorre starred with Karloff, Vincent Price and Basil Rathbone. One particularly interesting project which conforms to this casting practice was the series *Collector's Item* (1957), which paired Lorre with Vincent Price as a crime-fighting duo who pursued stolen or lost cultural artefacts. Lorre played an ex-con who used the tricks of the trade for the purposes of 'good' rather than 'evil', but the series' distance from the established horror personae of both Price and Lorre might explain why only two episodes were made and never broadcast.[6]

This association with classic Hollywood horror is conveyed in the most explicit terms in the 1962 episode of *Route 66* entitled 'Lizard's Leg and Owlet's Wing' (CBS, tx. 26 October 1962). In this episode, the itinerant male lead characters, Tod Stiles (Martin Milner) and Buzz Murdock (George

Maharis), find temporary work at a hotel on Route 66. Ostensibly, the hotel is holding an executive conference, but this is soon revealed to be a cover for a horror film convention. The convention is being run by Peter Lorre, Boris Karloff and Lon Chaney Jr, who all appear as fictionalized versions of themselves. The three actors are represented as famous horror stars that are attempting to find ideas for a new television show but cannot agree on a format, until Tod suggests that they revisit their horror past. Karloff dons his Frankenstein's Monster costume and Chaney Jr dresses as both the Wolf Man and the Hunchback of Notre Dame (one of Lon Chaney Sr's roles). Whilst, to some degree, this foregrounding of costume and grotesque appearance only emphasizes the lack of Lorre's iconic status within the cinematic genre, as he has no memorable horror film role to re-inhabit, the show works very hard to sidestep this issue. Instead, Lorre is presented as the *most* frightening horror star during a scene in which a female secretary fails to register anything abnormal about Karloff and Chaney Jr (who are in full costume), but screams and faints upon the merest glance at Lorre's grinning face.

In addition to American television's use of Lorre in horror contexts, many programmes also made specific reference to the individual characteristics associated with Lorre's persona. In many programmes, Lorre played figures with underlying psychotically murderous tendencies, including: Le Chiffre in 'Casino Royale' for *Climax!* (NBC, tx. 21 October 1954); Max Vorhees – a deceptively deranged stranger who ingratiates himself into a wealthy household – in 'A Promise to Murder' for *Climax!* (NBC, tx. 17 November 1955); and Willy – a bank robber who somewhat needlessly targets a blind woman – in 'Number Five Checked Out' for *Screen Directors' Playhouse* (NBC, tx. 18 January 1956). He was also cast in a number of roles which made use of the 'abnormal' or 'strange' elements of his image, such as an episode of *Studio 57* from 1955 entitled 'Young Couples Only' (DuMont, tx. 3 September 1955). In this episode, written by Richard Matheson, Lorre played a mysterious janitor who is revealed to be an alien (complete with a third eye in the back of his head) who plans to abduct young newly-weds to take back to his planet.

Perhaps the best known of the televisual roles which referenced and reinforced Lorre's sinister public image was an episode of *Alfred Hitchcock Presents* called 'Man from the South' (CBS, tx. 3 January 1960), adapted from a Roald Dahl story. Lorre plays Carlos, a mysterious man who encounters a penniless gambler (Steve McQueen). Carlos devises a bet: that the gambler will be unable to light his cigarette lighter successfully ten times in a row. If the gambler succeeds, he will win Carlos's car. However, if he loses, Carlos will remove his little finger with a cigar cutter. Throughout the show, Lorre's character is continually referred to in terms that mirror the perverse elements of the actor's public image: apart from the macabre challenge itself, he is also called a 'monster', 'pathetic' and 'sick'. Furthermore Carlos is shown to be both genuinely menacing and unnervingly childlike. The palpable threat is clearly demonstrated by the introduction of Carlos's wife: she intervenes in the bet after the seventh successful attempt to light the lighter. In revealing her own fingerless hands – the sight of which makes Carlos grin in an insanely childish manner – the bet is swiftly ended. The tense atmosphere is maintained as, after Lorre leaves the scene, the gambler reaches for a cigarette, only for his lighter to fail on the eighth attempt.

Lorre's appearances on American television conform to a number of the key features associated with his extra-filmic persona. Although there are some isolated examples of complex performances or characterizations, within the majority of Lorre's television work there can be discerned a proclivity towards repetition and self-parody. Somewhat ironically, many of the negative comments that are misleadingly applied to critiques of Lorre's cinematic work, such as the notion that the disillusioned actor came to rely upon lazy parodies of his own image in the later years of his career, are more applicable to his appearances on the small screen than to his film work from the same era, the 1950s through to 1964.

'Caricature'

As demonstrated by the figure of *Corpse Bride*'s 'Maggot' which opened this book, one of the most prolific and long-running methods of representing Lorre away from the cinema screen is through caricatures of the actor's extra-filmic persona. Regarding Lorre, my categorization of the term 'caricature' is admittedly quite a loose one, and here I am concerned with brief or exaggerated representations of the actor – visual or otherwise – that were created in isolation from the presence of Lorre himself. These include animations, impressions or impersonations, and references made to Lorre in songs, films, novels and advertisements. What these often incongruent representations share is the objective of using Lorre's extra-filmic persona as a form of shorthand to infer certain general characteristics, genre associations, or behavioural practices in texts which are independent of Lorre.

Caricatured versions of Peter Lorre have existed for seventy years and range enormously in tone, duration and 'accuracy'. There are examples of at least sixty-three caricatures created between 1937 and 2005. Caricatures of Lorre are a significant mode of representation to consider, not only because of the direct influence they had upon public perceptions regarding the actor during his own lifetime, but also because of their continuing presence within American (and British) popular culture. Caricatures can be seen to have played as significant a role as radio in this regard during the formative years of his career in Hollywood. Furthermore, because they are not reliant upon the continuing presence of the actor, the existence of Lorre-based caricatures continued after his death in 1964 and can be considered one of the main explanations as to why the persona of 'Peter Lorre' is still widely recognized today.

It is no coincidence that the first documented 'caricature' (or more accurately, impersonation) of Lorre occurred in 1937, the year in which alternative discourses surrounding public perceptions of the actor begin to recede in favour of one dominant coherent image. As such, the impersonation from that year can possibly be credited with helping to solidify (along with representations in printed media) the actor's extra-filmic persona. The impersonation occurs within *One in a Million* (1937), a film produced by Twentieth Century-Fox as a star vehicle for the ice-skating star, Sonja Henie. The studio had only recently employed Peter Lorre under a long-term contract, and so the inclusion of this caricatured version of the actor within this film can be seen as a means of publicizing their new acquisition in the form of an easily marketable image. Again, whilst to a large degree it may be possible to credit Twentieth Century-Fox with pioneering the inceptive elements of Lorre's cohesive persona, it was also developing independently elsewhere, and so Lorre's short time at the studio, along with the lack of archival evidence on this topic, make it difficult wholly to assign 'authorship' to Darryl Zanuck or Fox's publicity team.

The impersonation in *One in a Million* is unrelated to the plot or to Henie's character, and is performed by the vaudevillian team, the Ritz Brothers. Momentarily diverting from the main love story, the three men perform a comedy number on roller skates entitled 'We're the Horror Boys of Hollywood', in which they are each dressed as Boris Karloff (in costume as Frankenstein's Monster), Charles Laughton (in costume as Captain Bligh) and Peter Lorre. Despite the explicit reference to 'horror' in the title of the song, the number itself repeatedly undermines its assertion that Lorre is a 'horror boy'. Much like the *Route 66* episode, Peter Lorre's costuming is highly problematic as it makes no reference to any of the actor's roles. Instead of borrowing the distinctive, and potentially iconic, bald look of Lorre's recent film appearance in MGM's *Mad Love* (1935), the Ritz Brothers' 'Peter Lorre' wears an outfit that has no relation to any role played by the actor in his film career to this point. It is comprised a dark suit, a slicked-back and long-fringed hairstyle, dark lipstick and an earring.

In addition to this visual aspect, Lorre's lack of iconic status is also compounded by the spoken introduction to the song, in which 'Boris Karloff' has to explain to 'Charles Laughton' and, by implication, to the film's audience, exactly who Peter Lorre is. (The horror status of Charles Laughton's Captain Bligh is equally as questionable.) Despite this, the song is explicit in its insistence that Lorre *is* an icon of horror cinema. The chorus defines all three actors in this way as the Ritz Brothers sing, 'We're the Horror Boys of Hollywood … / We do bad things and we do them good … / We never get kisses / We just get the hisses'. Furthermore, the solo verse given to 'Peter Lorre' introduces the subject of 'typecasting' and the limiting nature of Lorre's own apparently 'horrific' screen work as 'Lorre' sings: 'Stop it, stop it! I tell you, it's not me! It's the parts they give me! Every time I appear in a scene, there's a shot, a scream, and somebody is MURDERED!'

This assertion of Lorre's position as one of the horror genre's great monsters was continually reinforced through other caricatures created during his lifetime. Most were able to expand upon the Ritz Brothers' version in their inclusion of specific personal characteristics pertaining to the extra-filmic persona of the actor, partly because the majority of them were created during the 1940s – a decade in which Lorre's image became firmly established and defined, partially through radio. This included Paul Frees' impression of Lorre on the Spike Jones radio show, which spoofed the popular romantic song, 'My Old Flame', in the guise of Peter Lorre's 'monstrous' persona. Frees (as Lorre) would sing, 'My old flame / I can't even remember her name / I'll have to look through my collection of human heads … My old flame / My new lovers all seem so tame / They won't even let me strangle them!' (*Spotlight Revue*. CBS, tx. 10 December 1948).[7]

The most recognizable caricatures of Lorre were the animated caricatures created by Warner Bros.' animation department. These images were the ones that proved to be indelible in the mind of Tim Burton (and others), and their popularity and longevity means that they have been one of the most significant factors in shaping perceptions surrounding Lorre. Cartoon representations of Lorre were included in five Looney Tunes or Merrie Melodies animations between 1941 and 1947. This was virtually the same period that Lorre was under contract at the studio, and, although many contemporary celebrities were parodied in Warner Bros.' animations, the studio's ownership of the rights to the actor's image undoubtedly played a part in this increased presence (Clark 1995: 23–24). However, 'ownership' remains difficult to gage in this context. Recent Warner Bros. productions – *Carrotblanca* (1995), *Looney Tunes: Back in Action* (2003) and *Corpse Bride* (2005) – continue to use the Lorre caricature, implying some sort of continued ownership of the right to the image, especially in the texts which nostalgically revisit and rework the studio's past achievements. However, its unmitigated proliferation elsewhere since the 1940s suggests otherwise. Additionally, Robert Clampett, one of the animators instrumental in the construction of Warner Bros.' caricature, took the image with him when he moved to Columbia in 1945, and in 1947 he directed the animation *Cockatoos for Two*, in which this version of 'Peter Lorre' played a featured role.

Each Warner Bros. caricature developed a key aspect of Lorre's public image: *Hollywood Steps Out* (1941) depicts Lorre as a perverse voyeur; *Horton Hatches the Egg* (1942) associates the actor with a bizarre death (suicide); and *Hare-Raising Hare* (1946) and *Birth of a Notion* (1947) reconstruct Lorre as an evil scientist. Only *Racketeer Rabbit* (1946) remains separate from this image to some degree in its depiction of him as a thuggish gangster. In addition to this, the exaggerated caricatured appearance of Lorre within these Looney Tunes cartoons was instrumental in defining how Lorre was perceived in visual terms in the years that followed. The

Figure 7.1 *One in a Million* (1937).

Figure 7.2 *Hair-Raising Hare* (1946).

Warner Bros. animators reconstructed Lorre with a small body and over-sized head, slicked down black hair, huge eyes with heavy lids, fleshy lips, and rotten teeth. Additionally, his voice (as impersonated by Mel Blanc) was a strangulated nasal whine which often emitted a deranged giggle. The debt owed by the 2005 'Maggot' to these cartoons is clear.

This particular representation only corresponded with the actual physical appearance of the actor during a brief period in 1940. Prior to this, Lorre was significantly overweight and 'baby-faced', and during 1941 his own rotten teeth were replaced which markedly altered his facial appearance. However, it is this grotesque caricatured representation that became the template for the visual and aural caricatures of Lorre which followed. Many of the more modern examples have become increasingly abstracted from the reality of Lorre's demeanour. They rarely resemble Lorre himself, but have taken the Warner Bros. caricature as their main point of reference. In addition to *Corpse Bride*, this is most noticeable in the caricatures in *Carrotblanca* and *Looney Tunes: Back in Action*, which are explicit pastiches of the Looney Tunes cartoons, but an abstraction of the original Warner Bros. version can also be seen in examples such as *The Brave Little Toaster* (1987). As such, visual and aural cues which often signify the actor's extra-filmic persona in more recent caricatured representations (including animated and live-action examples) have, in many cases, been created from echoes of past animated caricatures rather than from specific film appearances by Lorre during his Hollywood career.

The number of caricatured representations of Peter Lorre increased dramatically after the actor's death in 1964. The nature and range of references also widened, and whilst some can be seen as caricaturing Lorre's extra-filmic persona, others are parodies of film roles that Lorre played. His appearance as Joel Cairo in *The Maltese Falcon* (1941) and his association with Sydney Greenstreet form a significant number of Lorre caricatures. Parodies of the Lorre and Greenstreet double act occur in *The Avengers* (1968), *Scooby-Doo* (1970), *The Return of the Pink Panther* (1975) and *Duckman: Private Dick / Family Man* (1994); and references to Cairo can be found in the impersonations of the character by Dom Deluise in *The Cheap Detective* (1978) and George Costigan in 'The Greek Interpreter', an episode of *The Adventures of Sherlock Holmes* (1985).

The majority of the remaining 'caricatures' reference the extra-filmic persona which is not anchored in specific roles. Again, horror iconography dominates the allusions made to Lorre. Examples such as the puppet, 'Yetch', in *Mad Monster Party* (1967), or the cartoon, 'Igor', in *The Electric Company* (1969) have helped to associate the actor with the role of the deranged sidekick to a Frankenstein-like mad scientist (a role famously played on-screen by Dwight Frye and Bela Lugosi, but never by Lorre).[8] Parodies of Lorre are also used to create a general sense of unease or danger, such as the use of Lorre in a campaign by the American Heart and Lung Association in which 'Lorre', making use of the actor's iconic prop, played the role of the cigarette. 'Caricatures' also quickly convey unsavoury or psychotic behaviour, such as the script direction in *Godspell* (1973) to deliver a line 'in the style of Peter Lorre'; or demonstrate the repugnance or grotesque nature of a particular character via voice or appearance, as in *Chip 'n' Dale Rescue Rangers* (1989) or *Count Duckula* (1988).

A survey of the caricatures which parody Lorre's extra-filmic persona also reveals that this type of image is especially prevalent within texts whose primary audiences are families or children. Out of the sixty-three caricatures recorded, at least thirty-six (57 per cent) were found in programmes that were specifically designed to be consumed by younger audiences and can be categorized as 'comic' in nature. Apart from the examples already mentioned, notable allusions made to Lorre include those made on the following American and British television programmes: *The Dick Tracy Show* (1961), *The Flintstones* (1964), *Stingray* (1964), *Fraggle Rock* (1983), *Transformers* (1984), *The Ren and Stimpy Show* (1990), *The Tick* (1994), *The Simpsons* (1998), and *Jackie Chan Adventures* (2002). The young age at which audiences were (and still are) subjected to references made to Lorre have helped to ensure the continuing presence within mainstream popular culture of the actor's extra-filmic persona, and build upon the connections between younger audiences, youth cultures and Lorre that began with his film roles of the 1950s and 1960s.

These brief sketches highlight both the transmedial career of Peter Lorre, and the manner in which the actor's horror-based public persona should primarily be defined as 'extra-filmic' through the way it was constructed and maintained away from the cinema screen. In many cases, especially within the platforms of radio and publicity material, their content paradoxically insists upon the close relationship between image and cinema. In doing so, they also implicitly suggest the need to identify and to separate the constituent elements that comprised Peter Lorre's career (and indeed, the different elements that work towards the creation of a 'Hollywood' career in general) in order to fully understand his value to his employers as a performer, distinct from his presence within popular culture.

Notes

1. For example: Harry Brand 1937; Ken Whitlow, undated, but circa 1940; Jay Chapman, undated, but circa 1941; Anonymous, Universal, 1942; Anonymous, Universal, 1946; Anonymous, Universal, 1955.
2. Lorre was represented by the William Morris Agency throughout the 1940s and also by the smaller Sam Jaffe Agency in the mid-1950s. He was also represented by Paul Kohner circa 1953.
3. Lorre was only optioned to appear in four horror films that failed to reach production. Source: King Hanson 1993a,b.
4. For an extended version of this discussion see Thomas 2008.
5. With the exception of *Mystery Playhouse No.5*, which was a repeat of his appearance on *Inner Sanctum*'s episode from 1944, 'Death is a Joker', Lorre never appeared within the main story.
6. Although elements associated with Price's persona are referenced in the role, such as the association between the actor and 'high culture'. See Heffernan 2004.
7. Lorre also guested as 'himself' on this broadcast, appearing once Frees had impersonated him.
8. Frye played 'Fritz' in *Frankenstein* (Dir. James Whale, Universal, 1931) and 'Karl' in *Bride of Frankenstein* (Dir. James Whale, Universal, 1935). Lugosi played 'Ygor' in *Son of Frankenstein* (Dir. Rowland V. Lee, Universal, 1935).

CONCLUSION

In his book, *Acting in the Cinema*, James Naremore (1988: 63) commented that 'Peter Lorre was roughly correct when he described the work of movie acting as "face-making"'. Whilst Naremore uses the phrase in a neutral and purely descriptive context to outline what he observes are the inherent physical and gestural qualities of screen acting, the agenda that lay behind Lorre's repeated application of the phrase was purposefully negative. The term revealed the actor's apparently disparaging views regarding his own career as Lorre publicly characterized certain examples of his own screen work as 'just' making faces. This statement was firmly directed at examples taken from his work in Hollywood – the implication being that Lorre performed to a higher standard away from the restrictions of this mainstream commercial industry. From this, one can deduce that Lorre believed that there was something lacking in both his own performative labour and the conditions of his employment within the Hollywood filmmaking industry, in comparison to his experiences in European cinema and theatre.

Lorre's own negative perspective has been shared by wider critical and evaluative discourses surrounding the actor and his work. As I have explored, the figure of Peter Lorre has been defined in a variety of ways which are reliant to a large degree upon devaluing or misunderstanding the bulk of his screen work: the insistence that he was typecast in a series of similarly limiting roles; the reductive approach which equates his film labour with his extra-filmic persona; the need to discover the 'reality' of the émigré artist behind the 'image' of the screen monster; the belief that his performance in *M* was never bettered, only parodied; or that he allowed Hollywood to waste his considerable talents in meagre supporting roles. These approaches construct Lorre as a tragic figure whose artistry was corrupted by an unforgiving commercial system of production.

I have argued throughout this book that this type of approach offers a limited acknowledgement of the potential complexities of screen performance and classical Hollywood employment practices. Lorre illustrates the full range of these complexities: the relationship between the Hollywood labour market (and Hollywood's relationship with European markets), different performative practices, the construction of star status and star personae, and modes of representation that surround public individuals and identities, both within divergent media forms and also wider cultural, ideological and economic concerns. An emphasis upon Lorre reveals a tightly defined and easily recognizable public persona which has been credited as 'typecasting' the actor as a 'monstrous other'. The reduction of Lorre to a consistent 'image type' is typical of the way in which filmmaking and cultural industries handle stars and other performers.

Typecasting and the clear demarcation of image and identity play highly functional roles. These functions can be explored from two perspectives: the cultural and the economic. It is the former that has been traditionally invoked in relation to Lorre, rigidly defining him as 'Lorre-the-émigré', and reading his public image as Hollywood's appropriation of European cultural and cinematic heritage for its own ideological ends. From this perspective, Lorre's recognizable persona constructs the actor in stereotypical terms, whereby 'Peter Lorre' immediately signifies the abnormal, the outsider, the 'Un-American'. He becomes representative of the figure 'who does not belong' – a discourse that has been foregrounded within more traditional studies of émigrés. The function of this Hollywood persona was (and is) highly malleable and useful within public and social discourses as it easily represents the 'grotesque other' – via Lorre – within American media forms.

However, concepts surrounding the perceived stability of cultural space, nation and 'belonging' are increasingly being questioned around the émigré figure, and Lorre illustrates many of these shifting boundaries with his difficult-to-place national identity, his integration within the studio system, his changing cultural associations, and his transnational and transmedial career (Bergfelder 2007b: 7). As such, he can be seen as emblematic of further critical discourse that considers the political economy of the actor within filmmaking contexts, particularly Hollywood economies. From this perspective, the concept of 'typecasting' remains hugely important. But rather than being explained only in terms of cultural stereotyping and how Hollywood (as a singular homogeneous cultural entity) might perpetuate particular dominant social images and relations, 'typecasting' is reconnected to its industrial function. In doing so, the specific nature of the public image or 'extra-filmic persona' becomes less significant, definitions of typecasting are altered, and different components of the 'Hollywood' industry are acknowledged.

As a system of production based around a labour market, the Hollywood filmmaking industry was (and is) reliant upon such strategies that seek to manage and delineate between individual labour and skill sets. Discourses which primarily define the relationship between industry and individual in terms of employers and employees recognize the need to develop consistent and marketable star personae, but discuss the position of the 'actor-as-employee' in markedly different terms than the sociological role they (and their image) might reflect. Here, typecasting becomes a necessary practice of the casting process that the majority of actors are subjected to, possibly even regardless of the cultural implications that they may convey (Robertson Wojcik 2003). The production and maintenance of a coherent identity (on the part of the actor) remains vitally important, not only as a means of conveying a certain social role, but also as a means of exercising and guaranteeing quality control within an immense pool of labour. A 'robust public identity' enables the 'multitalented' to be filtered out from the 'unskilled'; the former are employed and the latter are discarded as 'nonentities' (Zuckerman et al. 2003).

Furthermore, distinguishing between historical contexts (Hollywood during the studio system and afterwards) enables significant intricacies within labour management, typecasting, and risk investment in the industry to be acknowledged. Ezra W. Zuckerman (2005) argues that studio-era Hollywood illustrates the dichotomy between these factors: on the one hand, the studio system closely controlled actors' labour via long-term contracts, but this significant and relatively secure investment in human capital also allowed for experimentation and development in the way studios handled actors' engagements on-screen. Once this system began to disappear during the 1950s, the need for low-risk, short-term investment in actors' labour grew, as did an increased reliance upon typecasting and public image.

There is a close correlation between these economic and historical contexts and the development of Lorre's screen career. Different circumstances within his employment (within Hollywood and elsewhere, at specific studios and under certain producers or directors) impacted upon his film work and screen performances in a variety of ways, resulting in a body of work that was disparate and (within the context of mainstream cinema) often highly experimental. However, present throughout the majority of Lorre's Hollywood career is the constructed image of 'Peter Lorre', the monstrous and murderous extra-filmic persona. This image was highly marketable and profitable, and contributed immensely to Lorre's popularity and star status. It created a sense of coherence around the actor that disguised the absence of such continuity within his screen employment. The image was a construction of the heterogeneous entertainment industry based in and around Hollywood – not created on the cinema screen, not of one studio in particular, and not even limited to one media form. Instead Lorre's star persona illustrates the diversity of media forms and modes of representations within 'Hollywood' during the studio system. It also illustrates a central paradox of studio-era Hollywood: it was an inherently contradictory system that generated space for security, freedom and performative experimentation, but also maintained tight control over its investment in actors' labour via employee/employer relationships and in the way the industry incorporated and used other media outlets.

By its nature as a capitalist system, discourses within studio-era Hollywood where Lorre worked overplayed the role of the consumer and the product offered for consumption whilst downplaying the production process itself. This relationship can be clearly demonstrated through the manner in which the career of Peter Lorre was managed during his years as a Hollywood performer, most notably in the gap that existed between his screen work and his public image, and the subsequent insistence within Hollywood discourses that there was no such disparity. Throughout Lorre's Hollywood career, various promotional strategies on the part of numerous employers were in place which emphasized the homogeneity between the actor's work, image and history. This can also be discerned in the words of the actor himself, and whilst in private, Lorre may well have been a singularly disillusioned actor, his publicly released statements to that effect – including 'face-making' – equally conform to the remit of promotional discourses which constructed the actor as a 'known commodity' via his persona. It is this public representation of 'coherence' that has informed critical analyses of the actor.

During the course of this book I redefined Lorre's persona as one shaped via 'extra-filmic' means. Because of my overall focus upon the cinematic labour of the actor and his position within various filmmaking contexts, I have to some degree sidelined a more detailed exploration of this type of persona. However, it has not been my intention to dismiss Lorre's public image; instead I have concentrated on the ways in which an over-reliance upon it can impinge upon readings of screen labour and performance. The 'extra-filmic' nature of personae from the classical era, such as Lorre's, would merit further exploration – as images in their own right (away from film roles), and because of the manner in which performers' personae could be constructed through transmedial contexts. I have explored more thoroughly Lorre's work on American radio elsewhere, but a more general investigation into the details of the employment strategies behind, and the reception of, this form of broadcasting based around the performances of established Hollywood celebrities would be useful (Thomas 2008). It is also possible that a further consideration of the potential role played by the agent in the maintenance of the consistency of their clients' personae within the Hollywood studio system may be equally significant.

Despite these limitations, a sustained investigation into Lorre's position within the Hollywood production process enables the acknowledgement that important facets of actors' careers may be otherwise obscured by the dominance of their public identity. With specific regard to Lorre, we can observe a highly complex negotiation occurring between employee and employer in terms of casting practices, extra-filmic promotion and publicity, employment strategies, and transnational and transmedial careers – all of which had a significant impact upon screen performance itself. Rather than perceiving Lorre's career as severely compromised by an unforgiving Hollywood system that misused his talents – as Vincent Price does in the quotation which opened this book – there is much evidence available in the terms of Lorre's employment which suggests that the actor was treated with a substantial amount of respect by the various studios that he worked for throughout his career in terms of the wide variety of roles he was assigned and the acknowledgement of his performative skills through the preferential formal treatment afforded to him within his films. The studios' methods of publicizing Lorre were restrictive in their insistence upon the nature of Lorre's typecasting and public image, but the other conditions of his employment were far more flexible and allowed for (and perhaps even relied upon) a certain degree of experimentation. This form of employment was equally reliant upon the promotion of Lorre as typecast by his 'extra-filmic' persona because of the coherence this marketable identity gave to the actor's otherwise inconsistent career.

Lorre's screen performances demonstrate that even within less than ideal circumstances – such as his supporting status or his employment in low-budget or low-brow filmmaking – he consistently utilized complex performative techniques which belied the apparent simplicity of the roles themselves (albeit with varying results) and showed him to be a perceptive and flexible screen performer capable of significant creative agency, particularly within controlled systems of production. Within Lorre's career as a whole between Europe and Hollywood – from the 1920s to the 1960s – a persistent engagement with acting techniques can be discerned, which allowed him to either adapt to or challenge the environment in which he was working, and as such Lorre's own judgement of acting as just 'face-making' should be recognized as a highly inaccurate pronouncement on his own achievements.

The dismissal of film acting as little more than an extended opportunity for an actor to 'make faces' is a fundamental misunderstanding of the process of screen performance itself and also of the conditions which affect performance, such as formal filmic treatment or labour positions. Naremore may be correct in highlighting the overtly physical basis of screen acting, in which isolated images of performers using basic and easily recognizable gestures with specific cultural meanings are edited together to allow for a transparent mode of characterization, but a sustained overview of a film actor's career, such as Lorre's, also reveals that screen performance can be much more complex than this equation. Lorre's performances are more than a mere succession of 'correct' expressions determined to a large degree by an external controlling force – be it Fritz Lang, Bertolt Brecht, Warner Bros., or Lorre's own public image.

Instead it is more relevant to characterize the screen performances discussed here in light of a more precise understanding of their industrial and performative contexts, both in Hollywood and Germany. Lorre's individual performances are worth exploring in their wider contexts, partly because they are difficult to define according to one singular pattern – such as their apparent recycling of the actor's nefarious public image, or the reduction of Lorre's life to a series of simplistic oppositions between 'Europe' and 'Hollywood', 'artistic visions' and 'commercial pressures', and 'person' and 'persona'. A comprehensive understanding of Lorre's screen career reveals that studio-era film performances were not necessarily simplistic or transparent, and that a number of objectives lay behind them, and consequently, they lent themselves to a range of interpretations. Lorre's performances were constructed through the changing labour status occupied by the actor during his international career; and they utilized a pluralistic tone (often within the same film) which enabled a move between naturalistic and nonnaturalistic techniques within specific aesthetic frameworks, such as the naturalism conventionally practised within Hollywood. In doing so, they depicted the complex relationship created and controlled by the actor between themselves, their character and their audience; the purposeful employment of physical and vocal techniques in order to achieve this; and the collaborative nature of performance, between the needs of the individual actor, the remaining cast, the filmmakers, producers and the industry as a whole. Considering Lorre's transmedial and international career through an extended study which focuses on the actor as a central point of investigation not only illustrates the inconsistencies within screen performance, but also demonstrates its potential for complexity and mutability according to various determining factors – from transnational cultural identities, labour conditions and marketing strategies, through to theatrical experiences and theoretical or historical discourses.

BIBLIOGRAPHY

Abrams, Leslie H. 1988. 'Two Birds of a Feather: Hammett's and Huston's *The Maltese Falcon*'. *Literature/Film Quarterly* 16(2): 112–18.

Alley, Kenneth D. 1997. '*Passage to Marseille*: A Case of Unjust Neglect'. *Literature/Film Quarterly* 25(3): 198–203.

Anonymous. 1934. 'Review of *The Man Who Knew Too Much*'. *The Times* 10 December: 12.

Anonymous. 1935. 'Review of *The Man Who Knew Too Much*'. *Picturegoer* February: 24.

Anonymous. 1935. 'Review of *The Man Who Knew Too Much*'. *The Times* 27 April: 2.

Anonymous. 1935. 'Review of *Hands of Orlac* (Mad Love)'. *The Times* 5 August: 8.

Anonymous. 1935. 'Peter Lorre, Tactician'. *New York Times* 3 November: 5.

Anonymous. 1935. 'Review of *The Man Who Knew Too Much*'. *Monthly Film Bulletin* 1(12): 116.

Anonymous. 1935. 'Review of *Hands of Orlac* (Mad Love)'. *Monthly Film Bulletin* 2(19): 103.

Anonymous. 1935. 'Review of *Crime and Punishment*'. *Monthly Film Bulletin* 2(23): 193.

Anonymous. 1936. 'Review of *Crime and Punishment*'. *The Times* 16 March: 10.

Anonymous. 1936. 'Review of *Crime and Punishment*'. *Film Pictorial* 9 May: 5.

Anonymous. 1937. 'Review of *Crack Up*'. *Monthly Film Bulletin* 4(38): 33.

Anonymous. 1937. 'Review of *Nancy Steele is Missing*'. *Film Weekly* 19(455): 29.

Anonymous. 1937. 'Review of *Nancy Steele is Missing*'. *Monthly Film Bulletin* 4(40).

Anonymous. 1937. 'Review of *Lancer Spy*'. *Monthly Film Bulletin* 4(47).

Anonymous. 1937. 'Review of *Crack Up*'. *The Times* 1 March: 12.

Anonymous. 1938. 'Review of *Lancer Spy*'. *The Times* 21 February: 12.

Anonymous. 1938. 'Review of *Thank You Mr Moto*'. *Monthly Film Bulletin* 5(49): 19.

Anonymous. 1938. 'Review of *Mr Moto Takes a Chance*'. *Monthly Film Bulletin* 5(50): 42.

Anonymous. 1938. 'Review of *I'll Give a Million*'. *Monthly Film Bulletin* 5(56).

Anonymous. 1938. 'Review of *Mysterious Mr Moto*'. *Monthly Film Bulletin* 5(57): 222.

Anonymous. 1938. 'Review of *Thank You Mr Moto'*. *The Times* 18 July: 10.

Anonymous. 1939. 'Review of *Think Fast Mr Moto'*. *The Times* 13 February: 10.

Anonymous. 1940. 'The New Pictures'. *Time Magazine* 2 December.

Anonymous. 1941. 'Review of *The Face Behind the Mask'*. *Monthly Film Bulletin* 8(90): 68.

Anonymous. 1941. 'Review of *You'll Find Out'*. *Monthly Film Bulletin* 8(86): 20.

Anonymous. 1941. 'Review of *Mr District Attorney'*. *Monthly Film Bulletin* 8(93): 118.

Anonymous. 1964. 'Obituary: Peter Lorre'. *New York Times* 24 March: 35.

Anonymous. 1985. 'Review of *Mad Love'*. *The Listener* 114(2930.10): 31.

Arnold, Edward. 1998. 'Lorenzo Goes to Hollywood', in B. Cardullo et al. (eds), *Playing to the Camera*. New Haven and London: Yale University Press: 74–78.

Astor, Mary. 1998. 'A Life on Film', in B. Cardullo et al. (eds), *Playing to the Camera*. New Haven and London: Yale University Press: 185–89.

Austin, Thomas and Martin Barker (eds). 2003. *Contemporary Hollywood Stardom*. London: Arnold.

Barefoot, Guy. 2001. *Gaslight Melodrama: From Victorian London to 1940s Hollywood*. New York and London: Continuum.

Baron, Cynthia. 1999. 'Crafting Film Performances: Acting in the Hollywood Studio Era', in A. Lovell and P. Krämer (eds), *Screen Acting*. London and New York: Routledge: 31–45.

—— 2004. 'Suiting up for Performance in John Woo's *The Killer'*, in C. Baron, D. Carson and F.P. Tomasulo (eds), *More than a Method: Trends and Traditions in Contemporary Film Performance*. Detroit: Wayne State University Press: 297–330.

Baron, Cynthia and Sharon Marie Carnicke. 2008. *Reframing Screen Performance*. University of Michigan Press.

Baron, Cynthia and Diane Carson. 2006. 'Analysing Performance and Meaning in Film'. *Journal of Film and Video* 58(1–2): 3–6.

Baron, Cynthia, Diane Carson and Frank P. Tomasulo (eds). 2004. *More Than a Method: Trends and Traditions in Contemporary Film Performance*. Detroit: Wayne State University Press.

Barrios, Richard. 2003. *Screened Out: Playing Gay in Hollywood from Edison to Stonewall*. London and New York: Routledge.

Beck, Calvin Thomas. 1975. *Heroes of the Horrors*. New York and London: Collier Books.

Beck, Jerry and Will Friedwald. 1989. *Looney Tunes and Merrie Melodies: A Complete Illustrated Guide to the Warner Bros. Cartoons*. New York: Henry Holt.

Behlmer, Rudy. 1985. *Inside Warner Bros. 1935–1951*. New York: Simon & Schuster.

Beltzer, Thomas. 2004. '*Crime and Punishment*: A Neglected Classic', *Senses of Cinema*.

Benaquist, Lawrence. 1982. 'Function and Index in Huston's *The Maltese Falcon'*. *Film Criticism* 6(2): 45–50.

Benjamin, Walter. 1973. *Understanding Brecht* (translated by Anna Bostock). London: NLB.

Bennett, Charles. 1978. 'Peter Lorre,' in D. Peary (ed.), *Close-Ups*. New York: Workman: 334–35.

Bentley, Eric. 1981. *The Brecht Commentaries*. New York: Grove.

Bentley, Eric (ed.). 1968. *The Theory of the Modern Stage*. London and New York: Penguin Books (Third Edition 1990).

Berenstein, Rhona. 2002. 'Horror for Sale: The Marketing and Reception of Classic Horror Cinema', in M. Jancovich (ed.), *The Horror Film Reader*. London and New York: Routledge: 137–49.

Berg, Gretchen. Originally published 1965. Reprinted in 2003. 'The Viennese Night: A Fritz Lang Confession', in B.K. Grant (ed.), *Fritz Lang: Interviews*. Jackson: University of Mississippi Press: 50–80.

Bergfelder, Tim. 2007a. 'German Cinema and Film Noir', in A. Spicer (ed.), *European Film Noir*. Manchester and New York: Manchester University Press: 138–63.

———— 2007b. '"Introduction: German-speaking Émigrés and British Cinema 1925–1950: Cultural Exchange, Exile and the Boundaries of National Cinema" Destination London', in T. Bergfelder and C. Cargnelli (eds), *Destination London: German-speaking Émigrés and British Cinema 1925–1950*. New York and Oxford: Berghahn Books: 1–23.

Bergfelder, Tim and Christian Cargnelli (eds). 2007. *Destination London: German-speaking Émigres and British Cinema 1925–1950*. New York and Oxford: Berghahn Books.

Beyer, Friedeman. 1988. *Peter Lorre: Seine Filme – sein Leben*. Munich: Heyne Verlag.

Birdwell, Michael E. 1999. *Celluloid Soldiers: Warner Bros.' Campaign against Nazism*. New York and London: New York University Press.

Biskind, Peter. 1984. *Seeing Is Believing: How Hollywood Taught Us to Stop Worrying and Love the Fifties*. London: Pluto Press.

Blatner, Adam. 1997. *Acting-In: Practical Applications of Psychodramatic Methods*. London: Free Association Books.

Bodroghkozy, Aniko. 2002. 'Reel Revolutionaries: An Examination of Hollywood's Cycle of 1960s Youth Rebellion Films'. *Cinema Journal* 41(3): 38–58.

Bogdanovich, Peter. 1997. *Who the Devil Made It: Conversations with Legendary Filmmakers*. New York: Alfred A. Knopf.

Brecht, Bertolt. 1968. 'On Experimental Theatre' (translated by John Willet), in E. Bentley (ed.), *The Theory of the Modern Stage*. London and New York: Penguin: 97–108.

———— 1931. 'The Question of Criteria for Judging Acting' (Originally published 8 March 1931), reprinted in J. Willet and R. Manheim (eds), 1979, *Bertolt Brecht: Collected Plays Vol. II Part I*. London: Eyre Methuen: 104–7.

———— 1970. 'Der Sumpf'/'The Swamp', in J. Willet and R. Manheim (eds), 1979, *Bertolt Brecht: Poems*. New York: Methuen: 418.

——— 1991. 'Short Description of a New Technique of Acting Which Produces an Alienation Effect', in J.G. Butler (ed.), *Star Texts*. Detroit: Wayne State University Press: 66–79.

Britton, Andrew. 1991. 'Stars and Genre', in C. Gledhill (ed.), *Stardom: Industry of Desire*. London and New York: Routledge: 198–206.

Brown, Krista A. 2006. 'The Troll Among Us', in P. Powrie and R. Stilwell (eds), *Changing Tunes*. London and Burlington, VT: Ashgate: 74–87.

Buchanan, Barbara J. 1935. 'Peter Lorre Talks about Real and Unreal Horror'. *Film Weekly* 14 December: 10.

Butler, Jeremy G. (ed.). 1991. *Star Texts*. Detroit: Wayne State University Press.

Cardullo, Bert, Harry Geduld, Ronald Gottesman and Leigh Woods (eds). 1998. *Playing to the Camera: Film Actors Discuss Their Craft*. New Haven and London: Yale University Press.

Carnicke, Sharon Marie. 1999. 'Lee Strasberg's Paradox of the Actor', in A. Lovell and P. Krämer (eds), *Screen Acting*. London and New York: Routledge: 75–87.

——— 2004. 'Screen Performance and Directors' Visions', in C. Baron, D. Carson and F. Tomasulo (eds), *More Than a Method: Trends and Traditions in Contemporary Film Performance*. Detroit: Wayne State University Press: 42–67.

——— 2006. 'The Material Poetry of Acting: "Objects of Attention", Performance Style and Gender'. *The Shining* and *Eyes Wide Shut*. *Journal of Film and Video* 58(1–2): 21–30.

Carson, Diane. 2004. 'Plain and Simple: Masculinity through John Sayles's Lens', in C. Baron, D. Carson and F. Tomasulo (eds), *More Than a Method: Trends and Traditions in Contemporary Film Performance*. Detroit: Wayne State University Press: 173–90.

Caspar, Drew. 2007. *Postwar Hollywood 1942–1962*. Malden: Blackwell.

Chamberlain, Dorothy and Robert Wilson (eds). 1997. *In the Spirit of Jazz: The Otis Ferguson Reader*. New York: Da Capo Press.

Chan, Anthony B. 2001. '"Yellowface": The Racial Branding of the Chinese in American Theatre or Media'. *Asian Profile* 29(2): 159–77.

Chung, Hye Seung. 2006. *Hollywood Asian: Philip Ahn and the Politics of Cross-Asian Performance*. Philadelphia: Temple University Press.

Clark, Danae. 1995. *Negotiating Hollywood: The Cultural Politics of Actors' Labor*. Minneapolis and London: University of Minnesota Press.

——— 2004. 'The Subject of Acting', in L. Fischer and M. Landy (eds), *Stars: The Film Reader*. New York and London: Routledge: 13–29.

Collins, Cindy Ruth. 1999. '*The Man Who Knew Too Much*', in G. Svehla and S. Svehla (eds), *Peter Lorre*. Baltimore: Midnight Marquee Press: 30–37.

Combs, Richard. 1985. 'German Hollywood'. *The Listener* 10 October: 31.

Cooke, Alistair (ed.). 1971. *Garbo and the Night Watchmen*. London: Secker & Warburg.

Corman, Roger (with Jim Jerome). 1990. *How I Made a Hundred Movies in Hollywood and Never Lost a Dime*. London: Muller.

Courtney, Richard. 1973. 'Theatre and Spontaneity'. *The Journal of Aesthetics and Art Criticism*: 79–88.

Crafton, Donald. 1998. 'The View from Termite Terrace: Caricature and Parody in Warner Bros. Animation', in K.S. Sandler (ed.), *Reading the Rabbit: Explorations in Warner Brothers Animation*. New Brunswick, New Jersey and London: Rutgers University Press: 121–36.

Cronyn, Hume. 1998. 'Notes on Film Acting', in B. Cardullo et al. (eds), *Playing to the Camera*. New Haven and London: Yale University Press: 193–200.

Crowther, Bosley. 1938. 'Mysterious Mr Moto of Devil's Island'. *New York Times* 19 September: 16.

Dalle Vacche, Angela. 1990. 'Representation, Spectacle, Performance in Bernardo Bertolucci's *The Conformist*', in C. Zucker (ed.), *Making Visible the Invisible*. New Jersey and London: The Scarecrow Press: 391–413.

Davies, Bette. 1998. 'The Actress Plays Her Part', in B. Cardullo et al. (eds), *Playing to the Camera*. New Haven and London: Yale University Press: 177–85.

DeCordova, Richard. 1986 (1995). 'Genre and Performance', in B.K. Grant (ed.), *Film Genre Reader II*. Austin: University of Texas Press: 129–39.

———— 1990. *Picture Personalities: The Emergence of the Star System in America*. Chicago: University of Illinois Press.

———— 1991. 'The Emergence of the Star System in America', in C. Gledhill (ed.), *Stardom: Industry of Desire*. London and New York: Routledge: 17–29.

Denzin, Norman K. 1995. *The Cinematic Society: The Voyeur's Gaze*. London, Thousand Oaks, and New Delhi: Sage.

Dick, Bernard F. (ed.). 1992a. *Columbia Pictures: Portrait of a Studio*. Lexington: University Press of Kentucky.

———— 1992b. 'The History of Columbia: From the Brothers Cohn to Sony Corp', in B.F. Dick (ed.), *Columbia Pictures: Portrait of a Studio*. Lexington: The University Press of Kentucky: 2–65.

Di Franco, J. Phillip (ed.). 1979. *The Movie World of Roger Corman*. New York and London: Chelsea House.

Doherty, Brigid. 2000. 'Test and Gestus in Brecht and Benjamin'. *MLN* 115(3): 442–48.

Doherty, Thomas. 1993. *Projections of War*. New York: Columbia University Press.

———— 1997. 'The Elusive Factoid: World War II Motivation at Warner Bros.?' *Film and History* 27(1–4): 120–22.

———— 2002. *Teenagers and Teenpics: The Juvenilization of American Movies in the 1950s*. Philadelphia: Temple University Press.

Douglas, Susan J. 1999 (2004). *Listening In: Radio and the American Imagination*. Minneapolis and London: University of Minnesota Press.

Drake, Philip. 2006. 'Reconceptualising Screen Performance'. *Journal of Film and Video* 58(1–2): 84–94.

Dyer, Peter John. 1964. 'Fugitive from Murder'. *Sight and Sound* 33: 125–27, 156.

Dyer, Richard. 1979 (1998). *Stars* (New Edition with supplementary chapter by Paul McDonald). London: BFI.

—— 1980. 'Stereotyping', in R. Dyer (ed.), *Gays on Film*. London: BFI: 27–39.

—— 1982 (1991). '*A Star Is Born* and the Construction of Authenticity', in C. Gledhill (ed.), 1991, *Stardom: Industry of Desire*. London and New York: Routledge: 132–40.

—— 1986. *Heavenly Bodies: Film Stars and Society*. London and New York: St Martin's Press.

—— 1993. *The Matter of Images: Essays on Representation*. London and New York: Routledge.

Dyer, Richard (ed.). 1980. *Gays on Film*. London: BFI.

Dyer MacCann, Richard. 1962. *Hollywood in Transition*. Boston: Houghton Mifflin Company.

Eddershaw, Margaret. 1996. *Performing Brecht*. London and New York: Routledge.

Eisner, Lotte. 1969. *The Haunted Screen*. Berkeley, Los Angeles: University of California Press.

—— 1976. *Fritz Lang*. London: Secker and Warburg.

Elhaney, Joe M.C. 2006. 'Howard Hawks: American Gesture'. *Journal of Film and Video* 58(1–2): 31–45.

Ellis, John. 1991. 'Stars as a Cinematic Phenomenon', in J.G. Butler (ed.), *Star Texts*. Detroit: Wayne State University Press: 300–15.

Elsaesser, Thomas. 2000. *Weimar Cinema and After: Germany's Historical Imaginary*. London and New York: Routledge.

Erens, Patrica. 1980. 'Between Two Worlds: Jewish Images in American Film', in R.M. Miller (ed.), *The Kaleidoscopic Lens*. Englewood, NJ: Jerome S. Ozer: 114–34.

Ewen, Frederic. 1970. *Bertolt Brecht: His Life, His Art, His Times*. London: Calder & Boyars.

Eyles, Allen. 1964. '*The Maltese Falcon*'. *Films and Filming* 11(2): 45–50.

Falsetto, Mario. 1990. 'The Mad and the Beautiful: A Look at Two Performances in the Films of Stanley Kubrick', in C. Zucker (ed.), *Making Visible the Invisible*. New Jersey and London: The Scarecrow Press: 325–64.

Ferguson, Otis. 1936 (1997). 'Hollywood's Gift to Broadway', in D. Chamberlain and R. Wilson (eds), 1997, *In The Spirit of Jazz*. New York: Da Capo Press: 146–50.

—— 1936 (1971). 'Wings Over Nothing', in A. Cooke (ed.), 1971, *Garbo and the Night Watchmen*. London: Secker & Warburg: 209–12.

Fischer, Dennis. 1999. '*The Mask of Dimitrios*', in G. Svehla and S. Svehla (eds), *Peter Lorre*. Baltimore: Midnight Marquee Press: 170–79.

Fischer, Lucy and Marcia Landy (eds). 2004. *Stars: The Film Reader*. New York and London: Routledge.

Fonda, Henry. Originally published 1966. Reprinted in 1998. 'Reflections on Forty Years of Make-Believe', in B. Cardullo et al. (eds), 1998, *Playing to the Camera*. New Haven and London: Yale University Press: 210–19.

Fraenkel, Heinrich. 1938. 'Pop-Eyed Villain'. *Film Weekly* 20(514): 30.

French, Philip. 1969. *The Movie Moguls*. London: Penguin.

Friedman, Lester (ed.). 1991. *Unspeakable Images: Ethnicity and the American Cinema*. Urbana: University of Illinois Press.

Friedrich, Otto. 1986. *City of Nets: A Portrait of Hollywood in the 1940s*. London: Headline.

Frischauer, Willi. 1953. 'Mr Murder'. *Picturegoer* 30 May: 9.

Fuegi, John. 1987. *Bertolt Brecht: Chaos According to Plan*. Cambridge and New York: Cambridge University Press.

Fujiwara, Chris. 2004. 'You Despise Me, Don't You? Peter Lorre at the Harvard Film Archive'. *Boston Phoenix*.

Gale, Stephen H. 1996. 'The Maltese Falcon: Melodrama or Film Noir?' *Literature/Film Quarterly* 24(2): 145–47.

Garncarz, Joseph. 2006. 'The Ultimate Irony: Jews Playing Nazis in Hollywood', in A. Phillips and G. Vincendeau (eds), *Journeys of Desire: European Actors in Hollywood*. London: BFI: 103–14.

Garnham, Nicholas. 1968. *'M': A Film by Fritz Lang*. New York: Simon and Schuster.

Gemünden, Gerd. 2003. 'From "Mr M" to "Mr Murder": Peter Lorre and the Actor in Exile', in R. Halle and M. McCarthy (eds), *Light Motives*. Detroit: Wayne State University Press: 85–107.

George, Manfred. 1951. 'Peter Lorre Returns to the German Cinema'. *New York Times* 23 September: 113.

Geraghty, Christine. 2000. 'Re-examining Stardom: Questions of Texts, Bodies and Performance', in C. Gledhill and L. Williams (eds), *Reinventing Film Studies*. London: Arnold: 183–201.

Gledhill, Christine (ed.). 1991. *Stardom: Industry of Desire*. London and New York: Routledge.

Gledhill, Christine and Linda Williams (eds). 2000. *Reinventing Film Studies*. London: Arnold.

Gomery, Douglas. 1980. 'Economic Struggle and Hollywood Imperialism: Europe Converts to Sound'. *Yale French Studies* (60): 80–93.

——— 2005. *The Hollywood Studio System: A History*. London: BFI.

Gordon, Robert. 2006. *The Purpose of Playing: Modern Acting Theories in Perspective*. Ann Arbour: University of Michigan Press.

Gow, Gordon. 1973. '16mm: *Der Verlorene*'. *Films and Filming* 20(2): 69–70.

Grant, Barry Keith (ed.). 1986 (1995). *Film Genre Reader II* (Revised Edition). Austin: University of Texas Press.

——— 2003. *Fritz Lang: Interviews*. Jackson: University Press of Mississippi.

Greene, Graham. 1935 (1995). Review: '*The Hands of Orlac*', in D. Parkinson (ed.), 1995, *Mornings in the Dark*. London and New York: Penguin: 16.

——— 1936 (1995). 'The Genius of Peter Lorre', in D. Parkinson (ed.), 1995, *Mornings in the Dark*. London and New York: Penguin Books: 403–4.

——— 1936 (1995). '*Crime and Punishment*', in D. Parkinson (ed.), 1995, *Mornings in the Dark*. London and New York: Penguin Books: 85.

Gunning, Tom. 2000. *The Films of Fritz Lang: Allegories of Vision and Modernity*. London: BFI.

Hadley Garcia, George. 1983. 'The Mysterious Peter Lorre'. *Hollywood Studio Magazine* 16(9): 18–19.

Halle, Randall and Margaret McCarthy (eds). 2003. *Light Motives: German Popular Film in Perspective*. Detroit: Wayne State University Press.

Hand, Richard J. 2006. *Terror on the Air! Horror Radio in America 1931–1952*. Jefferson, NC and London: McFarland.

Hantke, Steffen (ed.). 2007. *Caligari's Heirs: The German Cinema of Fear After 1945*. Lanham, MD: Scarecrow Press.

Harmetz, Aljean. 1993. *Round Up the Usual Suspects: The Making of Casablanca – Bogart, Bergman and World War II*. London: Weidenfeld & Nicolson.

Hart, Henry. Originally published in 1956. Reprinted in 2003. 'Fritz Lang Today', in B.K. Grant (ed.), 2003, *Fritz Lang: Interviews*. Jackson: University of Mississippi Press: 13–15.

Hayman, Ronald. 1969. *Techniques of Acting*. London: Methuen.

———— 1983. *Brecht: A Biography*. Oxford and New York: Oxford University Press.

Heffernan, Kevin. 2004. *Ghouls, Gimmicks and Gold: Horror Films and the American Movie Business 1953–1968*. Durham and London: Duke University Press.

Higson, Andrew. 1991. 'Film Acting and Independent Cinema', in J.G. Butler (ed.), *Star Texts*. Detroit: Wayne State University Press: 155–81.

Higson, Andrew and Richard Maltby (eds). 1999. *Film Europe and Film America: Cinema, Commerce and Cutural Exchange 1920–1939*. Exeter: University of Exeter Press.

Hilmes, Michele. 1999. *Hollywood and Broadcasting: From Radio to Cable*. Chicago: University of Illinois Press.

———— 2001. *Only Connect: A Cultural History of Broadcasting in the United States*. Belmont, CA: Wadsworth.

Hilmes, Michele and Jason Loviglio (eds). 2002. *Radio Reader: Essays in the Cultural History of Radio*. New York: Routledge.

Hirschhorn, Clive. 1979. *The Warner Bros. Story*. London: Octopus.

Hoberman, J. 2005. 'Strange Bird'. *Film Comment* 41(6): 40–41.

Hollinger, Karen. 2006. *The Actress: Hollywood Acting and the Female Star*. New York and London: Routledge.

Horak, Jan-Christopher. 2005. 'Sauerkraut & Sausages with a Little Goulash: Germans in Hollywood, 1927'. *Film History* 17(1–2): 241–60.

Ito, Robert B. 1997. 'A Certain Slant: A Brief History of Hollywood Yellowface'. *Bright Lights Film Journal* 18.

Izod, John. 1988. *Hollywood and the Box Office: 1885–1986*. London: Macmillan Press.

Jancovich, Mark. 1996. *Rational Fears: American Horror in the 1950s*. Manchester and New York: Manchester University Press.

Jancovich, Mark (ed.). 2002. *The Horror Film Reader*. London and New York: Routledge.

Jarvie, Ian C. 1991. 'Stars and Ethnicity: Hollywood and the United States, 1932–51', in L. Friedman (ed.), *Unspeakable Images: Ethnicity and the American Cinema*. Urbana: University of Illinois Press: 82–111.

Jelinek, Elfriede. 2005. 'The Joker' (translated by P.J. Blumenthal). *Film Comment* 41(6): 38–39.

Jewell, Robert B. 1984. 'Hollywood and Radio: Competition and Partnership in the 1930s'. *Historical Journal of Film, Radio and Television* 4(2): 125–41.

Kael, Pauline. 1974. *The Citizen Kane Book*. New York: Bantam Books.

Kaes, Anton. 2000. *M*. London: BFI.

Kapczynski, Jennifer M. 2003. 'Homeward Bound: Peter Lorre's *The Lost Man* and the End of Exile'. *New German Critique* 89: 145–71.

Kawin, Bruce. 1986 (1995). 'Children of the Light', in B.K. Grant (ed.), *Film Genre Reader II*. Austin: University of Texas: 308–29.

Keane, Marian. 1990. 'The Great Profile: How Do We Know the Actor from the Acting?', in C. Zucker (ed.), *Making Visible the Invisible*. Metuchen, NJ and London: The Scarecrow Press: 167–97.

———— 1993. 'Dyer Straits: Theoretical Issues in Studies of Film Acting'. *Post Script* 12(2): 29–39.

Kerr, Paul (ed.). 1986. *The Hollywood Film Industry*. London and New York: Routledge and Kegan Paul.

Keser, Robert. 2007, '*Der Verlorene*'. *Senses of Cinema* 45.

Kiebuzunska, Christine. 1988. *Revolutionaries in the Theater: Meyerhold, Brecht and Witkiewicz*. Ann Arbour: UMI Research Press.

King, Barry. 1985. 'Articulating Stardom'. *Screen* 26(5): 27–50.

———— 1986. 'Stardom as an Occupation', in P. Kerr (ed.), *The Hollywood Film Industry*. London and New York: Routledge: 154–84.

———— 1987. 'The Star and the Commodity: Notes Towards a Performance Theory of Stardom'. *Cultural Studies* 1(2): 145–61.

King Hanson, Patricia (Executive Editor). 1993a. *American Film Institute Catalog: Feature Films 1931–1940*. Berkeley, Los Angeles and Oxford: University of California Press.

———— 1993b. *American Film Institute Catalog: Feature Films 1941–1950*. Berkeley, Los Angeles and Oxford: University of California Press.

Kiss, Robert J. 2006. 'Peter Lorre', in A. Phillips and G. Vincendeau (eds), *Journeys of Desire*. London: BFI: 343.

Koepnick, Lutz. 2002. *The Dark Mirror: German Cinema between Hitler and Hollywood*. Berkeley, Los Angeles and London: University of California Press.

Koppes, Clayton R. and Gregory D. Black. 1997. *Hollywood Goes to War*. New York and London: Macmillan.

Kozloff, Sarah. 2000. *Overhearing Film Dialogue*. Berkeley: University of California Press.

Kracauer, Siegfried. 1947. *From Caligari to Hitler*. London: Denis Dobson Ltd.

Krutnik, Frank. 1991. *In a Lonely Street: Film Noir, Genre, Masculinity*. London and New York: Routledge.

Kuhns, David F. 1997. *German Expressionist Theatre*. Cambridge: Cambridge University Press.

Kuleshov, Lev. 1974. *Kuleshov on Film: Writings by Lev Kuleshov* (translated and edited by Ronald Levaco). Berkeley, Los Angeles and London: University of California Press.

―――― 1991. 'The Training of the Actor', in J.G. Butler (ed.), *Star Texts*. Detroit: Wayne State University Press: 51–65.

Larue, Johanne and Carole Zucker. 1990. 'James Dean: The Pose of Reality? *East of Eden* and the Method Performance', in C. Zucker (ed.), *Making Visible the Invisible*. New Jersey and London: The Scarecrow Press: 295–324

Lev, Peter. 2000. *The Fifties: Transforming the Screen 1950–1959*. New York: Scribners.

Levin, Meyer. 1935 (1971). '*Crime and Punishment*' in A. Cooke (ed.), 1971, *Garbo and the Night Watchmen*. London: Secker & Warburg: 97–102.

Lovell, Alan. 2003. 'I Went in Search of Deborah Kerr, Jodie Foster, and Julianne Moore but got Waylaid', in T. Austin and M. Barker (eds), *Contemporary Hollywood Stardom*. London: Arnold: 259–70.

Lovell, Alan and Peter Krämer (eds). 1999. *Screen Acting*. London and New York: Routledge.

Loviglio, Jason. 2004. 'Radio in Wartime: The Politics of Propaganda, Race and the American Way in the Second World War'. *American Quarterly* 56(4): 1079–87.

Luft, Herbert G. 1960. 'Peter Lorre: Began his Film Career as a Psychopath and May End it as a Clown'. *Films in Review* 11(5): 278–84.

Lyon, James K. 1980. *Bertolt Brecht in America*. Princeton: Princeton University Press.

MacDonald, J. Fred. 1979. *Don't Touch That Dial! Radio Programming in American Life from 1920 to 1960*. Chicago: Nelson-Hall.

MacDougall, Robert. 1999. 'Red, Brown and Yellow Perils: Images of the American Enemy in the 1940s and 1950s'. *Journal of Popular Culture* 32(4): 59–75.

MacNab, Geoffrey. 2000. *Searching For Stars: Rethinking British Cinema*. London and New York: Cassell.

―――― 2006. 'Sympathy for the Devil'. *The Independent* 21 April: 10–11.

Magarshack, David. 1968 (1990). 'Stanislavsky', in E. Bentley (ed.), *The Theory of the Modern Stage*. London and New York: Penguin: 219–74.

Maltby, Richard. 2003. *Hollywood Cinema* (Second Edition). Malden, MA: Blackwell.

Marchetti, Gina. 1995. *Romance and The Yellow Peril: Race, Sex and Discursive Strategies on Hollywood Film*. Berkeley: University of California Press.

Marineau, Rene F. 1989. *Jacob Levy Moreno: 1889–1974*. Tavistock, London and New York: Routledge.

Maxwell, James. 1989. *'La Belle Dame Sans Merci* and the Neurotic Knight: Characterisation in *The Maltese Falcon'. Literature/Film Quarterly* 17(4): 253–60.

Mayer, David. 1999. 'Acting in Silent Film: Which Legacy of the Theatre?', in A. Lovell and P. Krämer (eds), *Screen Acting*. London and New York: Routledge: 10–30.

McCullough, Christopher. 2004. 'Peter Lorre (and his Friend Bert Brecht): *Entfremdung* in Hollywood?', in J. Milling and M. Banham (eds), *Extraordinary Actors*. Exeter: University of Exeter: 164–75.

McDonald, Paul. 1998. 'Supplementary Chapter: Reconceptualising Stardom', in R. Dyer, *Stars*. London: BFI: 175–200.

——— 2000. *The Star System: Hollywood and the Production of Popular Identities*. London: Wallflower.

——— 2004. 'Why Study Film Acting? Some Opening Reflections', in C. Baron, D. Carson and F. Tomasulo (eds), *More than a Method: Trends and Traditions in Contemporary Film Performance*. Detroit: Wayne State University Press: 23–41.

McGee, Mark Thomas. 1984. *Fast and Furious: The Story of American International Pictures*. Jefferson, North Carolina and London: McFarland.

McGilligan, Patrick. 1997. *Fritz Lang: The Nature of the Beast*. New York and London: Faber and Faber.

McLean, Adrienne. 1992. '"I'm a Cansino": Transformation, Ethnicity and Authenticity in the Construction of Rita Hayworth, American Love Goddess'. *Journal of Film and Video* 44(3–4): 8–26

——— 2003. '"New Films in Story Form": Movie Story Magazines and Spectatorship'. *Cinema Journal* 42(3): 3–26.

——— 2004. *Being Rita Hayworth: Labour, Identity and Hollywood Stardom*. New Brunswick, New Jersey and London: Rutgers University Press.

McTeague, James. 1994. *Playwrights and Acting: Acting Methodologies for Brecht, Ionesco, Pinter and Shephard*. Westport, Connecticut and London: Greenwood Press.

Meyer-Dinkgräfe, Daniel. 2001. *Approaches to Acting*. London and New York: Continuum.

Miller, Don. 1973. *'B' Movies*. New York: Curtis Books.

Miller, R.M. (ed.). 1980. *The Kaleidoscopic Lens: How Hollywood Views Ethnic Groups*. Englewood, NJ: Jerome S Ozer.

Milling, Jane and Martin Banham (eds). 2004. *Extraordinary Actors: Essays on Popular Performers*. Exeter: University of Exeter Press.

Mitter, Shomit. 1992. *Systems of Rehearsal: Stanislavsky, Brecht, Grotowski and Brook*. London and New York: Routledge.

Moon, Krystyn R. 2005. *Yellowface: Creating the Chinese in American Popular Music and Performance 1850s–1920s*. New Brunswick, NJ: Rutgers University Press.

Moreno, Jacob Levi. 1946. *Psychodrama*. Vols. 1&2. Beacon, New York: Beacon House.

—— 1947 (Third Edition 1983). *The Theatre of Spontaneity*. Beacon, New York: Beacon House.

—— 1951. *Sociometry, Experimental Method and the Science of Society: An Approach to a New Political Orientation*. Beacon, New York: Beacon House.

Moreno, Joseph. 2006. 'The Deeds of My Father, William L. Moreno'. *British Journal of Psychodrama and Sociodrama* 21(1): 37–45.

Morin, Edgar. 1960. *The Stars* (translated by Richard Howard). London: John Calder; and New York: Grove Press.

Morris, Gary. 1993. 'Beyond the Beach: Social and Formal Aspects of AIP's Beach Party Movies'. *Journal of Popular Film and Television* 6(1): 2–11.

Morrison, James. 1998. *Passport to Hollywood*. New York: State University of New York Press.

Naremore, James. 1988. *Acting in the Cinema*. Berkeley, Los Angeles and New York: University of California Press.

—— 1998. *More than Night: Film Noir in its Contexts*. Berkeley, Los Angeles and London: University of California Press.

Negra, Diane. 2001. 'Immigrant Stardom in Imperial America: Pola Negri and the Problem of Typology'. *Camera Obscura* 16(3): 159–95.

Newham, John K. 1937. 'Comedy Menace: A Portrait of Peter Lorre'. *Film Weekly* 19(455), 3 July: 14.

Nga, Thi Thanh. 1995. 'The Long March from Wong to Woo: Asians in Hollywood'. *Cineaste* 21(4): 38–40.

Omasta, Michael, Brigitte Mayer and Elisabeth Streit. 2004. *Peter Lorre: Ein Fremder im Paradies*. Vienna: Paul Zsolnay.

Orgeron, Marsha. 2003. 'Making *It* in Hollywood: Clara Bow, Fandom and Consumer Culture'. *Cinema Journal* 42(4): 76–97.

Ormrod, Joan. (2002). 'Issues of Gender in *Muscle Beach Party*'. *Scope* Online Journal.

Ottinger, Ulrike. 2000. 'Peter Lorre: *Der Verlorene*', in European Coordination of Film Festivals (ed.), 15 by 15, The European Film Heritage, Brussels.

Parkinson, David. 1995. *Mornings in the Dark: The Graham Greene Film Reader*. London and New York: Penguin Books.

Patterson, Michael. 1981. *The Revolution in German Theatre 1900–1933*. Boston, London and Henley: Routledge and Kegan Paul.

Pearson, Roberta E. 1990. '"O'er Step not the Modesty of Nature": A Semiotic Approach to Acting in the Griffith Biographs', in C. Zucker (ed.), *Making Visible the Invisible*. New Jersey and London: The Scarecrow Press: 1–27.

Peary, Danny (ed.). 1978. *Close-Ups: Intimate Profiles of Movie-stars by Co-stars, Directors, Screen Writers and Friends*. New York: Workman.

Phillips, Alastair. 2002a. '*Screen* Dossier: European Actors in Hollywood'. *Screen* 43(2): 167–74.

———— 2002b. 'Changing Bodies/Changing Voices'. *Screen* 43(2): 187–200.

Phillips, Alastair and Ginette Vincendeau. 2006. 'Film Trade, Global Culture and Transnational Cinema: An Introduction', in A. Phillips and G. Vincendeau (eds), *Journeys of Desire: European Actors in Hollywood, A Critical Companion*. London: BFI: 3–20.

Phillips, Alastair and Ginette Vincendeau (eds). 2006. *Journeys of Desire: European Actors in Hollywood*. London: BFI.

Phillips, Gene D. Originally published 1975. Reprinted in 2003. 'Fritz Lang Remembers', in B.K. Grant (ed.), *Fritz Lang: Interviews*. Jackson: University of Mississippi Press: 175–87.

Polan, Dana. 2002. 'Methodological Reflections on the Study of the Émigré Actor'. *Screen* 43(2): 178–86.

Powrie, Phil and Robyn Stilwell (eds). 2006. *Changing Tunes: The Use of Pre-Existing Music in Film*. London and Burlington, VT: Ashgate Publishing.

Prawer, S.S. 1980. *Caligari's Children: The Film as Tale of Terror*. Oxford, New York, Toronto and Melbourne: Oxford University Press.

Price, Michael. 1999. 'The Lost One', in G. Svehla and S. Svehla (eds), *Peter Lorre*. Baltimore: Midnight Marquee Press: 216–19.

Price, Vincent. 1981. 'Introduction', in S. Youngkin, J. Bigwood, and R. Cabana Jr, *The Films of Peter Lorre*. Secaucus, NJ: Citadel: 15.

Prince, Stephen and Wayne E. Hensley. 1992. 'The Kuleshov Effect: Recreating the Classic Experiment'. *Cinema Journal* 31(2): 59–75.

Pudovkin, V.I. 1991. 'Film Acting', in J.G. Butler (ed.), *Star Texts*. Detroit: Wayne State University Press: 34–41.

———— 1998. 'Stanislavsky's System in the Cinema', in B. Cardullo et al. (eds), *Playing to the Camera*. New Haven and London: Yale University Press: 130–37.

Rajewsky, Irina O. 2005. 'Intermediality, Intertextuality, and Remediation: A Literary Perspective on Intermediality'. *Intermédialités/Intermedialities* (6): 43–64.

Ray, Robert B. 1985. *A Certain Tendency of the Hollywood Cinema: 1930–80*. Princeton: Princeton University Press.

Reimer, Robert C. and Carol J. Reimer. 1992. *The Nazi-Retro Film: How German Narrative Cinema Remembers the Past*. New York: Twayne Publishers.

Robertson Wojcik, Pamela. 2003. 'Typecasting'. *Criticism* 45(2): 223–49.

———— 2006. 'The Sound of Film Acting'. *Journal of Film and Video* 58(1–2): 71–83.

Robertson Wojcik, Pamela (ed.). 2004. *Movie Acting: The Film Reader*. New York and London: Routledge.

Rogin, Michael. 1996. *Blackface, White Noise: Jewish Immigrants in the Hollywood Melting Pot*. Berkeley, Los Angeles and London: University of California Press.

Roof, Judith. 2002. *All About Thelma and Eve: Sidekicks and Third Wheels*. Urbana: University of Illinois.

Russell Taylor, John. 1983. *Strangers in Paradise*. London: Faber and Faber.

Russo, Vito. 1981 (1987). *The Celluloid Closet: Homosexuality in the Movies* (Revised Edition). New York and Toronto: Harper & Row.

Salisbury, Mark (ed.). 1995 (2006). *Burton on Burton* (Revised Edition). London: Faber and Faber.

Sandler, Kevin S. 1998. *Reading the Rabbit: Explorations in Warner Bros. Animation*. New Brunswick, NJ: Rutgers.

Sarris, Andrew. 1960. 'El and M'. *Village Voice* 1 September: 6–8.

———— 1966. *The Films of Josef von Sternberg*. New York: The Museum of Modern Art.

Saunders, Thomas J. 1999. 'Germany and Film Europe', in A. Higson and R. Maltby (eds), *Film Europe and Film America: Cinema, Commerce and Cutural Exchange 1920–1939*. Exeter: University of Exeter Press: 157–80.

Scheiffele, Ebherhard and David Kaye. 2002. 'Using Psychodrama to Expose Intolerance towards Homosexuality'. *The British Journal of Psychodrama and Sociodrama* 17(2): 19–35.

Sellier, Geneviève. 2002. 'Danielle Darrieux, Michele Morgan and Micheline Presle in Hollywood: The Threat to French Identity'. *Screen* 43(2): 201–14.

Sennett, Ted. 1979. *Masters of Menace: Greenstreet and Lorre*. New York: E.P. Dutton Books.

Sennwald, Andre. 1935. 'Poet of the Damned'. *New York Times* 31 March: 3.

———— 1935. 'Review of *Mad Love*'. *New York Times* 5 August: 12.

———— 1935. 'The Screen' (Review of *Crime and Punishment*). *New York Times* 22 November: 18.

———— 1935. 'Review of *Crime and Punishment*'. *New York Times* 24 November: 5.

Sergi, Gianluca. 1999. 'Actors and the Sound Gang', in A. Lovell and P. Krämer (eds), *Screen Acting*. London and New York: Routledge: 126–37.

Sharp, Anne. 2000. *The Peter Lorre Companion*. Xlibris.

———— 2003. *Walking the Shark: A Peter Lorre Book*. Xlibris.

Shary, Timothy. 2005. *American Youth on Screen*. London and New York: Wallflower Press.

Shindler, Colin. 1979. *Hollywood Goes to War*. Boston and Henley: Routledge & Kegan.

Shingler, Martin. 2006. 'Breathtaking: Bette Davis's Performance at the End of *Now Voyager*'. *Journal of Film and Video* 58(1–2): 46–58.

Shipman, David. 1972. *The Great Movie Stars: The International Years*. London: Angus and Robertson.

Skal, David J. 1993 (2001). *The Monster Show: A Cultural History of Horror* (Revised Edition). New York and London: Faber and Faber.

Smith, Don G. 1999. '*Crime and Punishment*', in G. Svehla and S. Svehla (eds), *Peter Lorre*. Baltimore: Midnight Marquee Press: 38–45.

Spicer, Andrew (ed.). 2007. *European Film Noir*. Manchester and New York: Manchester University Press.

Stacey, Jackie. 1994. *Star Gazing: Hollywood Cinema and Female Spectatorship*. London: Routledge.

Staiger, Janet. 1991. 'Seeing Stars', in C. Gledhill (ed.), *Stardom: Industry of Desire*. London and New York: Routledge: 3–16.

Stanislavsky, Constantin. 1991. 'When Acting is an Art', in J.G. Butler (ed.), *Star Texts*. Detroit: Wayne State University Press: 18–33.

Sterling, Christopher H. and John M. Kittross. 1990. *Stay Tuned: A Concise History of American Broadcasting* (Second Edition). Belmont, CA: Wadsworth.

Sumelian, Leon. 1936. 'Sh! Meet Peter Lorre – the Menacing Man'. *Motion Picture Weekly* June: 51–52.

Svehla, Gary J. and Susan Svehla (eds). 1999. *Peter Lorre*. Baltimore: Midnight Marquee Press.

Tasker, Yvonne (ed.). 2004. *Action and Adventure Cinema*. London and New York: Routledge.

Thomas, Sarah. 2008. 'A "Star" of the Airwaves: Peter Lorre's Appearances in American Radio'. *The Radio Journal* 6(1): 143–55.

Thomson, David. 1977. 'The Look on an Actor's Face'. *Sight and Sound* 46: 240–44.

――――― 1981. 'Bits and Pieces: Character Actors'. *Film Comment* 17(3): 11–19.

――――― 2002. *The New Biographical Dictionary of Film*. London: Little Brown.

――――― 2005. 'The M Factor'. *The New Republic* 28 September: 32–36.

Thornton, Steven. 1999. '*Mad Love*', in G. Svehla and S. Svehla (eds), *Peter Lorre*. Baltimore: Midnight Marquee Press: 46–59.

Tomasulo, Frank P. 2004. '"The Sounds of Silence": Modernist Acting in Michelangelo Antonioni's *Blow Up*', in C. Baron, D. Carson and F. Tomasulo (eds), *More Than a Method: Trends and Traditions in Contemporary Film Performance*. Detroit: Wayne State University Press: 94–125.

Tomlinson, Doug. 1990. 'Performance in the Films of Robert Bresson: The Aesthetics of Denial', in C. Zucker (ed.), *Making Visible the Invisible*. New Jersey and London: The Scarecrow Press: 365–90.

Tudor, Andrew. 1989. *Monsters and Mad Scientists: A Cultural History of the Horror Movie*. Oxford: Basil Blackwell.

Tyler, Parker. 1962. *Classics of the Foreign Film*. New York: Citadel.

Valinoti, Raymond J. 2005. 'Master of Menace Meets French Expressionist: The Films of Peter Lorre and Robert Florey'. *Films of the Golden Age* (42): 83–85.

Vasey, Ruth. 1997. *The World According to Hollywood, 1918–1939*. Exeter: University of Exeter Press.

Viera, Maria. 2004. 'Playing with Performance: Directorial and Performance Style in John Cassavetes's *Opening Night*', in C. Baron, D. Carson and F. Tomasulo (eds), *More Than a Method: Trends and Traditions in Contemporary Film Performance*. Detroit: Wayne State University Press: 153–72.

Vincendeau, Ginette. 2000. *Stars and Stardom in French Cinema*. London and New York: Continuum.

Vincent, William. 1992. 'Rita Hayworth at Columbia 1941–45', in B.F. Dick (ed.), *Columbia Pictures*. Lexington: University of Kentucky Press: 118–30.

Vineberg, Steve. 1991. *Method Actors: Three Generations of an American Acting Style*. New York: Schirmer Books.

Walker, Alexander. 1970. *Stardom: The Hollywood Phenomenon*. London: Penguin.

Waugh, Thomas. 1990. '"Acting to Play Oneself": Notes on Performance in Documentary', in C. Zucker (ed.), *Making Visible the Invisible*. New Jersey and London: The Scarecrow Press: 64–91.

Whiteclay Chambers II, John. 2006. 'The Movies and the Antiwar Debate in America 1930–1941'. *Film and History* 36(1): 44–57.

Wilkins, Paul. 1999. *Psychodrama*. London, Thousand Oaks and New Delhi: Sage Publications.

Willett, John. 1964. *Brecht on Theatre: The Development of an Aesthetic*. New York: Jill and Wang.

—— 1988. *The Theatre of the Weimar Republic*. New York and London: Holmes & Meier.

Willett, John and Ralph Manheim (eds). 1979a. *Bertolt Brecht: Poems 1913–1956*. New York: Methuen.

—— 1979b. *Bertolt Brecht Collected Plays: Volume Two Part One*. London: Eyre Methuen.

Williams, Tony. 2007. 'Peter Lorre's *Der Verlorene*: Trauma and Recent Historical Memory', in S. Hantke (ed.), *Caligari's Heirs: The German Cinema of Fear After 1945*. Lanham, MD: Scarecrow Press: 17–36.

Wilson, Robert (ed.). 1971. *The Film Criticism of Otis Ferguson*. Philadelphia: Temple University Press.

Worland, Rick. 1997. 'OWI Meets the Monsters: Hollywood Horror Films and War Propaganda 1942–1945'. *Cinema Journal* 37(1): 47–65.

—— 2003. 'Faces Behind the Mask: Vincent Price, Dr Phibes and the Horror Genre in Transition'. *Post Script* 22(2): 20–33.

Wright Wexman, Virginia. 1999. 'Kinesics and Film Acting: Humphrey Bogart in *The Maltese Falcon* and *The Big Sleep*', in J.G. Butler (ed.)., *Star Texts*. Detroit: Wayne State University Press: 203–13.

Youngkin, Stephen D. 2005. *The Lost One: A Life of Peter Lorre*. Lexington: University of Kentucky Press.

Youngkin, Stephen D., James Bigwood and Raymond Cabana Jr. 1981. *The Films of Peter Lorre*. Secaucus, NJ: Citadel.

Youngkin, Stephen D. and Felix Hofman (eds). 1998. *Peter Lorre: Portrait des Schauspielers auf der Flucht*. Munich: Bellville.

Zucker, Carole. 1993a. 'Introduction: Film Acting'. *Post Script* 12(2): 3–4.

—— 1993b. 'The Concept of "Excess" in Film Acting: Notes Towards an Understanding of Non-naturalistic Performance'. *Post Script* 12(2): 54–62.

———— 1999. 'An Interview with Ian Richardson: Making Friends with the Camera', in A. Lovell and P. Krämer (eds), *Screen Acting*. London and New York: Routledge: 152–64.

———— 2004. 'Passionate Engagement: Performance in the Films of Neil Jordon', in C. Baron, D. Carson and F. Tomasulo (eds), *More Than a Method: Trends and Traditions in Contemporary Film Performance*. Detroit: Wayne State University Press: 192–216.

Zucker, Carole (ed.). 1990. *Making Visible the Invisible*. New Jersey and London: The Scarecrow Press.

Zuckerman, Ezra W., Tai-Young Kim, Kalinda Ukanwa and James von Rittmann. 2003. 'Robust Identities or Nonentities? Typecasting in the Feature-Film Labor Market'. *American Journal of Sociology* 108(5): 1018–73.

Zuckerman, Ezra W. 2005. 'Typecasting and Generalism in Firm and Market: Genre-Based Career Concentration in the Feature Film Industry, 1933–1995'. *Research in the Sociology of Organizations* (23): 173–216.

Archival Resources

British Film Institute Library, London, UK

Anonymous. 1935. 'Peter Lorre', Studio Biography, Columbia Pictures.

Anonymous. 1942. 'Peter Lorre', Studio Biography, Universal.

Anonymous. 1946. 'Peter Lorre', Studio Biography, Universal.

Anonymous. 1954. 'Peter Lorre', Studio Biography, Walt Disney Studios.

Anonymous. 1955. 'Peter Lorre', Studio Biography, Universal.

Brand, Harry. 1937. 'Peter Lorre', Studio Biography, Twentieth-Century Fox.

Obituary. 1964. 'Gentle Villain Dies: Peter Lorre is Found by his Housekeeper'. *Evening News* 24 March.

Obituary. 1964. 'Peter Lorre Dies in Hollywood'. *The Guardian* 24 March.

Obituary. 1964. 'Peter Lorre Dies'. *Daily Mail* 24 March.

Obituary. 1964.'The Sad Faced Man of Menace is Dead'. *Daily Express* 24 March.

Margaret Herrick Library, Academy of Motion Picture Arts and Sciences, Los Angeles, USA

Beat the Devil. 1952. Production files and correspondence files.

Crime and Punishment. 1934–35. Production Code Administration files and clippings file.

The Cross of Lorraine. 1943–44. Production Code Administration files and clippings file.

The Face Behind the Mask. 1941. Production Code Administration files and clippings file.

Island of Doomed Men. 1940. Production Code Administration files and clippings file.

Mad Love. 1935. Production Code Administration files and clippings file. Paul Kohner correspondence and clippings file.

This Gun for Hire. 1936–40. Paramount Studios Production files.

Anonymous. 1935. 'Review of *Mad Love*'. *Hollywood Reporter* 27 June.

Anonymous. 1935. 'Review of *Mad Love*'. *Motion Picture Herald* 29 June.

Anonymous. 1937.'Lorre Prefers Roles of Villains'. *Detroit Free Press* 4 January.

Anonymous. 1938. 'Hollywood-by-the-Way'. *The Family Circle* 8 July: 12.

Anonymous. 1937. 'Review of *M*'. *New York Herald-Tribune* 27 July.

Anonymous. 1940. 'Review of *Island of Doomed Men*'. *Variety* 27 May.

Anonymous. 1941. 'Review of *The Face Behind the Mask*'. *Variety* 12 February.

Anonymous. 1941. 'Review of *The Face Behind the Mask*'. *Motion Picture Herald* 15 February.

Anonymous. 1941. 'Review of *The Face Behind the Mask*'. *Hollywood Reporter* 24 April.

Anonymous. 1946. 'Peter Lorre Interviewed by his Stand In, Russel Coles'. Studio Biography, Paramount.

Anonymous. 1957. 'Only Human: Peter Lorre's Menacing Exterior Masks a Gentle Soul'. *TV Guide* 2 November.

Brand, Harry. 1936–40. 'Peter Lorre' Studio Biographies, Twentieth-Century Fox.

Di Castri, Daphne. 1981. 'Peter Lorre: When He Was Bad – He Was Very Good'. *Hollywood Studio Magazine* November.

Fidler, Jimmy. 1938. 'Movie Medley'. *Chicago Sun-Times* 10 July.

Hall, Gladys. 1937. 'Are You Insane?' (typed draft copy). *Screenland* 2 October.

Lorre, Peter. Unknown date. 'The Role I Liked Best' (extended draft version).

——— 1946. 'The Role I Liked Best'. *Saturday Evening Post*.

Lynn, Hilary. 1936. 'He'd Rather Act than Eat: Talent and Temperament – and a Prankster too – that's Lorre'. *Modern Screen* 12(2), January.

McNamee, Gregory. 2005. 'The Lost One'. *Hollywood Reporter* 13 October.

Price, Vincent. 1964. 'A Great Actor's Tribute to a Great Actor'. *American International Pictures Magazine* April: 4.

Soter, Tom. 1985. 'Lorre: A Melodrama'. *Video* October.

Straker, Jean. 1936. 'Such a Modest Murderer'. *Film Pictorial* 9 May.

Strauss, Theodore. 1940. 'Review of *Island of Doomed Men*'. *New York Times* 10 June.

Tildersley, Alice L. 1937. Untitled article. *Post* 25 April.

Weiler, A.H. 1944. 'Mild-Mannered Villain'. *New York Times* 25 June.

Warner Bros. Archive, University of Southern California, Los Angeles, USA

All Through the Night. 1941. Production file, pressbook, clippings file.
Arsenic and Old Lace. 1942. Production file, pressbook, clippings file.
Background to Danger. 1943. Production file, pressbook, clippings file.
Casablanca. 1942. Production file, clippings file.
The Constant Nymph. 1943. Production file, pressbook, press releases.
Crack Up. 1936. Production file and scripts.
The Maltese Falcon. 1941. Production file, final shooting script, pressbook, clippings file, actor biographies.
The Maltese Falcon: Stephen Karnot. 1949. 'Character Analysis of Sam Spade'. Warner Bros. Studios, July.
Napoleon. 1935. Production file.
Passage to Marseille. 1943. Production file, pressbook.
Peter Lorre payroll records. 1941–45.
Peter Lorre legal files. 1941–46. Free Lancers single-picture contracts, multiple-picture contracts.
Anonymous. 1942. 'Review of *Casablanca*'. *Hollywood Reporter* August 12.
Anonymous. 1943. 'Being Typed as Menace Brought Success to Lorre'. *Chicago Daily News* 29 May.
Anonymous. 1943. 'Cherubic Lorre: He Puts the Charm in his Murders'. *New York Herald-Tribune* 27 June 1943.

INDEX